JOURNEY
TO
RUSSIA

JOURNEY TO RUSSIA

Miroslav Krleža

Translated from the original by
WILL FIRTH with an introduction by
DRAGANA OBRADOVIĆ

SAN—
DORF
PAS—
SAGE

TITLE OF THE ORIGINAL EDITION
Izlet u Rusiju

Copyright © Miroslav Krleža
—Hrvatska akademija
znanosti i umjetnosti, 2021

English translation © 2021 Will Firth

COVER AND LAYOUT DESIGN
Nikša Eršek

PUBLISHED BY
Sandorf Passage
South Portland, Maine, United States

IMPRINT OF
Sandorf
Severinska 30, Zagreb, Croatia
sandorf.hr | contact@sandorf.hr

Sandorf Passage books are
available to the trade through
Independent Publishers Group:
ipgbook.com | (800) 888-4741.

This translation was made possible by
a grant from the City of Zagreb. It was
also supported by the Writers' House in
Pazin, the Croatian Writers' Society,
the European Society of Authors, and
the Dutch Foundation for Literature.

h,d,p,
hrvatsko društvo pisaca
croatian writers society

The CIP record is available in the
computer catalog of the National and
University Library in Zagreb under
the number 000980467.

Library of Congress Control Number:
2020940943

ISBN
978-9-53351-029-3

Printed in Znanje, Zagreb

schwob

HIŽA OD
BESID
CASA
DEGLI
SCRITTORI

CONTENTS

> *What is imperialism?*
> *The wars and crises of imperialism over the last fifty years*
> *The power of monopolies, cartels, and finance capital*
> *The imperialism of Great Britain*
> *The rivalry of imperialist groups and Anglo-German relations*
> *The result of imperialism—anarchy*
> *The results of the Russian Revolution*
> *In a nutshell*

Introduction

Journey to Russia by Miroslav Krleža (1893–1981) is a collection of impressionistic essays about the author's trip to the Soviet Union from the fall of 1924 until the spring of 1925. The current edition contains the majority of pieces that appeared in the first edition of *Journey to Russia* published in 1926. This translation is based on the 2013 Croatian edition published by Novi Liber in Zagreb, which does not include the opening stages of the trip through Vienna and Dresden. The essays collected here cover Krleža's journey by train from Berlin through the Baltic states to Moscow, with a diversion to an unnamed outpost in the Soviet north.

Krleža undertook the journey in his early thirties, at a time when he was a rising literary talent in Zagreb, then part of the Kingdom of Serbs, Croats, and Slovenes (i.e. the first Yugoslavia). He was starting to establish himself as a poet, dramatist, essayist, and editor of two left-leaning cultural journals, *Plamen* (*Flame*) and later *Književna republika* (*Literary Republic*), with his longtime friend and colleague August Cesarec (1893–1941). Sympathetic to social democratic movements of the pre-World War I period and critical of the Austro-Hungarian military campaign he was forced to participate in as a colonial subject, Krleža was increasingly drawn to the politics of the left. He joined Zagreb's first Communist cell in 1919, committed to the politics of class emancipation and social equality.

In the 1920s, the Kingdom of Serbs, Croats, and Slovenes was a hostile environment for Communists, as the left posed a significant threat to the fragile monarchy. Together with the legacy of South Slavic social democratic movements of the late nineteenth and early twentieth centuries, the events of the 1917 October Revolution in Russia contributed to the evolution and development of Communist political thought in the Balkans. Thousands of young soldiers who had fought as subjects of the Austro-Hungarian empire on the Galician front, and who had been taken as prisoners of war, were liberated by the Russians in 1917. They brought the revolutionary movement with them upon their return home. In an attempt to thwart the energized political program that would jeopardize the country's monarchic parliamentary democracy, the Constituent Assembly of the Kingdom of Serbs, Croats, and Slovenes passed a proclamation in 1920 illegalizing operations of the Communist Party of Yugoslavia. Its members found themselves at risk of arrest and deportation. Given the open hostility toward Communist thinkers and activists, culture became an important arena for discussion about politics, thrusting leftist literary journals—such as those published by Krleža and Cesarec—into prominence.[*] *Journey to Russia* is part of this history, as the majority of the essays that comprise the book were initially published in *Književna republika*.

When Krleža undertook his trip to the Soviet Union, he left behind a domestic climate of paranoia, fear, and enmity toward ideas of communism. Very little was known about the Soviet Union, though there was much negative speculation. Yet despite the mystique and enigmatic exoticism often attached to the imaginary geography of Russia, and the language of heightened yearning he himself uses with regard to the place, Krleža exhibits, above all, a proximity to the region. This is signaled in the naming of his work: Krleža does not so much travel to faraway Russia as go on an outing, an excursion (*izlet* in Croatian). In doing so, he rejects the established "political topography" of Europe as the geopolitical space that offers a civilizational order to emulate, to adopt.[**] Rather, it is the Soviet Union that symbolizes future-oriented politics of class liberation, a clear antithesis to the bourgeois, decadent world of capitalist Europe. Europe is failing, writes Krleža, listing its signs of solipsism, decadence, and its intersecting crises of philosophy, art, and politics: "Creative skill and art are transformed into decoration and mechanized art production. (From the *Secession to Dada*, the bluff rules Europe.)"

"Where does Europe begin and Asia end?" he asks from Berlin, en route to Moscow. The terms used to explore this question call to mind various political and symbolic geographies, animated by dichotomous properties—for example, colonized Asia is described as "impoverished" and "plebian." This constellation of economic and cultural underdevelopment produced by large-scale, long-term oppression is equally relevant for the

[*]   See James M. Robertson, "Literature, revolution, and national aesthetics on the interwar Yugoslav left," *Nationalities Papers*, DOI: 10.1080/00905992.2017.1341471.

[**]   Katarina Peović Vuković, "Izlet u Rusiju. Krležina dijalogičnost i ljevica," *Književna smotra: časopis za svjetsku književnost*, 45:169–170 (2013), 3.

post-imperial legacy of the Balkans, a theme Krleža would return to frequently in his writing. Yet Asia is not for him a static signifier of otherness whose difference can be assimilated through the capitalist order and transformed into progress. Instead, in Asia, as in Europe, "class struggle rages in sooty factories." During the 1920s, Asia represented the site of rising revolutionary, anti-colonial struggle of peoples who were striving for political emancipation. The 1920 Congress of the People of the East in Azerbaijan is emblematic of the broader support for proletarian struggle by the Communist International. It was a time when, as Krleža notes, "social relationships [were] shaken like geological deposits."

In *Journey to Russia*, politics coalesce with Krleža's interest in people and their social relations so that his observations about communism breathe with lived experience. Yet there are passages where he simply sets out the axioms of state socialism and its historical developments in order to correct many of the tendentious lies and misconceptions propagated in his home country about the Soviet Union. These passages, however, also serve as an important political education for readers: Krleža capably clarifies the systemic exploitation in capitalism (and its military consequences) and further argues for the importance and necessity of class equality and the rise of the proletariat. Away from theoretical reflections, his observations of life in the Soviet Union register the pressures and the difficulties of life under socialism. He is not so blinded by political idealization not to realize the challenges posed by comprehensively overhauling social organization. This does not, however, displace the optimism unleashed by early twentieth-century visions of Marxism, especially in terms of what it has to offer in the class struggle against colonial imperialism.

On the whole, the travelogue traffics in multiple genres from essay to essay: at times Krleža commits to socio-historical analyses with a pronounced political argument, in others he narrates within the confines of a dramatic, dialogic structure that would not be out of place in his own plays and novels. He also exhibits an aesthetic-theoretical strain, such as in his discussion of the alchemy produced by the interactions between memory and the senses—reflections no doubt influenced by Proust. This is abundantly evident in the essay "Entering Moscow," where a physical description of the city is delayed by Krleža's meditation on the power of the senses to access otherwise unknown emotions or truths: "Sadness manifests itself in color, smell, or sound, and therefore it cannot simply be reflected by the photographic lens." This is in part a rejection of discourses of vision and the technological apparatus of the photographic lens, but it is equally about the complexity of real-life phenomena. These literary essays plunge the reader into a world where reality is described only through the faculties of the senses. This is coupled with Krleža's idiosyncratic, inimitable style of syntactically complex sentences that coil around themselves, deepening metaphors and analogies, sometimes over a whole paragraph. This has the effect of blurring the passage of time, which is indexed through seasonal features (the deep winter of the distant north, or the first winds of spring in Moscow) and subordinates the more coherent signs of the itinerary he has planned. Indeed, Krleža's travelogue eschews some of the classic narrative motifs that indicate the protagonist's evolution, trajectory, and return.

Krleža clearly belongs to literary modernism, though poetically he shares much more with the expressionist lineage than other forms of the avant-garde, like Dadaism and Surrealism. He rejected pure aestheticism in the arts and was a vocal critic of certain Croatian and Serbian writers who adopted European literary models and used them to espouse a romantic nationalism that mythologized the common people and their way of life. The 1930s brought him into conflict with the official policies of the Communist Party of Yugoslavia. As an advocate of authorial freedom, he was critical of the aestheticism program of socialist realism that would result in state interference in literature—an echo of doctrinaire Stalinist policy. His disagreement with proponents of this literary-cultural program culminated in what is known as the "conflict on the left" that eventually led to his expulsion from the Communist Party of Yugoslavia. However, the Tito-Stalin split in 1948—after which Yugoslavia forged its political path autonomously from the Soviet Union—was crucial in welcoming Krleža back into the core of the cultural and political elite. A turning point in his return to favor was his contribution to the debates about the role of the state and its administration of literature. In 1952, at the Third Congress of Writers held in

Ljubljana, he delivered a Party-approved speech that signaled the end of socialist realism in Yugoslavia.

Almost a century of turbulent global history separates us from the events of 1925, the most important of which—in the context of Krleža's travelogue—is the fall of the Soviet Union and the end of state socialism in Eastern Europe and Central Asia. The social order that Krleža describes as coming into being is no longer in existence. Yet Krleža's political and ideological explorations in the text are not entirely irrelevant to contemporary readers. In particular, Krleža's descriptions of the bourgeois patricians of the early twentieth century are eerily similar to contemporary neoliberal ruling elites. His statement that "the state is only a decorative sham in its pretense to 'belong to the people,' when in fact it is an exponent of the bank" cannot fail to resonate in the twenty-first century, in the aftermath of a global recession and rise in ethno-nationalist populism that appeals to those disenfranchised by the economic system.

Will Firth's translation of *Journey to Russia* is a significant achievement not only because Krleža has been insufficiently translated into English, despite being the most important twentieth-century Croatian writer, but also because it is the first opportunity for readers to encounter Krleža as an essayist. He was a prolific literary critic and commentator, and Firth's translation of *Journey to Russia* provides a sense of the author's inseparable poetic and political concerns.

DRAGANA OBRADOVIĆ
Associate Professor, Department of Slavic Languages and Literatures, University of Toronto

BERLIN

As a picture, Berlin changed several lyrical images in the magic lantern of my consciousness, and I could write a whole little history of my own Berlin panorama. From my earliest childhood, I was captivated by the concept of Berlin in Adolph von Menzel's composition "Departure of King Wilhelm I for the Army, 1871." Menzel was an honorary citizen of the German capital, privy councilor of the Emperor who united Germany, a professor of the Royal Prussian Academy of Fine Arts, and a Great Master of the civil class of the *Pour le Mérite*. So his representations of things and events were naturally filled with pathos, as were the times he lived in, the anecdotes he aggrandized with his brush, and the laurels they celebrated him with.

Like in a Georg von Ompteda novel, the gentlemen of the time hunted game in their red *parforce* tailcoats and rested, with fans in hand, beneath tapestries and Venetian candlesticks in Makart-style interiors: Persian carpets, crystal, metals, onyx, carnelian, dripstones, conches, feathers of birds of paradise, portraits of gentlefolk in pale pastel, translucent silks; through the glass of the balcony door, a view onto an English landscape garden; gallooned servants serve "five-o'clock tea" when the clock tower of the count's palace pathetically strikes the first half of the fifth hour.

As court artist, Menzel painted the circles of the empire's nobility in the discharge of their highest martial functions: as generals on the battlefield and courtiers in the role of supreme masters of ceremony at the Court, in festive lighting beneath the domes against the backdrop of long purple drapes and marble columns.

That painter glorified the whole eighteenth century (so fruitful for the development of human thought) as a Prussian royal barracks. His cycles of lithographs sang the exploits of the army and the battles of Prussian King Frederick, called "the Great," and thus Menzel's exaltations of courtly life in Potsdam such as "Frederick the Great's Table at Sanssouci" and "The Flute Concert at Sanssouci" are decorations that conjure up all the Philistine optical illusions about the beauty of courtly life, even today, despite this democratic age. In Menzel's instrumentation we hear the lyrical overtone of longing for the wonderful days at

Sanssouci palace, which the age of the factory and its chimneys have, unfortunately, carried away forever.

Children are poisoned with militaristic legends, according to a perverse plan, and since our childhoods were spent in semicolonial circumstances, the battle glory of the Germanic overlords manifested itself as an ongoing motif of visual propaganda, whose sole purpose was to deceive children's consciousness with ornamental lies about a higher purpose of military conflagrations.

The first martial rumble of army drums in my childhood came to me through Menzel's painting "Frederick the Great at the Battle of Hochkirch." Reading August Šenoa and fighting my way through the absurdity of the Seven Years' War with his Maria-Theresia grenadiers, I saw all those battles through Menzel's eyes and I think it was from him that I learned that one of the victors at Waterloo came charging into battle on a white horse, just in the nick of time.

Menzel painted court dinners in the brilliant illumination of bright, orange-red candlesticks, and when he depicted the Prussian king and his circles, he made the already pliant and molluscan spines of the lower-order counts, barons, baronesses, and princelings bend to apish servility. Menzel's discreet jingle of guards' spurs and the rustle of long silk trains over the parquet floors of the court give you a sense of the devout soul of a loyal subject, that of a liveried servant, a poor soul narcotized by the pestilent aroma of the court setting.

As a boy, I imagined Berlin to be a city of Menzel's princes, counts, and countess—and all the countesses were circus riders, equestriennes of the prestigious Spanish Riding School. In her black costume that cascaded over her legs in thick folds, with a top hat and a coiffure à la Empress Elisabeth, and in knightly gloves, my plebeian image of a countess coincided with that circus countess because the first living, blue-blooded lady I had the honor to see beneath the greenish tarpaulins of a small provincial arena was that circus countess on her white horse: an exciting drama in the form of a pantomime, where the countess sets out in secret through the dark forest, with flashes of lightning in the night, escorted by an old servant, to a rendezvous full of uncertainty, to the beat of the Stefanie

Polka by Drum Major von Czibulka, of the imperial Austrian and royal Hungarian army.

The Countess, corseted with an old-fashioned bodice, powdered, and bathed (a real supernatural goddess!), reared up with her Arabian thoroughbred to dance a pirouette, a capriole, and then a lançade—all that in the sawdust-covered circus ring, that theater of theaters, whose emotive intensity would never be eclipsed by any later trick on the boards. The Countess was riding to a secret tryst with a mysterious cavalier, but on the path she was waylaid by bandits; there was a panicky exchange of pistol shots, the smell of gunpowder, a frantic gallop around the arena, and everything passed into a mad crescendo of applause and a clownish grimace on the face of the lady, like a menace, before she fell down dead.

For me, Berlin remained that kind of unearthly circus pantomime: the Lipizzan drill of the Spanish Riding School, officers in gold and silver, the boulevard "Unter den Linden" ablaze with a medley of imperial banners, coachmen with derbies and cockades, and the boisterous rejoicing of the people that war had broken out and the spirits of Odin and Barbarossa had risen from the dead (Menzel: "Departure of King Wilhelm I for the Army, 1871").

With typical Menzelesque splendor, the "imperial and royal" countish circus set out to the two-quarter time of Czibulka's polka on its fiendish cavalcade in 1914... From the esteemed Spanish Riding School with its white baroque horses, from pirouettes and pessades to the left and right, a headlong gallop cavorted to a mad rhythm: the whirlwind of their passing blew off all the wigs and top hats, the maddened horses threw Berlin's counts and countesses out of their saddles, the circus sheet billowed in the gunpowder smoke, and an acrobat grinned to dirgeful music in the center of the arena—a shell had taken off his lower jaw, and his Stuart collar was drenched with blood.

When Wilhelm II threw down the gauntlet, a turbid spring of all our suppressed forebodings flowed from Berlin, and since then, for ten years, not a day has passed without our thoughts being in touch with that distant and unknown city. The press intimidated us every day with stupid phrases about the "Baghdad Railway" and the "drive to the East," but no one in our region, apart from the Croatian politician Frano Supilo, attached any particular significance to those follies.

When the terrifying reality of those phrases actually appeared in our city in the form of mobilization orders for the "imperial and royal" army and a burning pogrom on the streets in July 1914, I remember looking at the chaos left behind in the streets—slashed bags of flour, boxes of quality candies in the mud, petroleum, cookies, blue vitriol, pickled gherkins, and risotto—and I was aghast, as if we were menaced by an armor-clad specter of a giant Teutonic knight who was crushing all the paper towers of our Philistine views on the world, people, and politics. The German Knights Templar, from Ulrich von Jungingen to Paul Hindenburg at Tannenberg, the colonizers of "our Slavic, Polabian original homeland," arose like a specter above Herder's dove-like Slavic world, and all our faith in Illyrian illusions about the destiny of the Slavic masses from Mount Učka by the Adriatic to Vladivostok evaporated in the whistling of the storm, which swept away forever not only Berlin's counts but also Petrograd's boyars.

In the scope of that chivalrous Slavo-Germanic clash of arms I had the honor of making my appearance in the forest of spears and banners beneath the black Teutonic cross as a very modest supernumerary when the Austro-German legions, on their historical road to Baghdad, got bogged down in Galicia, near Kolomyia and Rava-Ruska on the Dnieper. After Bregalnica, listening to the roar of the German artillery, I realized once more that war is an aberrant phenomenon from the perspective of a civilized man. There is no link between all the things a man hopes for and thinks are elements of his convictions, and this futile din of weapons—none at all. Nevertheless, contemporary man still lives illuminated by the gleaming blades of swords and he dies to the clang of armor and sabers according to the logic of unsheathed knives, and a continuous roar of artillery follows his cannibalistic frenzy under the stars.

That was early August 1916, one evening on the railroad line between Stanisławow and Delyatin, not far from the village of Grabovac, above the channel of the Bistrica River overgrown with thickets of willow—the terrifying days of the Brusilov Offensive, when that Russian general halted the movement of his masses in the moment of the Austrian army's total collapse, when not a single Austrian broom would have stood up against him all the way to Vienna. Those days, the Austrian army roamed the roads of Galicia like phantoms at death's door, and the belief prevailed among the demoralized troops that the game was over. Men rebelled by throwing aside their weapons and gear, on the verge of a mass revolt, as is prone to happen when tired and hungry soldiers are retreating with their backs to the enemy guns.

Faced with the inevitable collapse of the Austrian forces, the German high command flung its own units into the vacuum that gaped in front of the Austrian positions in order to raise the morale of the marauders and halt the catastrophe.

Carried along in the confusion of that demoralized scrum, I stood early that evening beside a wooden pontoon bridge over the Bistrica, watching the Austrian infantry slog in endless lines down the road, bloodstained, dirty, and torn—and the old lyrical motif of Austrian border-troops' retreats under Habsburg banners came to me as a motif of my own poetry, that wretched whining and complaining in the smoke of historical campfires. The creak of wheels, the neighing of hungry and thirsty horses, mass graves, a wretched gypsy procession that clinked with its harnesses and empty cans, spooning malodorous gruel under the smoke-stained canvas of their tent, all in a hail of bullets, when a human head is worth no more than a cat's.

In the twilight, when the red and green signal lights on the wooden bridge over the Bistrica had already been lit, the cavalry division of General von Gallwitz from Berlin came roaring over the boards and beams of the pioneers' bridge. The horses were well-fed and well-groomed, with shining hindquarters. The helmets, straps and belts, swords and guns, all spick-and-span and bright, and the uhlans' slim lances with pennons aflutter, the thunder of sturdy mares on the bridge, in contrast with the disheveled, demoralized misery of the Austrian marauders-cum-desperados, were nothing short of imperious. The division of General von Gallwitz from Berlin!

I watched the Berlin horsemen that same evening by the light of the campfire as they received their mail, read newspapers, browsed through magazines, brewed coffee in red-enameled pots, spread jam on hot white rolls, ironed their breeches and dolmans, cleaned their metal buttons, starched their collars, polished their boots, and since then every one of my associations with Berlin has been inseparably connected with that cavalcade of General von Gallwitz.

Amid the total collapse of an Empire, those Berlin uhlans appeared like a veritable blast of Odin's horn! They were so illustrious, and they bit into their bread and ironed their breeches with such self-assurance and haughtiness that I was seized by fear at the thought that those lancers really could make Berlin a victorious capital. The forgotten world of Menzel's images came back to me that evening in the Galician village of Cuciłów, and I was overcome by a dread of Berlin and its uhlans, and by the terrible thought that our frontiersman fate on the Empire's Ottoman border might still threaten us in decades to come. When I found myself in Berlin eight years later, I saw bold election posters on every street corner showing the burnished steel helmet of Gallwitz's uhlans being threatened by a red fist, beseeching voters: *Smash it!*

It was first light as we approached Berlin. Morning fires were lit beneath roofs in the grey veil of dawn, the smoke streamed up, and our train, with burning, orange-illuminated windows, thundered across cleared land and through pinewoods like a pub that goes on carousing at dawn without turning off the lights. Stations, towns, and villages in little forests and hollows were still in heavy black slumber; startled stokers shuffled yawning and leaden heavily along the platforms, woken by the express train. Waiters laid breakfast services in station restaurants, spread white tablecloths, carried silver jugs of hot coffee, and on the parallel track trains thundered past from the opposite direction in huge clouds of steam, shot through with red-and-green nighttime signal lights, in a rain of fiery sparks, like furious mammoths. I kept trying to find a way to curl up into a ball, shut my eyes, and fall asleep for two or three minutes to get some respite from the long night, when you are shaken up after sitting through the night, from the voices and the many impressions, and simply cannot settle down in the cantilena of sleep, when your eyelids close by themselves from thirst for a drop of morphine.

The tired moment of dawn, turbidly ashen grey like the cataract of a blind person, when your sore and swollen eyelids sting, when the train's grinding of iron and vortex of ghastly noise take all the dozing passengers across that mysterious border between darkness and the light of day. Still dirtied with night and drowsy from the heavy smell of the stuffy compartment, the grotesque grimaces and gaping galoshes of human mouths snore, and a man in the corridor speaks audibly on the muddled shore of his twilight state and agitated anxiety seems to ring in his words. Objects are still sharp-edged and solid: threadbare pillows stuffed with horsehair that nibbles at your cheeks, a painted square of glass in the window rattles, steam engines fly past, trees and telegraph poles, a picture of reality blurs and evaporates, and its objects dissolve anew and mingle in your doze. Thoughts are still adrift, and from unnamed full-blooded verticals everything melts in a horizontal of neglect and weary indifference. Instead of a man who thinks, travels, and desires more, we have a snoring human body like some split-open sack that shakes to the rhythm of our inane coach, and the person opposite me in the compartment seemed not to have a head: an apparition in an empty, shabby coat—a strange, soft doll, slobbery and wheezing as if it was breathing through a thin glass tube.

A dozen cyclists raced along the road parallel to the track, both men and women; grey dust rose up in low clouds, and from there came the choleric barking of a small black dog. It protested against the engine and scooted up the embankment in its loud, megalomaniac rush, only then to retreat with its tail between its legs and trot off after the cyclists.

To the left and right, towns remained in the twilight sleep of dawn, when green lamps still flicker their tongues, and the shadows of morning were deep blue and clear. Our fast train drummed over iron bridges, past stations and outer suburbs, where on either side walls resounded beneath advertisements in different colors; we forged on alongside a concrete channel filled with grey and muddy water, where black, tarred barges rocked. Barefooted bargees milled around on the black decks, splashing them down with pails of black, tarry water. Gasworks and factories glowed in the first rays of daylight; industrial blocks enclosed by tall red-brick walls (like the yards of penitentiaries or abattoirs), stood empty. Ships, boats, bridges, locked churches—everything was grey and illuminated by the light of a new day that came on in the eastern mists ever more clearly, to the chatter of birds.

We traveled on an iron tangent with red signal lights, and only here and there an occasional glass door opened, and there in a garret someone opened a window, high up under the roof, above the sixth floor. A painter had his studio there, and everything smelled of turpentine and wet paintings. Crumpled, bright colorful scarves, room dividers with inwoven, fan-shaped tropical butterflies, silk scarves with warm and intimate female smells, the distant sound of morning bells, and the painter, up under the roof, above the city, closed his eyes and listened to the thunder of the express train.

Movement grew in the morning light, where the calls of the newsvendors echoed on the empty streets as they announced the greasy paper that stinks of rotary-press oil, soaked with blood and misfortunes.

Trains rumbled past on countless railroad lines toward the glass arch of Anhalter Bahnhof station, where the tide of the Berlin morning grew with the din of wheels, horns, and the ringing of tram bells.

When a man brooding at the window of a speeding train asks himself what happened to Menzel's Berlin, the Berlin of General von Gallwitz's cavalry division, he is lost in mists: life takes a course quite different to human thought and governed by harder laws. Because eighty years ago, a poet dreamed in these German cities, and in front of Cologne cathedral he imagined the cavalry of the future:

> *The future's merry cavalry*
> *In this cathedral should be housed,*

fantasizing about the furious end of the empire's legitimacy, under the folds of the black-red-and-gold banner,

> *A banner stands high above,*
> *Its color black, red, and gold,*

and today, eighty years later, nothing has changed. Today too, travelers' bags and suitcases are opened by inquisitive customs officers:

> *They sniffed everything, rummaged through*
> *Shirts, pants and handkerchiefs, for hidden*
> *Needle-point lace or for gems,*
> *And for books that were forbidden.*

You fools that search inside my trunk!
There's nothing for you to find:
The contraband that travels with me,
Is hidden in my mind.

I remembered Heinrich Heine (to whom there are no monuments in this country) and recalled the sheer endless polemics in German political life for and against the black-red-and-gold flag of the Weimar Republic, and then a mixture of tedium and sorrow came over me. The customs officers and the borders were still there, the people were still there, and the systems—everything was still there, and how many subjects had passed through these cities with ideas that had vanished like Solomonic smoke in the wind?

In the romantic and naïve interval of expectation between July 1830 and the revolution of February/March 1848, when European intellectuals were convinced that the gap between the idea of political and economic liberation and its realization was much smaller than experience had shown, Heine sang a socialist song:

A new song, a better song,
O friends, I speak to thee!
Here upon earth we shall full soon
A heavenly realm decree.

At that time, Bakunin was eking out a living in Dresden under the pseudonym of Jules Elysard: *Even in Russia, the boundless snow-covered kingdom so little known, and which perhaps also has a great future in store, even in Russia dark clouds are gathering, heralding storm. Oh, the air is sultry and pregnant with lightning.* That was a time when even Dostoyevsky was a rebel, and the atheist Schopenhauer got hot under the collar about Hegel's all-too-religious homilies. The first railroads were being marked out, but no one, except for a few lyrical poets, was aware that the shackling of the globe in iron chains represented an economic revolution. Liebig founded the first chemistry laboratory, Humboldt explained the iron law of natural will, Börne, Freiligrath, Laube, Büchner, and so many others undermined the authority and legitimacy of feudalism, and parallel to them all the moralistic hypotheses of nascent bourgeois power. That was the time of Marx, Stirner, Feuerbach, and Strauss, the time of the Young Germany group; since then, the wielders of power in Europe's bourgeois parliaments have mutated into countless variations, in headlong anarchy, and, as we see, there is still no coordination and order—everything is still violence, delusion, and disease.

I was traveling with two unionists, functionaries of the social democratic party apparatus—the Scheidemann-Noske political bureaucracy. They were returning from Vienna after attending the international trade union congress of the Amsterdam International, deeply impressed by the city, the speeches, and the great mass parade in front of the parliament, when over 100,000 umbrellas marched with the rhythm of disciplined proletarian battalions.

We talked all night about politics, socialism, and the problem of taking political power for the German masses, who constitute a compact democratic majority of fifteen million socialist votes. I could not agree in any way with the thesis that the German working class, which holds in its hand all transport, production, shipping, power stations, commodity production, factories—in other words all the economic elements of the machinery of state—that that class was allegedly still not capable, and politically and economically competent enough, to take the wheel of government into its hands.

We also spoke about the lawsuit of Professor Nicolai and Colonel Wilamowitz-Moellendorff of the general staff. Dr. Georg Friedrich Nicolai, a professor of medicine and a prominent pacifist, who reacted to the proclamation of German intellectuals at the beginning of the war in 1914 by issuing his own anti-war manifesto, and whose noncomformist and provocative stance saw him deprived of all civil honors, had been thrown into jail and sentenced to ten years of hard labor. That man, who had refused to be mobilized and act as a military doctor during the war because the systematic preparation of new cannon fodder contradicted the underlying Samaritan principle of a doctor who had taken the Hippocratic oath, that humanist, whose gesture roused the conscience of a good part of Europe's intellectuals, had been branded a good-for-nothing by an officer of the imperial general staff, and now he had lost a defamation suit before a court of the

Weimar Republic. The court absolved the general-staff officer Wilamowitz-Moellendorff of any blame because by calling the author of the famous anti-war book *The Biology of War* a good-for-nothing who betrayed his fatherland, he did not commit any offense punishable by the positive legislation of the Republic.

The court had recognized the right of an officer of the general staff to call the pacifist Professor Nicolai a blackguard, good-for-nothing, and traitor. Since that dramatic case was very topical I tried to draw the attention of those German unionists, whose democratic principles made them worry about taking power in the name of fifteen million proletarians, to the political dangers lurking in the German zeitgeist as revealed by the Nicolai-Wilamowitz-Moellendorff case.

"I don't know what fundamental concepts of democracy demand that a Junker be conceded the right to label humanists as traitors, blackguards, and good-for-nothings in the press. If the positive legislation of the Weimar Republic guarantees the right of Junkers to consider idealistic activists good-for-nothings, and if the republic's laws today are such that political verdicts pronounced under their auspices by a wartime court of the former empire are considered valid, then, to be sure, one cannot say that that's not democratic, but unfortunately—logically—it's just another variety of Junker democracy."

It turned out in the conversation with those politically blinkered fellows that the perception or non-perception of there being certain "open questions of democracy" is a matter of fine detail, since those nuances are determined by associations, and when those associations do not exist there are not even the requisite elements that could arouse democratic fantasy, and without fantasy nothing in the world exists, including democracy.

Wilamowitz-Moellendorff is a typical puppet of the general-staff, who thinks like a lifeless puppet in the spirit of his upbringing, his mentality, and his moral views on society, the nation, and the state, because he is made up of marionettish petty details: a Prussian general's dolman with tinsel medals, a little glass wheel in his eye, a huge, heavy cavalry saber at his side, Menzel's pathos about "The Flute Concert of Sanssouci," Frederick the Great, Clausewitz, Ludendorff, Hindenburg, "The Guard on the Rhine," Moltke, imperial banners, the tabloid *Berliner Zeitung am Mittag*,

Junkers' spiked helmets, hand grenades, gas masks, assault units, hurrah, hurrah, hurrah, and whoever thinks civilization is about more than sabers and cannons is a good-for-nothing, a cunning blackguard, and a traitor to his fatherland. Since Professor Nicolai demonstrated in his *Biology of War* that he is just such a creature who thinks that sabers and cannons belong to prehistory, that war is a cannibalistic absurdity and an aberrant phenomenon from the perspective of a civilized man, and that pacifism is the only worthy political orientation for contemporary man, Professor Nicolai's form of reasoning and logic represents a one-hundred percent negation of the moral and social ideals of a man like Wilamowitz-Moellendorff, and well may one ask: What democratic forum is competent to be an arbiter in that dispute?

"The court."

"Which court?"

"The court of the Weimar Republic, by all democratic principles."

"Alright, the court of the Weimar Republic, which by all democratic principles adjudicates the rhetorical duel between a general and a civilian, is equally burdened with outmoded legitimist prejudices. Such a democratic court obviously had no reason at all to consider the sentences it pronounced in wartime incorrect or unjust in peacetime."

A court must not doubt its own high objectivity and, thus, logically, respecting its own ruling, it was just being consistent to the original verdict when it found Professor Nicolai guilty of treason. The court therefore, quite logically, acknowledged the right of its irreproachable and richly decorated warrior Wilamowitz-Moellendorff to label a man condemned of high treason by the same court a traitor to his people. That is statist logic, and if the opposite had happened, i.e. if Wilamowitz-Moellendorff had been condemned, that would have been a revolution, and a democratic one into the bargain, but that is exactly what the German unionists are unable to follow logically in their thoughts.

We talked about the forthcoming elections for president of the republic and the candidacy of Marshal Hindenburg, for whom all the counts and countesses would vote, as well as all the German fairy-tale hunters, all the maids with their devoted noncommissioned officer sweethearts, all the foresters with their dachshunds, and all the footballers, Junkers, and cyclists, who are convinced that the stab-in-the-back myth—the notion that the Empire was betrayed by socialists and proletarians on the home front—is not a myth but a verified historical truth.

One of the union functionaries was a Rollandist. Romain Rolland's book *Above the Battle* fell into his hands with a five-year delay, and then he started asking why the German proletariat had not taken a Rollandist stance on the war question.

"It didn't do anything, because in a dramatic situation like the one Germany is in today, when the dark shadow of a man like Hindenburg looms over the republic, you ought to know what you want, and in Germany today no one apart from Wilamowitz-Moellendorff knows what he wants," I said. "He realizes that the situation has come to a head: it's a fatal juncture. It will be woe to the defeated, and therefore Wilamowitz-Moellendorff will vote for Hindenburg. But the Weimar Republic with its fifteen million proletarian votes doesn't know what it wants. German democracy today fails to see what was clear to Heine back in 1848:

> *The future's merry cavalry,*
> *In this cathedral should be housed,*
> *And if you're not willing, I'll use force:*
> *I'll club you till you're deloused!"*

Everything then got entangled in a futile competition to outwit one another. Eastern Orthodox, Marxist, and neo Marxist prattlings about the Proudhon-Marx conflict, or Lassalle-Bebel, Kautsky-Liebknecht, Rosa Luxemburg-Wilamowitz-Moellendorff or Hindenburg, Austro-Marxism or anarcho-syndicalism, Sorel-Mussolini-Bakunin, words and words in that stuffy and dirty compartment, in the smoke, in the tentative light of dawn.

Also traveling with us were a Bulgarian student and a German commercial traveler, who had been an artillery officer during the war, stationed with his battery near Jerusalem, and he was chatting with the Bulgarian student (who also seemed to have been a German artilleryman in the Holy Land during the war) about the gunnery positions around Jerusalem.

And there was a married couple. They had spent the whole time nibbling and eating, picking at chicken bones, opening crackly paper bags of various rolls, packets and sachets, opened cans of food, peeled oranges, unstopped and stopped bottles of mineral water, munched chocolate and biscuits, taking off shoes, putting on slippers, opening their suitcases to look for pillows, shawls, and scarves—in sum, feeling as comfortable as if they were at home, but for that little family our conversation was like flogging a dead horse, or even less than that: smoke in the wind.

Europe may think itself lucky to have citizens like that, for whom the Gethsemane batteries are just a faint memory, and to have such gluttonous eaters of bread, for whom anything inedible is about as interesting as a dead horse. Pure, primitive Asia.

Where does Europe begin and Asia end? That is far from easy to define: while the Zagreb cardinals' and bishops' Maksimir Park is definitely a piece of Biedermeier Europe, the village of Čulinec below Maksimir Park still slumbers in an old Slavic, archaic condition, with wooden architecture from ages prehistorical, and Čulinec and Banova Jaruga to the southeast are the immediate transition to China and India, snoring all the way to Bombay and distant Port Arthur. Straw roofs dominate the landscape via Vienna to Linz, and cows graze on the railroad embankments near Prague, like here, too, around Strizivojna-Vrpolje in eastern Croatia.

In Berlin, for example, you feel at every step that today's metropolitan way of life is still not so urbanized that one could speak of a definite and final victory of the City over Asia. Asia is a zone of atonal music in the shadow of demonic water closets, and state borders where liberal manuscripts represent contraband. But today in Asia, too, cigarettes are sold in silver foil, *The Merry Widow* fills the theaters, and class struggle rages in sooty factories just like in Europe.

Berlin is a city where automobiles hum like cockchafers and dogs are requested in writing to refrain from doing foul deeds on the lawns of public gardens; and while the discarded golden cigarette butt feels hopelessly lonesome on the gleaming asphalt like an entirely forgotten and rejected foreign body or, more perversely, an utterly despised thing, in that same Berlin disturbed by diesel fumes, coachmen shout "whoa-ha," and "giddyap" to their nags—just like their faraway and unfamiliar class brothers around Vyatka and Vologda, who have no concept that the world now moves on tires.

Berlin is not only a city of snobbish, fashionable hotels (with powdered, blonde young bellboys as a distraction for older gentlemen of a certain persuasion), but in this most ambitious of all European centers people also live in moldering rooms with antiquated, bedbug-ridden polished sofas, where old ladies rub camphor on swelling toothaches, and where it smells of garlic and ginger—old-fashioned remedies from Frederick's time.

The megalomaniac figures of many martial symbols and deities freeze on the facades and tympana of Berlin's palaces; naked Achilles in sharp profile with armor and a spear waves to a golden goddess, a stone beauty whose skirt is lifted indiscreetly by the wind so that we can glimpse a charming thigh beneath the rich folds of her peplos; she is fated to sit in boredom in the hopelessly hollow and inscrutable company of soot-covered knights' helmets on chimneys. And while the scene on the facades of this Berlin theater is certainly olympically decorative, the windows of the beer bars in pseudo-Renaissance palaces painted with grey oily molasses are covered with tawdry plebeian curtains of the cheapest showy fabric; if you press your inquisitive ear to the window pane of those underground hovels, you will hear the ticking of an antique grandfather clock and see primitives resting in their slippers by the fire, shredding their own cheap tobacco on a board over their knees with a blunt knife. At those subterranean levels of consciousness one can believe in almost anything, in the magic of supernatural secrets; fortune-tellers are esteemed here like supernatural beings; and in this city, whose environs still today bear names of Slavic origin such as Buckow, Doberlug, and Nowawes, there live newcomers from eastern lands and expanses, in whose brains the odor of ammoniac, cowsheds, cottage straw, and the raw smell of smoke rouses ancient recollections of the cattle-breeding prehistoric state that still blithely subsists today from Čulinec to the Don and Volga rivers, and no one racks their brains about the superfluous dilemmas that agitate Western minds: Will the West impose *The Merry Widow* on the East, or the East foist new social imperatives on the West?

I chatted with a blind beggar woman in the wealthy industrialists' neighborhood on Tiergarten Avenue. Her manner of expression was in no way different from that of a blind woman in front of any of our church gates. Unobtrusive mansions stand with the lowered curtains of "serene seclusion," greenhouses with palms and blooming magnolias, and there, in the snowy, foggy twilight, a blind woman begged for help in the name of some baroque saint or other, lamenting just like all our blind poor moan to an accordion on Čulinec bridge.

What contrasts there are in this unhappy civilization traveling toward its own destruction, so stupidly torn by its own contradictions, dwindling in the agony of self-laceration that no thinking person can see the end of. The moneybags owner of that marble villa in Berlin is basking on the terrace of some fancy Egyptian hotel at this very moment, sipping aperitifs and flirting all night to the greenish luminance of ancient Egyptian lamps of translucent calcite. The owner of such a mansion along Tiergarten Avenue has extended his mastery over the whole planet, and if he is a second-generation rentier he chatters like a talking parrot—François van Loo's miniatures prove most convincingly that sculpture does not have to be monumental!

The man is surprised that his counterpart has never heard of Van Loo, and he is horrified that there are such primitives who have no idea that he was a master of miniature sculpture in the second half of the seventeenth century. He owns a small Jesus figure by Van Loo: a tiny ivory cameo showing the Savior on the road to Emmaus, accompanied by two apostles. He bought it in Brussels at the auction of Baron de Gontreuille's collection for 180,000 gold francs, and for every such connoisseur of Van Loo's miniatures several hundred slaves work themselves to ruin at the galley oar or the lathe.

The gentle owners of foundries in the second or third generation, shielded from crude reality by their annuities, turn into bluestockings in the scope of perverse mental games, where desperately stultifying mantras are prized above all things—the hollower the more bewitching! When a moneybags like this talks about fabrics, he cannot avoid mentioning Roger van der Weyden's brocades. He is sad if there is not at least one rag around reminiscent of those brocades! Once, really and truly, he kissed a girl with the marzipan-pink flesh of a Geertgen newborn baby, but he would not have been able to kiss that young woman so intensely and for so endlessly long if the renowned academician von B. had not composed a Roger van der Weydenesque brocade for the veil above the canopy of his alcove. Without a Roger van der Weydenesque brocade the fellow simply cannot feel he is a man! Geertgen's marzipan of maidenly flesh and Weydenesque brocades are the only concerns of these beautiful minds, and they have no greater headaches than the aesthetic because those parrots squawk in tasteful cages as if they were reading Miloš Crnjanski's travelogues.

Berlin is therefore not only a city of Roger van der Weydenesque brocades and Geertgen's marzipan love, not only a city of snobs, Egyptian bronzes, and Dürer's graphics, but also of a whale, twenty-three meters long, that was shown to the populace of sansculottes and plebeians as a wonder of nature, on a wooden raft on the Spree River, in front of the imperial palace.

As evening approaches, the lanterns of yellow silk interwoven with gold appliqués are lit, and waiters in fine tailcoats serve lobster, salmon, candied fruit, and Argentinean peaches that proudly bear the name of an Australian prima donna. And in those illuminated rooms an arrogant band of apes sits together, boring each other with orations in the name of an imaginary elite about metropolitan worldviews, opinions on religion, politics, art, science, and life's undying values and truths, as if those authentic aristocrats of the spirit had discovered a unique and redeeming elixir of intellect. Wheezing old men, their skin peeling like mummies' wraps, shortsighted masked ladies with golden lorgnettes, bloated red Falstaffs among a mob of shabby, experienced whores—all of that is the metropolitan victory of European intellect over squalid, plebeian Asia, which drowns in the fetid underground of the big city's trash and gives rise to beings both noxious and dangerous from the perspective of the aesthetic elite, just as rat snouts are toxic for the harmony on moneybags' yachts.

That is Europe, when you stand in galoshes, in your warm impermeable, wrapped in rubber, and watch thousands and thousands of anemic beggars wandering the streets in the sleet, and the water gets into their poor proletarian footwear, and you can virtually feel those feet squelching in wet, torn, filthy rags. The European man stands on the rainy Berlin street, in the February dusk, in that river of peasant carts and automobiles, poor wretches, burglars, and imbeciles, in that torrent of interests and impulses, out in the wind, in the driving snow, amid the sweetish aroma of gasoline, and the bleating of women who ply their trade, and he analyzes the aesthetics of it all, of course. Because what choice do untalented ramblers carried along by the current of the big city have other than to reflect in lyrical prose on the transitory nature of the worlds and civilizations that pour down in the universe like rains from the heavens? That is a kind of pale, Stirneresque solipsism that dissolves the elemental movement in social milieus, cities, and futile civilizations into the raw mechanics of events.

Social relationships are shaken like geological deposits, and lyrical phantoms emerge at big-city street corners, staring into the formic promenade of passersby; they all flow past and vanish, constantly welling up like a mighty river when it roars in the fall, but everything collapses galactically in stellar cascades, and everything will disappear in the boundless cataracts that pound our poor Europe from the plateaus of Mongolia all the way to this soot-grey city. Mighty Asia has spilled beneath its walls, lapping at its bastions like a great flood, and the leaden sky above it stretches all the way to the Himalayas.

Night has fallen, and around the imperial palace and the university library at the forum everything is quiet. Egyptian eagles with golden platters of the sun on their heads sleep now in the museum halls, and the spaces of the Dutch Renaissance fade on murky brown canvases. Uncommonly vivid patterns on Persian carpets, lilies of Murano glass, golden chalices full of wine, silver bowls with fish and lemons cut into slices. Red crabs, snipes, hares, red thighs of venison in the northern half-light of quiet, covered rooms, where curtains are of purple fabric and windows seven-hued and framed with lead. Snobbish Europe, aesthetic aristocracy, madness amid crackbrained reality.

And here is the Asiatic counterpoint: a man from our climes who graduated in the sciences in Antwerp or Amsterdam, a polymath who lives at the height of his time, in garrets and studies crammed with folios and books, one such "northern reformer" of ours, thrown by a whirlwind back to the charnel house of his homeland, "the remains of the remains" (reliquiae reliquiarum), to the Ottoman border, in the Asiatic chaos of the early seventeenth century: What could he do in the Slovenian and Croatian lands between Koprivnica and Križevci, Ljubljana and Brežice, in the reflection of the everlasting fires and the roar of heavy guns?

Oh, our poor Illyrian reformers and enlighteners—the Trubars, Dalmatins, Vlačićs, Lupetinas, and Križanićs! What could they do then, and what can they do now, when machines crush the Balkan peasant shoe and foreign artillery bulldozes farmers' fields, when sequins and shining weapons will rattle just like they did yesterday, and when relations are still so vastly inhuman, barbarous, and non-European? What use are these bronze statues to us when cannons are still the "ultima ratio regum et populorum"?

Mommsen, Humboldt, and Helmholtz sit mute and solemn in the baroque courtyards, snow drizzles down on the marble togas of the great men, and the pale light of the gas lamps spills over their wise, stoney skulls, modeling them in soft, lyrical shadows. Massive chestnut trees drip under the wet snow like the legs of a mastodon, among the cannons and bronze generals of 1871. The silence of night. The black water of the Spree gleams ominously in the canals, trails of light glisten in the turbid mirror of the water, and tram bells and whining motor horns echo from the city center. The asphalt shines there, and a thick cream of slush melts in the torrent of automobile tires; red-green and golden advertisements flow, fiery ellipses whirl, seminude females shiver in the rainy February wind, draped with the fluffy plumes of exotic tropical birds. There are bars, lacquered Chinese boxes of debauchery, with balustrades and tempera nakedness (monkeys on blossoming cherry branches touch naked women in clusters of yellow mimosa), a swirling on the ballroom parquet to the wail of saxophones and bassoons. A pursy northern woman in a tartan skirt dances with an English girl in a purple dress with a white lace front. Drunken fat Hungarian women shriek, blacks yelp, saxophones shrill, drums boom, and all that purple plush, that scarlet, cadaverous patchwork of starched shirtfronts and idiots—all of that hustles and romps to the cannibalistic, sensual whistling of bagpipes that bleat under the armpit of a yellow-green, tubercular young man. The massif of the city center is empty, and from Alt-Berlin beyond the Spree comes the lyrical striking of an ancient clock in a solitary belfry. The windows of empty palaces gape blindly into the blackness. Everything is murky and covered in soot. Laurel wreaths beneath the feet of the Uniter of Germany, snowflakes rustle on the dry leaves and the moiré ribbons of the imperial tricolor. Lions bronzed and stiff, and high above the head of one flutters a black flag. The president of the German Republic, the social democrat Friedrich Ebert, has died, and I am traveling to the Neman River and the Vistula and beyond, to the Kremlin, where the tsarist monuments have been torn down, and in Andreyevsky Hall Mexicans and Chinese declaim in a elevated tone about wages and the eight-hour working day.

CHEERLESS LITHUANIA

With every kilometer you sense more and more of Asia as you travel from Berlin to Eydtkuhnen on the Lithuanian border. The station in Kant's Königsberg in the yellow, sooty morning light is as uninviting as that in Sisak in Croatia. From bordello'd Europe you return to the "Pannonian" zone, like traveling from the southern to the northern Balkans. After clean, covered stations with their names on royal blue porcelain signs, with orchestrions, fire extinguishers, and chocolate, you enter a region of roofless platforms, sooty repair sheds, a snowstorm blowing through the open doors of the coaches, puddles of beer, and the dollar as the only internationally recognized currency. At the stations there are white Polish eagles, a deep, amaranth red on the signs, the jingle of cavalrymen's spurs, greatcoats, Russia leather, boots, policemen, customs officers, borders, the international political situation in the form of provisional wooden sentry boxes, and a martial mood as if you were traveling through one enormous military camp without end: primitive field kitchens, sealed coaches, machine-gun-armed infantry, artillery, horses, more heavy guns. A man making his way from the Balkans to Moscow clears the obstacles like a horse at a steeplechase. The Balkan obstructions, the Austrian Christian-socialist quarantine, Masaryk's barrier, the Ebert-Noske-Stinnes-Weimar border regime, the Polish one with two-headed white eagles and uhlans' pennons, the East Prussian and Lithuanian checkpoints, and finally the Latvian border. The League of Nations has detached the Balkans from Russia with eight rows of barbed wire, and whoever does not believe there is a blockade of the Russian Revolution should start out on a trip to Moscow, that infectious center of the Bolshevik contagion, hemmed in with eight European quarantine zones, and that traveler will have the honor of witnessing them open suitcases eight times and confiscate all suspicious persons, thoughts, books, newspapers, and toilet paper, to stop anyone getting the foolish idea that they could smuggle any stunning, brand new information past the western-European cordon into "Sovdepia": about how the peoples on the Neman River, the Vistula, and the Baltic coast hate each other.

The farther away you go from the home of sleeping cars, rubber, and tinfoil, the more you enter a zone of the strange and the violent, of police-state nationalism, of green faces in need of sleep that yawn tired and wretched, exposed to the blows of fate, which is so stupidly inhumane, without any of the small, decorative lies and daily accessories: without rouge for the lips, without polish for the nails, without eau de cologne and perfume, without cigarettes with a golden cigarette holder, without morning coffee poisoned with the tainted press, without soccer and politics, without suitcases of cheap vulcanized leather, without an article of the latest Parisian fashion, without illustrated color magazines, and without religious and royalist propaganda. In a word, without the many puerile, cheap toys that the bazaar of European civilization uses to deceive its imbecilic, naïve, infantile clientele. In the provincial towns beyond the cordon sanitaire people work hungry out in the muddy fields without ice cream and without coffeehouses, among cows—that whole cattle breeding way of life, like in Čulinec, in foot rags and peasant sandals. After the standardized dummies in central-European textile store windows, which all chew their rolls at exactly eleven o'clock, smoke Batschari or Massary cigarettes, vote for the DNP (Deutschnationale Partei) or SPD (Sozialdemokratische Partei Deutschlands), new fellows from the field appear in the coach with the uncertain gait of suspicious poachers and smugglers, and a mixture of fear and uncertainty speaks from people's eyes instead of dull, Philistine vacuousness. Whereas the average passenger all the way to Königsberg and Eydtkuhnen travels third class in striking uniformity, with the same suitcase of vulcanized paper overflowing with thermos bottles, small silver boxes of chocolates, chats with his partners about the price of various goods or political programs (reproducing the line of their party newspaper like a phonograph), ever farther to the east the coach becomes populated by travelers who at first glance do not live any kind of ordered life, shades that do not move along the track of the same, uniform, conditioned way of life, but still decay in disorganized anguish and futile sighing, Asiatic and primitive. You can see it in everything: these travelers are racked by worries.

After leaving East Prussia at the border in Eydtkuhnen, the train crossed into the Republic of Lietuva near Virbalis. The old Duchy of Lithuania was a country without a capital because its historical center, Báthory's Vilnius, was in the hands of the Poles, it being the birthplace of Marshal Piłsudski, and the capital of Kaunas, an old Russian stronghold on the Neman River, looks more like an improvisation than the capital of a sovereign republic. In today's international concert, Lithuania is a stick of live dynamite under the entire Russian-Polish-German-Lithuanian-Jewish question. Given the unresolved problem of the Polish (Danzig) Corridor and the German-Polish Zone around the Vistula, the whole raison d'être of the Republic of Lithuania consists in it being a new quarantine zone in a system of buffer states, policed and guarded by supernumeraries of the Treaty of Versailles, in the famous British greatcoats of colonial khaki, that infernal outfit, in which Europe set out on the last stage of its historical path. Sad Lithuania, with its ruined cottages, carbonized hamlets, and fields between the scattered coppices reminds us in many ways of our dear homeland Croatia. Seven political dailies are published in Kaunas, and while agrarians and barons dominate the parliament, all of Lithuania left and right of the railroad track is furrowed with trenches, because several years previously the Lord of armies, in His great wisdom, decided to turn this ill-fated farmer's patch into one of Europe's battlefields.

Why the Old Butcher chose precisely poor Lithuania for a rendezvous of His champions and armies is hard to say, but, like our homeland, Lithuania too is proud of having been an outpost of Western civilization for centuries. From Buda to Kaunas, the semiliterate press barks absurdities about the "historical mission of these peoples," and in reality that mission appears as squalor and backwardness, illiteracy, and political violence. The mood of Kolomyia and Rozhnyatov takes hold of this man who saw war in Galicia: the graves of fallen heroes, with rotten crosses on which fat ravens caw, windmills, and a dirty curtain of light over a bleak and hungry plain—all of that is tiring in its monotony and causes anxiety. Putrid, yellowish clay, melting rags of snow, birches, turbid spills of water and distant forests, peasants with wind-reddened cheeks, who graze together with their cows, spitting and grumbling with pipe in mouth, the forlorn sorrow of a misty day, when the coaches steam oppressively like malodorous bathrooms—seeing this Lithuania just makes you want to die.

Sitting next to me on this train was a pregnant young woman with puffy cheeks and swollen, sensual lips. She clenched her fingers nervously, folding them over her knees, and that agitation and friction, and the flow of blood to her fingertips, made her nails seem even dirtier than they already were. Her nervous, perspiring hand searched for something in her muff. She wiped her face with a crumpled, grimy handkerchief, rubbed her eyes with her thumb knuckles, gave a deep and pained sigh, and leaned her head against the dirty, greenish glass of the coach's old-fashioned window, whose frame had been daubed with reddish-brown oil paint that still stank of fresh turpentine. It was a third-class coach of a Russian local train. Telephone poles traveled slowly by, meadows, plowed fields, dilapidated shanties in the distance, from which wet smoke rose but then sank to writhe along a muddy sideroad. The woman leaned her head wearily on the dirty glass, her gaze roaming forlornly after a murder of crows, and her eyes were red from tears. Her worn out and rancid traditional jacket, pulled in at the waist, was conspicuously trimmed with a shabby collar of tattered ginger catfur, and her muff was molting and dropping whole tufts of hair onto her skirt, which showed the rounded outlines of her womanly thigh. A wet green feather on the brim of her hat kept falling down into her face, with unfailing persistence, and from time to time, in the rhythm of the shaking train, she mechanically brushed it away, righted it, and tightened the knot in her abundant hair held together by a shining false diamond. Vis-à-vis, bent at the waist, huddled a sandy-haired man, some thirty years older than his partner, wearing a threadbare derby, worn-out galoshes, and a dilapidated, once elegant fur coat; he was propping himself up with his right forearm on his right knee and explaining some private matter to the young woman with a lively gesticulation of his fingers. The man's voice fluttered nervously. His bristly, red handlebar moustache moved about above his upper lip like a living thing as the words crawled from his mouth, as slimy as caterpillars. He spoke quietly, and that whisper revealed a tone of sweet, concealed lasciviousness and the false assurance that things were really not as they seemed.

Evidently the jerk was consoling and deceiving the young woman with flagrant lies, and she chewed chocolate and listened distrustfully to his sweet whisperings as her dreamy gaze wandered to the clouds over the distant forest. The man and woman were speaking Russian, and to all appearances it was about worries brought on by the new little Lithuanian, who had announced his coming but was not arriving under the happiest of circumstances (or so it seemed).

The man in the derby talked, talked, and talked, and, searching for new chocolate candies in the pockets of his coat, obsequiously peeled off the foil and handed them to his Dulcinea, who absent mindedly ate that smeary mixture of hazelnut and cocoa, sighed, cried, adjusted her broken feather, licked her lips, looked for something nervously in her muff, wiped her face with her handkerchief, and swallowed her tears. It was clear that she was in a predicament and did not believe much of what the old codger was babbling to her mellifluously and seductively about, and, which again, was so transparently cheap and stupid.

They were Russian émigrés, as it turned out later: he a former colonel in Petlyura's army, and she a tsarist general's daughter. He was a married man with five children, and she had been just eleven when the Revolution broke out, and so on, and so forth.

Some traders from Riga were chattering next to us, beside a respectable and rather fat Lithuanian lady with endless supplies of victuals, and a gentleman, who introduced himself as a "grease manufacturer and wholesale dealer in oil for icon lamps." The lady peeled oranges and hard-boiled eggs, cut a rich chocolate cake and pieces of ham, while Mr. Grease Manufacturer (a Russian émigré in a caftan) thundered against the Bolsheviks. Actually, he was not a grease manufacturer but a musician and composer by his own inner calling and talent. He only became a manufacturer of lubricants in emigration out of necessity. But he yearned for music, and from that longing he would finally die, without being able to attain his ideal. And who was to blame? Bolshevism.

"What kind of musician are you then?" asked a Lithuanian student, who was returning home from Germany on vacation.

"A clarinet virtuoso. I was the conductor of an army balalaika band in Kazan during Kolchak's advance toward the Volga. Then the Reds took me against my will and I conducted the very same band at the military music contest in the Bolshoi Theater in Moscow. But I couldn't stand the tyranny. You can't live a human life over there! Now I work well and have my own factory with twenty-seven workers. I'm the state purveyor of lubricants for the Railroads of the Republic of Lithuania." (When we arrived in Šiauliai, he would show us his factory, right next to the station.)

"You're from Serbia, aren't you, Sir?" the grease manufacturer asked yours truly, turning a servile smile toward me. As if he meant to say: It takes all sorts to make a world. And if someone was traveling with a regular Serbian passport he must be an orderly man, so it was innocuous to exchange opinions on politics and various other current questions with such a person. (Traveling all day long in the same coach, the innumerable passport checks meant that the other passengers knew who you were and where you were heading, because the passports were inspected collectively.)

"Yes, from Serbia!"

"Where exactly is Serbia?"

"On the Adriatic Sea."

"Ah yes, lovely. (You could tell he had no idea where the Adriatic was.) Serbia is an Orthodox country, isn't it?"

"Yes, it is."

"If it's Orthodox, there must be icons in Serbia."

"Oh yes, there are icons—plenty. When was ever there an Orthodox country without icons?"

"But do you have oil for the icons?"

"Yes, we do. Why wouldn't we have oil for the icons? Why do you ask?"

"I have one or two railroad tankers of first-class oil for icons, and that oil could potentially be transported to Serbia. What do you think? That's a nifty idea... Your Serbia is somewhere near Hungary, right? I have a relative in Pest, on my late mother's side—an uncle, I guess, although he was her half-brother. Hungary isn't far away either, just on the other side of Poland, yes? Two tankers of first-class oil at the current price in Riga? Done! Well, shall we do business?"

"Why not transport your oil to Russia? Russia is also an Orthodox country, and much closer than Serbia."

"The Jews are in power in Russia today and there's no Orthodoxy anymore," the supplier of lubricants for the State Railroads of the Republic of Lithuania replied curtly and gloomily.

"You're traveling to Moscow, right?" came a voice from the other side of the coach, and everything suggested that the question was directed at me.

"Yes, to Moscow."

"Now I see why you washed your hands with eau de cologne, ha ha ha!"

"What do you mean?"

"You know very well what I mean! I mean it exactly as I mean it."

The stranger accentuated those last words loudly and nervously, and then he headed toward me. He was manifestly a psychopath, of unusually tall stature, dark complexion, in a black blazer, with a thin black tie done up sloppily, in the shape of a flattened figure eight, the knots dangling in front of his worn-out shirt. The man stood out with his height and dark, gleaming eyes, which bore pastel-blue, wrinkled eyelids that gave him the look of a strange, sick bird. Nervously and wheezingly, he blew out smoke through his rotten black teeth, removed his pince-nez, and, without removing his uncommonly dirty, greasy glove, wiped his eyes, as if he was afflicted with conjunctivitis or a trachoma.

Everything got into an enigmatic tangle at that point. Ten or fifteen minutes earlier I had indeed washed my hands with eau de cologne, because there was no water in the coach's washroom. So just then I could not comprehend what that madman wanted to say.

"Sorry, what's your point?"

"We know very well who we have here. Blood flows over there in rivers, and here you are washing your hands in eau de cologne. You must be doing very well for yourself!"

"What blood? What are you talking about?" I defended myself from the gangly fellow with my arm and realized there was going to be a fight.

"Ugh, shame on you! Here you wash your hands in eau de cologne, while over there blood flows! Ugh! You should be ashamed of yourself! Down with the Jews! Jews out!"

He spat hysterically and provocatively. I wanted to punch him in his pince-nez, and in our tussle we bumped the Russian ex-colonel in his old derby, who was in intimate dialog with the young pregnant woman. Interrupted while dealing with his private problem, and now irritated, he jumped to his feet and started to shout.

"You've taken everything from us, you've robbed us, and now you're even provoking us! Go back to where you came from or I'll kill you! I'll kill you like a dog! Get you gone, do you hear me, you Jewish cur!"

"Shame on you!" the hysterical fellow with the pince-nez spat, and a tumult filled the coach. The fat lady shouted incoherently with her mouth full, her teeth all yellow from yolk, and that thick golden mash distorted her big face into a carnival grimace of an apparition that muttered, as if she was deaf and dumb. Mr. Grease Manufacturer, i.e. the purveyor of oil for Orthodox icons, looked as darkly as a black cloud, and lightning flashed in the eyes of the unhappy young woman with the collar of old ginger cat fur, once so endearing in her sadness, and now with a gaze full of hatred, as if I personally were to blame for her pregnancy and for her not being the wife of a tsarist cavalry colonel—her, a general's daughter and former lady of the court. As if I were to blame for the misfortune of the untalented balalaika guy, who today sells his lubricant to Lithuania, and for the schizoid madman in his derby, who had lost his mind and was no longer drilling boys in Greek irregular verbs. I found myself surrounded by a mass of shady characters ready for any kind of madness, since it had turned out that I personally was the cause of their predicaments.

Just when an ugly scene seemed inescapable, help came unexpectedly from a young, confident Lithuanian railroader. Pushing his way into the thick of things he started talking to the people in Lithuanian, and so, word after word, I was able to extricate myself from the mêlée like a coward and disappear into the next coach, where a fire flickered in a tall cast-iron stove and coal fumes pervaded the space.

It had been a clear case of all against one. Both the psychopath, a Greek and Latin teacher from Tartu, and Petlyura's colonel, and the balalaika guy from Šiauliai, and the fat lady from Riga—all of them corresponded to our own Balkan psychopaths, teachers, soda manufacturers, tamburitza players, and corpulent ladies, that whole, democratic Philistine company that is unable to tell cause from effect. My second, the Lithuanian railroader, explained to me later that the mad, hysterical school teacher, an émigré good-for-nothing, was a police agent provocateur, whose task—or even his profession—was to provoke scenes on the trains.

"So you're traveling to the Union?" It was the first time I had heard the word "Union" from a living person. The Union of Soviet Socialist Republics. The USSR. It really sounded very good. Full of pathos, in fact.

"Yes, to the Union!"

"I served in the Red Army. I'm Lithuanian and was a gunner in the tsarist army in Galicia in 1917, on the Russian front. All of us became Red there! I came back to Lithuania three years ago. I have a wife and two children."

The Lithuanian Red Army railroader went on to tell me about Lithuania and its parliament, where socialism was represented by four social democrats, who did not count for very much. "It won't last long. The country is being bankrolled by the British, and sooner or later it will join the Union."

Twilight spread its wings over Lithuania. Countless graves of fallen heroes, lines and lines of trenches across the fields, here and there the occasional fortified artillery position, and grey clouds from which snow started to scintillate. Villagers alighted slowly and clumsily at the stations with bags, sacks, and canvas bundles, and at one fairly large station, illuminated by acetylene lights, there stood a company of infantry—a welcoming party with a band. Customs officers, mounted gendarmes with huge, heavy, clanging cavalry sabers, young ladies on the station's promenade, and a general who arrived with our train and was welcomed by the infantry company with a small black pony and a large drum on its left-hand side. A command rang out in Lithuanian, the Lithuanian national anthem was played to the beating of the drum, and the general with gold braid and red trousers inspected the line of the honor guard. The train set off slowly, and for a long while the reverberations of the helicon could still be heard in the dwindling light, like a death march under a grey sky full of ravens. Oil lamps were lit in the coaches and burned with a trembling light, their wicks smoking like wet cigars.

Riga! Jews in black caftans stroked their curly beards; legendary Russian muzhiks sipped and grumbled as they dried their damp peasant rags in the warm reek; and a shortsighted, humble woman, quiet and cowering like a wet chicken, lit a candle at the window and browsed the black-edged booklet *Prussianism and Socialism* by Oswald Spengler.

A schoolteacher, yes. An ethnic German who had become interested in Spengler when he held a lecture in the city the previous year on invitation of the Courlandic German Bund. "But everyone was disappointed with the gentleman," she would say. "He is a boring, elderly professor with illusions of grandeur, who earned a pretty fee with his lecture. The Courlandic German Bund had to pay for his trip in a sleeping car, first class, all the way from Munich to Riga and back, and on top of that even the door receipts, and then he came, read from his papers for half an hour, and at the banquet did not speak a single word with anyone the whole evening. A disagreeable, opinionated fool!"

IN THE SLEEPING CAR FROM
RIGA TO MOSCOW

Riga shimmered like the illuminated stage of a cheerful romantic opera with its play of greenish lights, with the mighty girders of its bridges—black galleons—and its tall Courlandic four-story buildings. Snow was falling. The bells of sledges, streetlights wrapped in cotton wool, the laughter of passersby, the snowball fights of children, the calls of the coachmen, the whistle and screech of engines beneath the glazed roof of Baltic Station, ladies with old-fashioned pelts over their shoulders, in fur hats, like portraits on Postimpressionist paintings, Russian porters in white aprons, the call of Russian engines like the horn of a ship lifting anchor, the bright medley of lights, the thronging travelers—all of that flowed together boisterously like a fairground scherzo from a bona fide Stravinsky ballet.

The Moscow train was ready and waiting at Moscow Station, heated and brightly lit, with liveried conductors busily putting fresh linen on the beds in the *wagons-lits* compartments. Russian sleeping cars are wider and more comfortable than international ones: here they serve tea, there is hot running water in the washrooms so all the passengers can "rinse off the spilt blood," and thick puffs of steam blow out from under the wheels, reducing the coefficient of fear before the incertitudes of the cold Russian night. In a word, these Russian coaches stood before us at the beginning of the journey at the station in Riga like a promise full of illusions after my negative Lithuanian and Latvian experiences. The conductor of the coach, in a black Russian overshirt, assured us that a Russian dining car would be hitched to the train the next day in Zilupe on the Russian-Latvian border, and at the same time he explained to an Englishman the difference between a "lit" and a "lat." A "lit" is the Lithuanian currency and a "lat" is Latvian. Riga is the capital of the Republic of Latvia, and a lat is a little more valuable than a lit, but neither of them is worth very much.

The Kingdom of Serbs, Croats, and Slovenes had not deigned to recognize Lithuania or Latvia, so I had to pay the Republic of Latvia around 800 dinars for a transit visa, with no right to sojourn. Tired from the trip and a sleepless night, yet curious to see the city Richard Wagner fled from because of his debts, I went to see the head of the station police to get permission for a twenty-four hour stay. There, on the Baltic coast, I had the honor of convincing myself once more that policemen's brains are disinclined to make even the slightest concessions. Was this some damn international rule? The Nordic giant sitting before me, a Mr. Lotiš, like Wallenstein's blustering Bramarbas in the Thirty Years' War, gnawed on a goose leg and explained to me in a mash of Latvian and Russian that I was asking the impossible and my request was ridiculous. Unable to reach an agreement with this gentleman, I resigned completely.

My argument was that the esteemed Republic of Latvia could at least take me in on a stormy, snowy night, after having so amiably made me pay 800 dinars. The counterargument from that big boor of a police officer was that the rulebook laid down clearly and logically what was allowed and what wasn't; therefore he could not sign anything he had no right to. I must never forget how I was plagued that whole evening by wondering why each and every police station stinks not only of that mentality but also of human substance; I also wondered why all the world's police forces, since they watch over the moral and bodily integrity of their citizens, have not created bright and clean institutions, a kind of modern Prytaneion in accord with the ideals of their calling. That police intermezzo thoroughly spoiled my mood—a cheerfully intoned, snowy overture—and I dreamed all night of an imaginary city in the springtime where almond trees flowered and golden weathercocks creaked on the rooftops by the gleaming silver sea, while here I was being chased by black hunchbacks; they were hot on my heels, and I dreaded the touch of their fiendish claws.

The ensemble in our coach was a colorful company made up of characters from all latitudes of our little globe.

By far the most elegant personality among the passengers was a Persian minister—a man of dark brown complexion, with a distinguished Oriental air—who also had his entourage with him: two ladies and a fourteen-year-old boy, who proudly sported his grey bowler hat. The minister's bodyguard-cum-servant, a colossus who could almost have been from the Balkans, served tea to him, the young master and the ladies, made coffee, shaved the minister, translated his orders, and generally acted as an intermediary between His Eminence and the vulgar plebeian rabble, i.e. almost everyone else.

The compartment next to the Persian minister, who inhabited two singles with his son and the ladies like a kind of open apartment, was occupied by Mr. Eierstangler, an industrial magnate and silk manufacturer from Shanghai, and his wife. Mr. Eierstangler was returning from Berlin to Shanghai on the Trans-Baikal line with his secretary and wife after a three-month stay in Europe. Madam Eierstangler, with slanting Mongolian eyes and an endless mass of toiletries and gadgets (nécessaires, vials and bottles, pads and pillows, rubber hot-water bottles, slippers, kimonos in a range of colors, etc.), was a boring and pampered lady, most literally, who spent days on end lethargically leafing through an Ullstein illustrated magazine; and then there was Mr. Secretary, a nondescript lackey, with a finely twirled moustache like a hussar. He traveled in the next, "hard-class" coach (third-class) and therefore did not show up very much, evidently happy that his master was not paying him much attention. The Eierstanglers drank their own German mineral water, disinfected the water for washing, used Lysol, carbolic soap and alcohol, and searched all day for bedbugs, although, as if to spite them, not one critter dared to show a leg; the Eierstanglers had a real and terrible fear of typhus, dysentery, and scabies; they nibbled hygienically packed cookies, washed their hands in their own private rubber basin, and peeled and ate apples all day as an aid to digestion. To my subjective amusement, these rich hypochondriacs played the phonograph all day, being experienced travelers skilled at killing time—and to think what gargantuan expanses still gaped before them, all the way to Manchuria! But they traveled in style in this "express," and it was obviously not the first time they had laid solitaire, tra-la-la'd tedious German couplets, made their own lemonades and anxiously wrapped themselves in shawls, looking after themselves nervously and frenetically, as if they had been through some ordeal.

I shared the neighboring compartment with a Russian NEPman* On the opposite side, in a single, there moaned and

---

* A NEPman is a beneficiary of the "New Economic Policy" of 1921; the term has more or less the same meaning as grafter, conman, smuggler, and contrabandist. The word has become international because I even heard the expression "Neplokal" being used in Berlin to refer to the clubs of war profiteers and currency smugglers.

wheezed an old hypochondriac: an asthmatic who suffered from paralysis, tuberculosis, and generally ruined health. He was returning to China to die after spending a year at a German sanatorium. He too had made his fortune in the fabled Orient; he was a German by origin and had done business in China for thirty years; now he snored and wheezed loudly the whole journey long, as if he was breathing through a tube. He rummaged through his luggage, searching for little bottles of poisonous medicines, swallowed dynamite and nitroglycerine, groaned all night in the corridor, struggled to open the double-sealed windows and basically behaved like one of those very dear and likeable traveling companions we don't forget in a hurry, not only because of our manifest lack of Samaritan love for our fellow man, but also due to a certain cannibalistic logic: Why is this living corpse hanging around and riding the trains when he's a certain candidate for death—as if he were going to live forever—when he has every chance of being thrown out of the train like an old sack this side of Tobolsk?

As well as two or three Russians and a German aeronaut heading to Chita, the passengers in that coach included an Armenian jeweler from Salonika, a man in black silk pajamas with an attractive French actress (returning from Paris), two English commercial travelers, and four German workers' delegates on their way to the Plenum of the International in Moscow. One member of their delegation had been taken off the train by the German border police back in Eydtkuhnen and another was arrested in Riga. All four of them were big-boned, manly figures—delegates from the Ruhr miners and the Hamburg dockers; likeable, self-educated Party men, calm and austere, with the skill of logical argumentation, intelligent views on the international situation, and the fantastic naïvety of the first revolutionary generation, which had next to no appreciation of the gulf between political plans and their realization.

When we crossed from Latvia into Russia and stopped at the border post in Sebezh, the situation in our coach changed somewhat. The border police detained His Eminence, the Persian minister, and his entourage, which caused alarm in our audience of millionaires. On his own initiative, Mr. Eierstangler threw a copy of the *Berliner Tagblatt* out of the coach, followed by a copy of the *Rigasche Rundschau* (a German daily that has been published in Riga for fifty-six years), lest the operatives of the State Political Administration (GPU) find him in possession of that counterrevolutionary mouthpiece.

Mr. Eierstangler's nervous gesture was altogether superfluous because there was nothing in that rubbishy paper that could have made him feel the need to conceal his political compass. But he renounced his orientation within a minute of crossing into hell, just like Peter renounced Christ in Caiaphas's peristyle. And when a rooster suddenly crowed in a henhouse somewhere in Sebezh, I couldn't suppress an ironic smile at the expense of this low-life traveling companion. The Hamburg workers' delegates, who had been treated as politically suspicious and made to get out at every station along the way to be searched, were relieved and delighted to see a young Red Army guard standing beneath the windows of our coach and looking on good-naturedly as the European travelers and foreigners threw newspapers out the windows to rid themselves of compromising political ballast. Madam Eierstangler, with the lackluster aloofness of an unfriendly Siamese cat, now smiled benignly at the Hamburg delegates in a bid to strike up a conversation with them on various topics; she became very amiable, even intrusive, although mixing with the common riffraff had been furthest from her mind on the journey to Riga whenever she had had to pass through the plebeian coaches like a vision from Hades. Madam Eierstangler offered her "dear and engaging compatriots" English luxury cigarettes ("Le Khédive," from Egypt) and spoke to them about solidarity among travelers, who were linked by destiny on such a long journey; she declared herself a companionable and congenial lady—did I hear right?—and took a most avid interest in the life of Hamburg's waterfront workers and the concerns of their union, which she sincerely hoped they would resolve to their utmost satisfaction in Moscow.

"The impoverished waterfront workers in China do not enjoy any union protection, unfortunately," she lamented, "and that's entirely the blame of the British, of course, who have compromised the mission of the white man in the Far East so completely and utterly."

The jeweler, a Turkish Armenian from Salonika, explained that he was a native of Georgia and sympathized with the Party, and in fact he had been a kind of émigré since 1905. The Communists sent an incredible 10,000 Ford motor tractors to Georgia every year—things had really taken off there, by all accounts, and could no longer be stopped. He portrayed Georgia in such a rosy light that I felt an urge to see that promised land, which, as Karl Kautsky deplored, had once groaned under the Russian yoke.

"I was in Odessa last spring when an American cargo ship arrived to unload Ford tractors," said the jeweler. "And you know what? When I saw all those vehicles stacked at the quay, I couldn't restrain myself. I cried. Just think: 10,000 tractors for this poor people, which until now has only known the scourge of tsarism. And now they have steam ploughs and schools! Oh, my good Lord!"

The pretty Parisian actress suddenly produced a porcelain puff box with a blue ribbon painted on the lid, and this narrow band encircling a hammer and sickle bore the stylized words: "Proletarians of all countries, unite!" Madam Eierstangler took an extraordinary liking to that puff box, especially to the decorative inscription on the top, and the lively blue made the slogan seem to float above the clouds. She took great interest in the possibility of acquiring such a charming object, which just goes to prove that even the most banal political propaganda can be executed tastefully, with artistic refinement.

At the station restaurant in Sebezh, Mr. Eierstangler effused about the great future of the USSR, which was apparent not only to proletarians but equally to all the world's capitalists. "There's no point denying it: one day the Trans-Baikal line will have been brought to the same degree of perfection as the American express train network, and when I can move his wares from Hamburg to Peking in fourteen days, the British Empire, which the sly English chandlers in their puritan deceit call the "Commonwealth," will be forced to close shop."

But all this cheap showmanship to avoid the light of day, so fatally reminiscent of little bugs' attempts to hide from a lamp, was definitely surpassed by the NEPman. My compartment-mate had caught my attention back at the Lithuanian consulate in Berlin. Chubby and rather short, he later arrived at the station in his own limousine wearing a beaver-fur coat and with a classy mistress at his side (also wearing beaver fur); this fellow spread an aura of self-confident, authentic affluence in the waiting room of the Lithuanian legation. The unknown lady accompanied him to the station (Friedrich-Strasse-Bahnhof); and there he was again in the corridor of the international coach last night, in printed silk pajamas with a colorful, foliate Louis Quinze flower pattern. He traveled to Riga in a single, but now he changed to a modest, second-class, two-berth compartment together with me. And there he was with an old man, a bearded Russian porter, talking about conscience and rates of pay and addressing the impoverished fellow in a condescending, would-be "comradely" way, like a noble chatting with one of his serfs back in the days of Tsar Alexander.

"What's your rate of pay?"

"Two lats, your grace."

"But what does your conscience say you should be getting, comrade?"

"It's got nothing to do with conscience, Sir. Two lats is what I get!"

"Your conscience, old boy, should tell you that half a lat is quite enough for you. There, you scoundrel, that's all you're getting. Now sheer off! What do I care about your rate of pay?"

So one "comrade" gave another half a lat, prompted by his "conscience," and then he started lamenting to the conductor of the coach that humanity had lost every moral compass and that the bandits here were out to fleece people at any price. I noticed that he boarded the Moscow-bound train in Riga without his beaver-fur coat and without his first-class suitcases covered with costly deerskin. Since I was in the top bunk, I saw in the mirror that he crossed himself before sleeping. The same actor who said goodbye to his mistress at the station in Berlin with an affectionate, "A bientôt, à tout à l'heure," who changed into a collarless black shirt in Riga and who crossed himself before going to sleep also bought all the Moscow newspapers and journals to see what was new at home because, allegedly, he hadn't been back for six months. He was a specialist in public insurance and had been in the West for advanced training, he said.

"You can't imagine how heart warming it is to be back! How good it is to see 'USSR' on the coaches in Russian. And how spirited the papers are here—there's no other press like it on earth… Just look at *Bezbozhnik* here. Is there a wittier atheist review anywhere in the world, I ask you? It really packs a punch and comes down hard on the NEPmen and other parasites in the

Soviet system. It's good and invigorating, like a tonic or a bracing northerly—it's healthy! Do have a look. And our coaches here: 'USSR,' wonderful, it's enough to make a grown man cry!"

He admired the country's name on the side of the coaches, read Stalin's lead article in *Izvestia* with delight, and acted like an out-and-out enthusiast of the new order, which he served eagerly and energetically, oh yes. Later I found out that my traveling companion was one of the big smooth operators of recent years and that he excelled in marketing Russian products at dumping prices in the West.

All of us met in the dining car and feasted on caviar, fish fillets au gratin on silver platters, game with savory sauces, and puddings. We drank tea and Yessentuki mineral water from the Caucasus, vodka and cognac. We smoked elegant, mild Russian cigarettes and listened to Mayakovsky on the phonograph. These were no longer the bordello songs from Mr. Eierstangler's small portable player, and it was no longer the hullabaloo of a jazz band—this was the authentic Mayakovsky, in the deep baritone of an old-fashioned reciter, from the horn of the old-fashioned phonograph in the dining car; Mayakovsky, who, like Mephisto, scoffs at the bourgeoisie and seems to foresee a better day dawning "for all comrade folks" on this unhappy planet.

Sadness manifests itself in color, smell, and sound, and therefore it simply cannot be reflected by the photographic lens. In addition to optical phenomena, the simultaneity of colors, smells, and sounds is uncommonly important in the sphere of sadness and gives rise to a certain dejected condition, often as salty as tears, bitter, and graphically unrealizable, and is more smell than sound, more color than form, more dream than reality, and more the shadow of an idea than a harshly spoken word. You can take fifty photographs of a particular funeral, but not one of them will reflect the intensity born of the smell of the extinguished candle, the putrid aroma of the corpse beneath the silver-black baldachin, or the echo of the first clod of earth when it bangs on top of the coffin like the final salute to a traveler leaving forever, never to return.

In Zavrtnica or Kanal near Zagreb, for example, many people live in conditions devoid of any comfort, in rotting wooden shanties covered with tar paper and the metal from old buckets, and when I looked at the hundreds and hundreds of photographs documenting this evident and inhuman poverty I often contemplated the secret of a certain "spiritual" sensation of color, smell, and sound, phenomena that are ultimately cosmic, because everything in the universe that appears in a human way does so as sound, color, or smell. The photographic plate captures only a certain quantity of visual details, but colors and smells are elements that model our moods, and those moods are later transfused into a perfect objectivization of those impressions, and thus a indefinite atmosphere arises in us that follows every intense sensation and experience like a shadow. But 300 photographs of the truly horrible housing situation in Zavrtnica or Kanal do not speak such a strong language as the voice of a newborn baby that cries alone in a dark room, in a space saturated with the putrid odor of a miasmic latrine, in a suffocating atmosphere of hopeless languor and the smell of blood and sweat, which slaves have exuded for centuries. The shabby, peeling oil cloths on rickety paupers' tables with chipped old cups and worn-out pots; the newspaper that lines those people's wretched apartments, those dens of damp and filth, the feather quilts, mice, vermin, and rubbish— who can create an image of them without color and smell? Colors and smells are part of life's secrets, and all romantic dreams are tied up with the great mystery of color and smell, and therefore photographic images of existential misfortune are so crushing in their rational negativity, the monotony and dullness of life in minus, and only the contrast with some color or smell opens up prospects in the mind's eye for the possibilities of beauty or horror that exist; thus a dramatic agitation occurs inside us, and we sense something that is already sad and wretched as much sadder and more wretched in the light of mysterious color, sound, or smell.

Of all secrets, smells are the saddest. The smell of an empty room in the early evening, when the objects are overcome by the dark and the hushed voices of passersby come from the street. The smell of tanned leather before the rain that blows in from the distance, from a provincial tannery at the end of the city, a burning tire, the damp wood in a pub—all those smells, like sounds, give rise to images in a man, and an enchanting reverberation of the music of colors, and melancholic and sad music rings in his ears, without which life would be grey, just like all dead objects are grey. Who could express the intensity of dull uniformity awoken in our memories by the smell of a classroom filled with the pungence of tar and parquet oil, a smell that accompanies us from our first days at school until today, when the memory of the dead beauty of childhood is our only remaining consolation?

During our first school days the anthracene ink on the paper of our new blue exercise books smelled mysterious and magical to us, and the smell of the warm, worn-down eraser from the old pencil box merged with the smell of the poor boys in coarse cloth and the clang of tin trays from the public soup kitchen into an indistinct, paltry instrumentalization of suffering and toothache, of long nightly vigils with a flickering memorial candle on the polished surface of an antique cupboard. Later everything smelled of gas lamps, women, and the crises of a young man's hard, dreary existence, roaming the mists that children wander through by the compass of their own noses, like whelps. It is sufficient for a half-open door to creak or a smell of parquet oil to inundate us for the recollections to begin humming in us again like the mournful motifs of a cello, and then infinite vistas open up onto burgeoning circles of hazy images that speak to us through the law of optical illusions of the kaleidoscope of reality, for the colors to burn brightly and astral bells to ring around us, and all that is nothing but a play of light and music, the smoke of a candle that goes out as soon as it has flared up. The parquet oil in the life of a man smells from those bygone days when children's bodies steamed in boots wet from snow, when the incandescent iron stove glowed rosily at the back of the classroom, and the children counted the days until Christmas Eve. In those festive holiday moments in the life of a child, parquet oil smells like a mysterious reminder that life is not a paradisical dream but tedium in sad classrooms, where cruel and inexorable equations with fractions reign together with cabalistic and unintelligible questions from the catechism.

Later, at university, the parquet oil smells like the dull fog between lectures in a stuffy, freshly painted seminar room, where the eye of a friar in the front row follows the speaker like a conditioned dog. A girl student, engrossed with her garter, absentmindedly wanders through God knows what distant landscapes, and a stammerer speaks, speaks, and speaks at the pulpit, while his shadow sways on the white wall, and everything merges in the pungent odor of parquet oil. Eyes smart from the early spring evening, fingers are numb from writing down so many wise sentences, and as the light of the gas lamp buzzes like a blowfly on the flypaper, the old factory of our mind produces our inane intelligence. A student in the back row unwraps his supper, and the skin can be heard coming off the saveloy, the transparent, reddish outer layer of the sausage rustles, and the seasoned meat smells of a poor, frugal student supper.

Endlessly boring, thick novels could be written about the problems of university in our country, infinite historico-cultural material with tables, statistics, and photographs could be amassed, and still nothing is more dismal than the rustling of the skin of a saveloy in the back row, that simple auditory effect, and the carbolized smell of parquet oil. (It is a pitiable country, where parquet floors are not polished but liberally impregnated with carbolized tar, and where they peel saveloys at lectures like famished troopers because, despite the Western-style spiritualization of our life, a saveloy is still a disproportionately stronger argument for hungry students' bellies than any food for thought, than any irregular verb or Ptolemaic hypothesis. All the economic and cultural circumstances of a predominantly rural environment can be discovered through one single, one could even say clandestine, peeling of a saveloy, and thus smells and sounds become symbols for entire emotive periods of our lives.)

No poverty can be expressed without color because color and light are constituents of scarcity, just as they are of abundance. On the beams of the February sun, colors, objects, human voices, movements, and buildings grow as if illuminated by Aladdin's lamp from *One Thousand and One Nights*. Surfaces of sky blue gleam in that moment with a pale green radiance of azure ice, and in the phosphorus illumination of the February afternoon sun, among the rubbish, rags, cans, and fences of a grey outer suburb, amid the wail of barracks' bugles, there comes the voice of an accordion, which becomes a poetic accompaniment of the afternoon's bright, lyrical concert. Windows shine in the ashy-golden light like retorts with a curious deadly elixir bubbling inside. In the somber spaces of human habitation, in those laboratories of poverty that stink of bedbugs and stale tobacco smoke, people spin their sad and fretful lives like spiders and poison themselves with their own smells and the magic lighting. What is the life of man really, if not the sorcery of colors and smells? From the blood-stained little shirt of the newborn baby to the dead matter on the catafalque, waxen, colorless, and cold, man travels through mists of carbolic fumes from elementary school to the asylum, from university to police lockups, where a clerkish twilight reigns, as boring as a line drawn with a ruler and as dull as a paragraph. As a child, man plays in dark and poorly lit pubs, where moisture drips from the vaults and spiders and centipedes crawl, he lives in rooms that smell of disintegrating furniture and oil lamps, walks in sooty cities amid sweetish clouds of horse urine and gasoline, and dies like a tailor's dummy, blackened from simple tallow candles. A sad vicious circle of colors, smells, and sounds!

On a warm afternoon in February, the sunlight plays a spring overture and the fiery bow of February vibrates ever more passionately. Movements and voices grow, and the monotonous accordion, the dull thuds of a soccer ball on the grassy patch between the red factory warehouses, the smell of greasy stoves, acid, and the smoke that has not yet found its escape and hovers around the squalid cottages on the outskirts—all of that turns to a light, lucid mirth. And jam-mouthed children with Prussian-blue,

watercolor eyes, and boring engines with their eternal meow-
ing, and once blank walls covered with naïve drawings—all of
that vibrates with a strange intensity in the sun's honey-golden
illumination.

I stood in front of a paltry second-hand clothing store
in an outer suburb, watching the mysterious play of colors and
sounds; so much sky blue splashed down in the sulfurous illumination of the spring afternoon that even the cheap oxhide shoes
of passersby began to shine, and the celestial blue spilled over
onto the finer leather of some pauper's boots like Chinese lacquer. The whole muddy brown, granite-paved street, washed by
the night's rain, babbled to the songs of the spring waters in the
gutters and canals. A policeman walked past, whistling a couplet
from *The Merry Widow*:

> All the world's in love with love
> And I love you.

And the missed melody of the hit operetta, the police tunic, the
greasy big hands reddened by the sun, and the nightstick—all of
that made a cheerful impression. As a shabby old carriage came
cantering past, a bright, crystal shaft of sun lit up the pair of old
white mares and the drunken driver. Its windows shone in the
light, and the tattered lining on its inside seemed like costly patterned wallpaper the color of pale cappuccino, a soft color like the
finest doeskin leather. A young, smiling lady was riding in it. That
young woman behind the bright glass, against the pale cappuccino lining, her beguiling, cattish smile, her right hand in a glacé
glove on the handle of her parasol, her gold-embroidered hat, an
old can of varnish in the streetside canal full of sunny reflection,
the water in the gutters, and a barber's sign rattling in the gentle
breeze—all those elements of light sang a song of dirty streets,
where hairdresser's signs chime like gongs.

I stood in front of that out-of-the-way clothing store, and
as the sun magically transformed the old carriage you could pal-
pably feel the light wreaking strange wonders with the entire
street, the sky, and the passersby.

For my taste, there is no plague on the world more infernal than second-hand clothing stores and pawnshops. They are

somber, dim places crammed with fabrics of an obscure smell, and there among the black and grey coats (that hang like disfigured corpses) a green gas light weeps, where orthodox Talmudists stalk and mutely record arcane figures in thick green folios of their balance books. The debts of beggars and paupers grow in those haunted tomes, and that wax museum of pale dolls, in cheap beggar's cloth full of holes, where the exiles from the ghetto whisper in hushed voices, dryly, always in dread, those panoramas of grief are home to my indefinite fear from earliest childhood: the fear of the curse of penury and misfortune.

But then with a cheerful rumble of the old horse-drawn carriage, as if Vesna herself, the Goddess of Spring, was riding along the muddy street in a golden straw hat to a rendezvous with pure, poetically naïve inspiration, the paltry clothing store appeared to me as a bright and cheerful apparition. The two blonde men in the shop window, their coarse hempen hair neatly parted, stood so straight in their starched shirts, so well mannered, like two genuine gentlemen, and the lips of the lady in the spring topcoat of vanilla-ice-cream beige, who flirtatiously smiled, escorted by her waxen cavaliers, flamed so charmingly and seductively, her Asta Nielsen hairstyle gleamed with such a sheen, and the boys and girls in navy blue sailor suits were so cheerful that I believed for a moment in the magic of the semblance as I do in reality itself. The movement of the carriage in the sun, the voice of an accordion, the reflection of the blue shine on the shoes of passersby, the young lady in the coach, the warm citrine color of the tailor's mannequins, and the gurgling water—all of that was narcotic, and the monumentally bad taste of those wax dolls shimmering with those pleasures whisked me away into a naïve fervor, such that I forgot the absurdity of the shop window I had hated for years.

That was just a diabolical instant of deception, because the very next moment a huge, thick cloud that seemed to be soaked with blue ink blotted out the sun, and within a second everything tarnished and grew hopelessly grey, like the winter landscapes in Flemish paintings. In the lightdark of the February afternoon, when the cawing of crows brings forebodings of menacing snow, the leaden light of the squalid street spilled and disappeared in the sad winter dullness. Morose people shuffled along the street in worn-out shoes under the weight of worries, their heads bent, ill-fated, without goal or purpose, with empty pockets, irritated like hyenas in a menagerie. In the shop window, comical dummies were exhibited in the full vacuity of their ghostly appearance. That cursed store again emanated the whole poverty of the stingy, anxious, eerily hushed voices from the shop, in the green gas light. The shabby old carriage rumbled lazily over the cobbles, and all the secret beauty was extinguished with the vanishing of the single warm pastel ray of February sun that emerged from behind the clouds and was snuffed out again.

Children are enchanters of smells, colors, and sounds, and they are the masters of discovering those shimmering secrets. Children are ingenious in the spiritualizing of phenomena, and no one can experience the joys of summer, the afternoon light, the musical beauty of the moon beneath crowns of chestnut trees, or a nighttime journey in a train more vividly and joyfully than a child. With their still unsullied sense of space, in the potpourri of colors and smells, children stand before events naïvely, and that original view is so valuable because it amounts to a direct opening of the curtains over the stage that forever appears to us as the secret of our own life. Hardboiled eggs on porcelain, dyed and painted at Easter, those oblong enigmas will never again have the roundness and aromatic radiance that they did in childhood. No ship will have sails as white as the one with which we plied the livingroom floor, and the smells of butter, honey, wine, warm bread, and baked apples with raisins—all those are enchantments that break down into boring, trite haptics in the hands of half-witted adults. Beauty vanishes later in life, it disappears like an illusion, and its potentials seem deceptive because beauty for adults consists of variations that are endlessly long, like a deadly boring organ fugue for humdrum church services, and people can hardly wait for the dreary liturgy of unspeakably boring verse to end. Adults, in their constant boredom, forget that life is a poem, which only reveals itself to the ear that can hear. Everyone mixes colors on the palette of his experiences according to his own personal traits, regardless of whether his mind shows an inclination toward painting or not. It is a great misfortune when minds are fatigued by drill and monotony, when they are tired of such painting and feel that bowing one's head to beauty is beneath the dignity of their solemn civil calling. Children are creators of genius who enjoy beauty in much stronger doses than adults, without the senile need to verbalize the splendor of colors and sounds they perceive, because children enjoy the treasures of beauty so candidly that none of them doubt that that cosmic panorama could one day be gone forever, never to come back. A child just needs a simple smooth surface in order to travel for years on the swirling lines on the cross section of a bright, polished board and to watch the reflections of a lamp that shines on the parquet floor like the reflection of a ship that vanishes into the opaque gloom under the divan. Parallel to their wise parents bogged in idiotic banality, who fight frantically over stubborn and often stupid details of so-called reality (so dreary, hopelessly grey and, in the end, so very poorly paid), children live in the spaces of their childhood like gifted creators. There is no dramaturgist who does not feel the sensations that a child experiences in the lingering dark between two armchairs, behind the drapes of a scarlet canopy or some old red skirt, and no one in their lives reads books with the same intensity as children leafing through old picture books. Children experience colors and sounds with a passion; they masterfully elevate the boom of a single string of the piano in the twilight of a somber room, the smells of fruit and cakes, coffee and spices, to enviable heights of enjoyment, and the attained potential of children's experience of beauty really could make a man embrace the phrase that we live in one of the most wisely constructed of all worlds.

Children are not religious, but they breathe in the smell of churches and their spaces so passionately that not one of the professional employees and supernumeraries of any church can feel the mystery of that place as deeply and intensely as a young boy in a white rochet and red surplice, who kneels with a copper thurible in his hand on the carpet in front of the silver-rimmed antependium on the marble altar. The baroque sculpture with a silver hanging (whose reliefs show kings in ermine and armored knights kneeling before the last of secrets), the smell of ancient dalmatics embroidered with golden lilies, the heavy brocades of the cope, the mystery of faded church banners—children breathe in all that like fish drink water. In churches later in life, a man takes in the moldy and brandy-bibbery smell of beggars, the blind, and epileptics, he looks with a "historico-cultural" eye for any dematerialized movement of the baroque saint on the altar, and he remembers a failed rendezvous in the half-light of the wormholed benches (that smell of the musk of old maidens). But never again will any church become the misty space of a grand cathedral with red and yellow sun-lit rosettes, marble saints and knights, and a solo-soprano of Schubert's "Ave Maria."

Man has forgotten in the course of his life that he enjoys the smell of frankincense, and now he finds that sacristies smell like spittoons filled with sawdust, and churches of beggars' rags, of cabbage, and of the deaf-mute sighs of idiots. Children swim in beauty, smells, and colors like dolphins. In childhood, beauty glitters kaleidoscopically with such intensity as one can imagine eternity shining, or a waterfall singing in the light of the sun. A child lives in a paradisical primeval state of abundance, feeling no stupid need to halt the surge and flow of all these occurrences. Man invented the plow after long famine and suffering, and art is full of the life giving pollen of flowers that have blossomed with such a wealth of colors, sounds, and smells that no vandalistic stupidity can destroy it. Goethe wrote about the optical analysis of colors, without devoting enough attention to the magical coloration of childhood, when a red ball cures us of a toothache or the despair of a rainy afternoon.

When we travel through unfamiliar spaces and cities we feel the sovereign power of colors and smells, and when we enter a city for the first time it makes a difference if it smells of freshly roasted coffee or if we are welcomed by bronze monuments with laurel wreaths and a solemn gesture of blessing from good augurs. It makes a difference at first contact with the new city if our gaze falls on a vagabond or beggar, or on a silver-trumpeted herald announcing the arrival of poets. Those are imprints that remain for a lifetime, and even on our deathbed, in the last spasm of memory, we are sure to hear a city with the joyful ringing of bells, with cheerful people, where they play billiards in brightly lit coffeehouses, while the other will be a boring mass of granite for us, with grey, dirty, dark streets, where little bells rattle on the doors of brandy bars, and dogs sniff and slink along with their tails between their legs amid universal languor and hunger. Melancholy, passion, joie de vivre, and weariness well up from colors

and smells like streams, and, when he travels, a man becomes ine-
briated by those childish secrets as he did long ago, traveling in-
doors from one cupboard to the next, from the divan to the stove.

So it was that my introduction to Moscow turned out to
be sad. The very moment I set foot in Moscow, on the terrace of
Vindavsky Station, in that very first second, the air felt dismal. It
smelled of snow. Crows cawed from the golden onion domes of
a Russian church, and it seemed as if rags had been incinerated
nearby: the air was heavy with the acrid smell of burning cloth.
A lady in black was sitting in front of the station in a convertible
automobile and she seemed to be unusually tall, perhaps because
she was actually standing in the open car; then she sat down, or
rather she let herself slump down on the back seat, wrapped herself nervously in her fur, and shouted at the chauffeur to drive.
Her face was pale, and her voice dark and ungracious. Its particular timbre, so unexpectedly sharp from the mouth of a beautiful
young woman, impressed me, so I was unable to concentrate all
my attention on the lady's stark figure; because now, I remember very clearly in retrospect that I stopped, bewildered by an
unusual new sight. A black-bearded man in a black caftan sat on
a one-horse sleigh with a white coffin on his knees. After seeing
that gravedigger, I was so surprised by that bizarre form of transport that I was torn between the stark lady and the man in black
with the white coffin on his knees. The next instant (or perhaps
at the same time, I can no longer separate things now), I knew
that the pale face of the strange lady in black was the epitome of
sadness, and I already stood spellbound by the symbolism of her
blackness, the color of her voice, and her ominous appearance.
The lady gave a sign to the driver with her black-gloved hand and
the car vanished in a big cloud of gasoline exhaust, leaving me as
if shot through with a vague, gloomy feeling from that demonic
smell of fire and death. That condition could not be called anxiety,
nor was it weariness like after a sleepless night, when people's
faces are green, like those of the drowned.

A smell of burning and a cheerless funeral, more a delicate spiderweb than a strong and distinct sensation of a misty
morning, when this man arrived in the city for the first time; his
consciousness, beset by strong smells and somber colors, closed
like the gills of a fish in muddy water. If there had not been that

enigmatic lady in black, if the sun had shone, if the burned rags had not smoked, if instead of the gravedigger in his caftan with the coffin I had seen girls smiling—an ordinary, most prosaic entry into the city would have become a triumph, just as easily as the shadow of stricken sadness appeared. Like when a jarringly wrong note is played on the guitar, I knew as I watched the blue cloud of fuming exhaust behind the convertible that it would require great mental exertion to overcome the fiendish magic of putrid smells and insipid colors. I sat helplessly in a sleigh, fearing to look to the left or right, so as not to see the beggars, broken windows, stray dogs, and ugly women, and that was not out of superstition but simply from the puerile fear that the first bad impressions of this Moscow morning could mar the personal inspiration that had come to me for years with the notion of this city as a panorama of bright horizons.

My hotel room smelled of burning and carbolic acid. Coarse rugs on a soldier's cot, a bleak, whitewashed room with bare walls—it all looked more like an asylum than a hotel. I was shaking with fever and, as I lay in bed, I frowned at the unfriendly, foreign, bearded man in the black-framed mirror on the wall, who was staring straight back at me. So as not to see that indiscreet foreigner in the mirror (a disagreeable person completely separate from my person), I got up and covered the mirror with a black cape. When I returned to the bed that black cape over the mirror began to trouble me because of the morbid symbolism of the black flag. Only when a dead body lies in a room are mirrors covered with black fabric. The pillowcases stank of pungent disinfectant, and the linen steamed with moisture beneath my sweaty, fever-stricken body. A man burst into the room twice, started to explain something and to bicker, so I got up to lock the door from the inside, but there was no key. On the way back to the bed, a splinter from one of the roughly sawed floorboards bored itself deep into my foot and as I was jabbing around with a needle, trying to get it out and bloodying my foot in the process, a chill shook me as I sat semi-naked in the unheated room, and my teeth chattered from the cold. The walls were icy and my breath fumed with every exhalation, and the whole hysterical atmosphere grew into a heightened delirium, where a man rambles in complete isolation. The little bottle of iodine tincture in my suitcase had leaked and stained my underwear and woolen sweater. The faces of deceased people began appearing to me in the shade of the closet: dead Hungarian cavalry officers were surprised that I had made it to Moscow. The iron pipes of the central heating started to crackle as if hot steam was about to flow along those wise arteries, but the sound disappeared again like an illusion, and icy silence filled the room again.

I lay there in intensive struggle with the unpleasant colors and smells until dusk, completely alone and deeply unhappy. A pale light came from the courtyard, where an electric lamp glowed faintly on a high, tarred post, and spilled intimately over the ceiling, giving the disagreeable room a little of the personal warmth of a human apartment in the early evening. A piano could be heard; the soft, warm, gentle notes of the piano diffused reminiscences of long-past, dead twilights, when you lay half asleep waiting for warm women, and the beating of your heart in your throat was all you could hear.

Finally a man appeared at the door to ask me why I hadn't come down. "A traveler arrives in a hospitable house and shuts himself in, as if he's died..."

I explained all my difficulties to the kind stranger, and in that way everything took on the tone of a lively anecdote, which ended with the welcoming comfort of vodka. The drink warmed me nicely, and so I sat there long in silence, and felt that good and agreeable colors were conquering the infernal. The tin roof of the two-story house on the other side of the courtyard, half-melted rags of snow, wooden fences, a barrel of frozen water—everything was covered in a soft white. That snowy, frozen barrel came from a painting of Brueghel's. It was snowing gently, and I brooded at length about the clean whiteness of the snow, feeling more peace and calm float down into me with every flake. Everything was quiet. In that harmony of colors and sounds, everything gracefully fell back into place.

We begin with Ciceronian pathos: all of Russia entered the Kremlin through the Spassky Gate, with cap in hand. The whole pageantry of the empire was connected with that Gate, and a ukase of the tsar demanded that every person entering it had to remove his hat and bow down before God and the tsar, both of whom kept court in this great Russian citadel for centuries. This seemed so absurd 150 years ago to Edward Daniel Clarke, an English traveler, that he passed through the Spassky Gate without taking off his hat—he was given short shrift and beaten bloody. Gallows stood in front of the Spassky Gate, and death penalties were carried out here in the name of the tsar; deacons and holy fathers traded the relics of saints here in the sixteenth century, and after a victorious war the tsars would enter their glorious capital city through the gate, as triumphant heroes. Processions of pilgrims from all parts of Russia converged on the Kremlin; the Impostor, Boris Godunov, Ivan the Terrible, and Napoleon all distinguished themselves on this stage, but today all that Ciceronian historical pathos has evaporated, so not even the tourist guide for foreigners speaks of the Kremlin in such theatrical language. Today everyone enters the Kremlin like Clarke did 150 years ago, with his head covered as the red flag of the Antichrist flutters from the Senate's dome. No icon lamps flicker today in front of the Novgorod icon of Christ Pantocrator or the Blagoveshchensk Mother of God, and here, if anywhere in the world, the Old Butcher lost one of his historical bastions with the fall of the Kremlin in 1917, as General Stessel had lost Port Arthur in 1905.

From Peter the Great's time to the October Revolution, seen from a Saint Petersburg perspective when the Romanovs had long forgotten that they were originally Muscovites, the Kremlin was but a distant mirage somewhere in the Russian provinces, having faded to a symbolic phrase in high school compositions and an element in Pan-Slavic toasts. "A big village"—that is how one spoke derisively of Moscow when the fate of the European world was made at tsarist balls in Petrograd. People would travel from Empire-style Saint Petersburg to the distant boyars' past to see the Tsar Cannon and Tsar Bell, and they returned from dusty Moscow glad to see the granite of Nevsky Prospect again; no cow bells chime as the animals head back from their watering places at the Moscow River, in the center of the city around Arbat, where Tolstoy lived in a little old wooden house surrounded by a fence, like in a provincial town. Today the Kremlin is the center of the USSR, and the magic formula of the "Third and last Rome" still haunts the Western anti-Bolshevik press like a newly arisen specter.

The Kremlin remains a symbol of the last five centuries of Russian history, and its curious beauty and distinctiveness are so proverbial that it can scarcely be described without waxing verbose and lyrical. The dark red, baked massifs of brick, typically fifteenth century, the golden Byzantine domes behind the Florentine fortification wall, the long galleries, and the rectangular, octagonal, and oval towers (each a work of architecture in its own right), golden weather vanes and towers, the contours of heavy walls with the gracility of the golden onion domes—all of that is a musical motif, partly sweet like a Tchaikovsky minuet and partly dramatic like a severed dog's head, that symbolic trophy of Ivan the Terrible, when remorsefully, in a monk's habit, with a dog's head like a medal on his breast, he proclaimed to the Russian people upon his triumphant return to Moscow that he had taken Kazan from the Mongols.

When seen for the first time from any angle, from the Moscow River or Red Square, the Kremlin resounds like the call of a trumpet, and one's gaze flits like a wind-borne bird from weathercock to weather vane, when the golden cupolas ring in the serene sky like verses from a legend that generations of Slavs have dreamed of for centuries. The contrast of gilded Byzantine domes with rustic fortification buttresses, the green of heavy, old Russian, Godunov-style hats covering individual towers (so ominously reminiscent of the primitive wooden towers dating back to the Rurik dynasty), all those winding lines and the ensemble of stone polygons, apple-topped bell towers and triangular facades, eaves and swallow-tailed merlons on the tops, dark, rainwashed ranges of bloodred brick—all of that flocks and spreads in the eyes of man like a cloud in the evening west. A wealth of gold, color, and boundless architectural passion! With its faded old Russian frescoes in the style of those in the Kiev Monastery, its haloed saints and angels, and the ingenious architectonics of the dominant theme, principally horizontal, which does not aspire to heights, nestling up against the Moscow River as if it had no intention of taking flight, the main inspiration of the architects was evidently Italian, although it still shines and the flickers as something Russian. That citadel of the Lord has today ceased to be a tsarist headquarters; it is no longer a tomb but a beacon. If the happy formula that connects dead antiquity with the bright illusions of distant future days has been discovered, then the Kremlin is precisely such a masterpiece that remains a unique architectural and political monument in history. The Gothic pyramidal spires on the Doric columns, the flat shells and rosettes as delicate as spiderwebs, crafted with the refinement of a virtuoso, the figures of Byzantine saints and ascetics, the gold-framed icons, the rich ornamentation of the sumptuous Gothic that spilled over into the Renaissance, the stone eagles and tsarinas, apostles, bears and birds, bells in belfries, and the Russian folk textile patterns on the moist arches of the portals so low that one has to walk through them with one's head bowed, as etiquette once dictated—all of that sings melodiously and richly, like the thirty-five Dutch bells in the Spassky Tower, as if everything in this world was ephemeral except for the poetic gift of man. If any architect was ever a poet, it was Aristotele Fioravanti.

In the rain and grey afternoon light, with cackling jackdaws over the lightning rods, with muddy, worn-out swards by the walls, with the smoky and melancholic backdrop of Moscow and its own massive iron-bound gates, the Kremlin can seem as gloomy as a real fortress. The large space of Red Square, which Silvije Kranjčević sang of so passionately after the Revolution of 1905–06, full of melting snow, crisscrossed by the tracks of automobile tires, the smell of fish, tar, and Russia leather from the department stores in Kitay-gorod, with sentries that pace monotonously atop the walls—all of that stands timelessly, as a symbol of centuries-old perspectives.

Groups of Easterners in colorful Persian and Bukharan gowns in front of Lenin's Mausoleum, a company of boys with red flags and drums, unsettled masses of passersby, axles creaking under the weight of wares—all of that is in motion and drones like at a fairground. A squadron of cavalry rides past, cars and trucks howl, barrels of salted fish are unloaded, vegetables, lamp oil, second-hand goods, and books are sold, and a moron waves a bottle as he bellows at the top of his lungs to an inquisitive crowd: a wonder of the twentieth century, here in the bottle of the seaman.

Riga and Avignon, the Torre Rotonda in Milan and the Ponte degli Scaligeri in Verona stand proudly like tombstones of old glory, also in the Italian rouge of burnt brick and with swallow-tailed merlons on the tops, but the Kremlin is the only Renaissance-style fortification today where flags still flutter and cannons point menacingly from the walls, in whose foundations are immured the skulls of 500 revolutionaries who fell in battles where heads still roll today.

At night, the Kremlin with its mighty red walls and towers radiates like the scenery in a fantastic Russian ballet with Bakst's decorations. The view from Prague Castle or Buda is reminiscent of Belgrade's Kalemegdan, and while the view from Prague Castle is intimate and sentimental like Smetana's *My Homeland*, and that from Belgrade does not reach to Zagreb, the view from the Kremlin's walls out to the wide, glistening Zamoskvorechye area beyond the river, in the quivering light of the green lamps, with the distant chiming of clocks on the plain—that view remains open, as Russian space itself is open. From the Kremlin's bell towers you can see to Vladivostok in one direction and to the Amazon River in the other.

Large glass quadrants of milky white shine in the black floods of the Moscow River near quayside factories. Their dynamotors hum, and ice floes pass through the illuminated squares of reflection and slip by into the blackness. The ice is breaking on Moscow River, spring is coming! A tram's lyre glides over the flat arches of the bridges, showering sparks, and the walls of the Kremlin's buildings are painted white and the golden cupolas gleam metallically. Blood red lamps on the southern rampart light up the sentry whose shadows pace mutely up and down, like Horatio's escort at Elsinore, when the spirit of the dead Danish king was meant to appear. The flush of the red flag flutters over the Senate's tower in the darkness; the red fabric illuminated by a powerful spotlight blazes like a flame, and that producer's trick dominates the entire fortification complex, all the Kremlin's eighteen towers, all the domes and bell towers, and the whole of Moscow like a beacon.

Below Saint Basil's Cathedral a nondescript dwelling is lit up—a very improvised shanty. Bearded men are drinking tea in that hovel and gesticulating animatedly. A young blonde woman gets up, opens the door, and tips a basin of water out onto the street. Silence. A train can be heard in the distance. A small dog gnaws at a bone beside me in the darkness. The Spassky Gate strikes a quarter past midnight, in two double octaves, and those thirty-two reverberations hum out over the palaces of Kitay-gorod, where churches with old Kazan icons stand near old boyars' houses, bright green and red like market stalls, all the way to Basmannaya Street on the one side and Tverskaya on the other.

At night, the monumentally simple, modestly whitewashed walls of the Assumption Cathedral, with the Cathedral of the Annunciation as the backdrop on the left and the Cathedral of the Archangel on the right, are a stage created for solemn performances and tsarist ceremonies. Clouds of frankincense once smoked here, and as the Kremlin's bells thundered like cannons, the regally vested tsar descended the stairway on the left of the scenery, on the path over to the Cathedral of the Archangel, to bow and kiss the icons. The red walls of those churches are whitewashed today, but the off-pink of the brickwork under the layer of lime is tinted light blue in the violet light of the electric lamps, making the saints and angels above the main portal, in the glow of the aureola, look like a tapestry interwoven with gold thread. That historico-cultural tsarist decorative center of the Orthodox Kremlin shines like a case of precious diamonds. And, even today, the Byzantine-Venetian churches have nooks and niches where time stands still and the occasional Byzantine light from days of yore darts its tongue. But in the brown and gold fabric of the church light in the center of the Kremlin, in the flickering of silver icon lamps, in the gold of iconostases on frescoes, on the gold of red and black icons, where saints and martyrs pray to the Lord in white dalmatics and white togas with decorative black crosses, in the tired spring light—here the center of the Kremlin citadel seems to have survived time untouched. With the glorious Prussian blue of the sky, as dark as the sea before the mistral, with the brassy yellow of the domes and the pathos of the colorful Russian palette with its naïve contrasts of folk textiles, the painter's motif is a little démodé, and unfortunately still artistically unrealized. On snowy evenings, without the warm pastel illumination of the sun, the pale-green lights in front of the ancient two-story houses dilute the colors, and then the black outlines of Napoleon's batteries from 1812, with cannonballs which lie piled up around the arsenal, seem like the mark of a chisel on a rough wood carving.

All that was built in the Kremlin during the reign of the last two or three tsars is in the spirit of tawdry parvenuism that one so often encounters in European palaces of the nineteenth century. The entire modern tsarist wing spoils the architectural harmony of the Kremlin complex, and the burgs in Vienna and Buda show a similarly disastrous impact. The portals of the new tsarist palace are framed in red marble, and the whole scenario of the tsar's residence has been set on this historical stage with the obvious intent of presenting the boyaresque luxury of a palace to the naïve populace on a millionaire's scale, as if an American monster movie was to be filmed here, designed to dazzle the broadest classes with the gold and wealth of its mosaics, marble, intarsias, and stuccowork.

Above the main steps: a monumental canvas with a massive golden frame, in the history-painting genre and the style of epigonic "Pilotyism," applied for touristic propaganda. In full illumination, surrounded by his retinue, His Imperial Majesty, Emperor and Autocrat of All Russias, Tsar Alexander III, receives a deputation of muzhiks, who bow their heads to the Tsar after the failed peasant revolts throughout the country: "Go back to your homes and do not believe the lies about the gifting of land. Property is sacrosanct!" Those words of the Tsar are carved on a yellow plaque beneath the frame of the painting. Today the Russian "muzhiks" keep stopping in front of that canvas, spelling out the Tsar's words of wisdom, and it seems they are glad that the lies about the gifting of land have become the truth. Where is the Tsar's inviolability of property today?

The white marble hall of the Order of St. George with furnishings in the orange-yellow colors of the sash of that high tsarist decoration, with an endless line of numbers of the tsarist regiments decorated with that highest medal from Narva to Port Arthur and Lvov, stands in front of generations like a tomb. A pyramid of wreaths is heaped in the middle of the hall for Nariman Narimanov, the deceased Chairman of the Central Executive Committee of the USSR, and through the glass of the monumental windows the two red letters "K" and "O" can be seen out in the hazy expanse of Zamoskvorechye on the chimney of the large Krasny Oktyabr (Red October) biscuit factory. The parquet floors crackle, and the shouting of youth echoes from the park in front of the palace: young artillerymen are playing soccer there and screaming at the top of their lungs, as if that noise was not in crass contradiction to the rules of tsarist pageantry, when due silence reigned in the gardens in front of such a hallowed residence—such as reigns in front of temples where demigods dwell.

The International is in session in large, golden Andreyevsky Hall. Typewriters chatter and hum, stenographists zip to and fro with sibilant serpentines of spoken sentences, gilded marble columns shine, reflections spill over the light blue, greenish tints of silk and the golden commander's chains of the Andreyevsky Order with the crucified body of Christ. Here incandescent crowns of rich candlesticks burn brightly, and over all the commotion, above the red tables and the chairman's canopy, high up above the gold-framed portal—a discreetly modest portrait of Karl Marx.

The International sits like the Vatican Council and has been holding conference on one and the same topic for forty years and more. The earth, one of the heaviest celestial bodies, wreathed in mists, revolves slowly, once in twenty-four hours. The heavy, foggy earth turns slowly, and through the mists pastel-green patches of ploughed fields can be glimpsed, cleared forests, and the filament-fine, discontinuous threads of civilization, like spiderwebs. Green brown continents, deep blue oceans, steamer lines, streaks of canals and railroads, progress. And while a constant ant-like teeming can be seen along those threads, with a dark red trail of blood, here from the vantage point of Andreyevsky Hall people speak into the distance, to the whole earth, and their words travel in waves over the entire globe like the flashes of a lighthouse.

A hundred-year-old Chinese man sits like a raven on a branch, chewing some sweet root and blinking his wise eyes like a tortoise. The venerable old man listens to the Kremlin's signals, and his bright eyes still twinkle from an inner fire. The subject is Shanghai, China, and Chinese flesh being cleaved wholesale by European Shylocks. Men from Azerbaijan and Bukhara talk of the British machine guns, and Berbers wave from the other side in deep solidarity with the unfortunates in Calcutta and Pakistan. A Mexican speaks about petroleum and the United States, and a tubercular Finn with very bad teeth drones on like a Lutheran about the eight-hour working day, Amsterdam, and wages. A Boris Godunov-type supernumerary wanders among the speakers—a muzhik with cropped hair and a bound book under his arm: Bukharin's ABC *of Communism*. A temperamental Calabrian gesticulates as he speaks about the poverty of his native region, where peasants still slave in semifeudal conditions, and a pale, tubercular woman leans against a gilded marble column and broods à la Chekhov about distant illusions, happy blue islands, on which humanity would disembark one day with certainty and mathematical precision. The hum of that swarm of orators buzzes monotonously from the antenna as if some strange, unknown insects from a faraway planet were scratching at the microphone or as if the wind was sounding in the telegraph wires. A man from India speaks, he is answered by Borneo and Skopje, and all those voices complain to each other how hard it is to live under inhumane circumstances, how idiotic it is to die an unnatural death, in droves, for others' interests on the battlefield, in the mines, in galleys, how incompatible it is with the dignity of man to live in slavery, and that the time has come for him to take the rudder of the ship into his own hands.

Those lives bear the whole weight of the mines and foundries; phosphoric acid eats away their eyelids and skin, red-hot iron burns their flesh, and a whole heavy world rests on the shoulders of these Atlantes. They debate about how to Archimedeally lift up the globe, cast off their burden, and begin to live like humans, finally instituting what should have been instituted long ago, in the early days of every civilization: that all men are equal, which has not been achieved until today due to the languidity of the human spirit. There is still much doubt in people's minds and much obscurity, because such blasphemous thoughts are opposed to all magic, and the task of escaping from shamanism, from the boyars' and moneybags' gold and blood, involves processes of such vast proportions that their movement, measured on the timescale of one human generation, is the movement of a snail.

Lenin, one of the greatest hypnotists in history, stands in spirit above the crimson canopy of Andreyevsky Hall, and all the speakers at the rostrum begin and end their speeches with quotes from him. *Dixit Lenin discipulis suis.*

The apostles of Leninism speak on an intercontinental scale about things that are in fact very simple and logical, and Malayans, Indo-Chinese, and Japanese attending Moscow's Oriental University follow those speeches from the back of the hall like an audience. Young Hungarians are sitting there too, Croatian boys and Albanians, together with Poles and Germans. And when one speaker's boring voice is reminiscent of a provincial archimandrite, two Russian schoolgirls leaf through their logarithm tables. Sine and cosine—just like we copied each other's homework during mass at high school!

This one-act play took place in one of the northern governorate cities, which has around 40,000 inhabitants; and if the occasional whistle of a steam engine from the dirty railroad station did not fill the air, even today you would expect Chichikov from Gogol's *Dead Souls* to appear at the end of the street with his famous troika. Wooden fences, crooked oil lamps, fat ravens perched on the wires between telephone poles, real Russian Biedermeier with wooden columns on the portals of two-story houses, and colorful flowered curtains on the windows. At the Hermitage Hotel, an ancien régime waiter looking like Tsar Nicholas with a white apron and soft, servile movements explains to foreigners that the city was once the residence of Ivan the Terrible and that the medieval nunnery has been converted into a club for a cavalry regiment that distinguished itself in the revolutionary civil wars everywhere from Perm in the Urals and Semipalatinsk to Arkhangelsk and Warsaw. Long, boring avenues between snowdrifts, the red bricks of a newly built electric power plant, and in the deep channel of the frozen river peasants can be seen breaking out green slabs of ice and loading them onto a low, wide sledge. Tracks wind over the white, icy mirror of the riverbed, worn and yellow from horses' urine; to the left and right of that bizarre road black, tarred barges and steamers rest frozen in the ice; small sooty chimneys emit smoke, and those pale wisps create the illusion that the ships are under steam and about to set off.

We arrived in that far-northern governorate city accompanied by Mr. Karl Diefenbach, the general manager, director, and chief stockholder of the export firm Karl Diefenbach AG, from Hamburg. A heavily built gentleman in his sixtieth year with rose-colored skin, fair complexion, a blonde, greying, straight, brush-like British-style moustache, with an uncommonly bright, starched and ironed shirtfront, priggishly clean, stiff collar and cuffs—general manager Diefenbach had three pet topics: the Battle of Sedan, Admiral von Tirpitz, and angina pectoris.

The gentleman from Hamburg, whose fortune was estimated at about ten million marks, was head of an international firm that exported lumber to India, the Levant, and the Mediterranean with its own ships, bought a fantastic quantity of different timber products to the value of many million gold marks from the Russian wholesale trust Gosek (acronym for "State Export

Complex") for the 1925–26 season, and so the fellow logically wanted to see the wares he had purchased before they were loaded in the spring. He was playing with the intention, back in Moscow, of signing for another consignment of dressed timber and thus pocketing new profits after this excursion.

Mr. Karl Diefenbach, who in the train browsed in an illustrated popular brochure about Flettner's rotor, and who passionately cited Von Liliencron, was actually quite guileless in his intellectual horizons. Forever naïve, he was surprised by the simplest of original thoughts that did not coincide with what he considered irrefutable truths. Whenever it was appropriate, or not, he would quote his dear Von Liliencron, and you just needed to see him reciting individual verses by his literary hero to assure yourself that illiteracy is not always the biggest hindrance to human intelligence and that today's international situation is in constant peril due to much greater dangers than illiteracy.

> I rode out ahead of the squadron,
> And harked in the mist: Is the coast clear?
> Far back the men and orders of baron,
> Muffled the jingle of horses and gear.

The enthusiastic reciter of this poetry, a cavalry captain of the reserve with an Iron Cross, 2nd Class, who did not take his cockade on this business trip out of tact, having earned that high decoration fighting Russian forces around the Masurian lakes, moved with great self-assurance in various fields of the mind, as do general managers who are unaware of the danger of such subtle adventures. He knew about Expressionism, Schönberg, and the Laban Dance School, but his main focus was on the development of the German merchant fleet and navy, in a way that in political vocabulary is vulgarly called "Tirpitz fascism." He explained to me in detail that Communards could never be victorious in Hamburg because the city was girdled by three, sound, well organized, red-white-and-black agrarian belts, where the villagers were good Teutonic farmers and there was no place for political escapades. He talked about the "colossal" Tirpitz, the ingenious organizer of the German fleet, who all of the British admirals should go into apprenticeship with.

"Tirpitz turned the 20,000 German naval officers into granite, solid rock, a perfect embodiment of what we call *Pflicht-gefühl*, that typically German sense of duty, which unfortunately is unknown to the British and Americans. Those Anglo-Saxons will die in war for profits, but not out of conviction. That's the first point. And then Tirpitz is the only world war admiral not to have been defeated."

"Come on, if your 'colossal' admiral is the only one unvan-quished, where is Tirpitz's great fleet now?" I asked Mr. Diefen-bach. His negation of obvious historical facts revealed an annoy-ing strength of resistance, I felt, which continued the struggle with a determination to win even though he had been sunk.

"What do you mean, 'where is Tirpitz's fleet'?" Mr. Diefen-bach replied with surprise. "It remained undefeated, every child knows that."

"But where is your admiral's invincible fleet today? Where is it plowing the waves? On which seas, under what flag?"

"The fleet was scuttled. The German crews sank it them-selves, that's common knowledge. Why do you ask? Haven't you heard of the German tragedy at Scapa Flow?"

"There we have it! Tirpitz's fleet is rusting 800 meters beneath the sea, while British admirals are plying the waves of every ocean. And those British admirals, you say, ought to go into apprenticeship with your colossal Tirpitz? Oh, Mr. General Man-ager, where are your wits? That must really be a superb admiral, whose fleet is at the bottom of the sea, and yet he can serve as a model of how to go from victory to victory."

My conversation with the gentleman from Hamburg pro-ceeded roughly in that paradoxical framework the whole last night in the sleeping car, where he passionately explained to me that socialism had already been implemented in Germany and that they did not need any kind of social revolution there.

"In Germany the rich are considered to be only interim managers of property, and there has been a de facto nationaliza-tion of wealth. What is happening in Russia now, we already had long ago, at the time of Frederick the Great. The degree of social consciousness in Germany was higher under the Prussian kings than it is in Russia today. To cut down a tree on a public avenue, or to break a window, basically to disrupt any small detail of public order is simply inconceivable there. When there is a sign that says something is 'verboten,' then it truly is 'verboten.' But not in this country. No one cares whether something is 'verboten' or not."

"Congratulations on the Germans' high level of social consciousness, Mr. General Manager, but I don't know if you're aware that Marx defines the degree of social consciousness quite differently."

"Marx was a Jew!"

The main official representative accompanying the gentleman from Hamburg was the director of Gosek, Pyotr Konstantinovich Andreyevsky, who lived in Siberia for three years as a student before joining the professional revolutionaries. He took cities from Yekaterinburg to Odessa in the revolutionary wars, which some call the Russian Civil War, and now he manages the state trust Gosek and holds an important Party position, just as he stood with his artillery batteries in a rain of shells manning equally important "positions" for the Party.

"It would be simpler to fight with a Browning in my hand," Pyotr Konstantinovich told me in connection with the difficulties and worries that cropped up left and right on the onerous path, on which human consciousness was being liberated from the thrall of historical inertia. "This is no small thing: a new society is being born on new foundations, all the established notions of private law and property have been turned upside down. The war was an armed struggle for victory and the demarcations were clear: you were either for the Soviets or for Wrangel, but today trouble lurks on every side, nothing but temptations left and right, and pockets are still pockets, and usually empty, material responsibility is greater than during the war, and today we have ballet, card games, the hippodrome, and all of us are flesh and blood. You know, three weeks ago a close friend of mine shot himself, a man who sacrificed the best fifteen years of his life for the cause of the Party. And then he shot himself because of money! He was the director of a bank; and then came women, cards, travel abroad, foreign currency, champagne—and crash!"

I traveled with Pyotr Konstantinovich Andreyevsky to this distant, former residence of Ivan the Terrible as a kind of entourage for Mr. Diefenbach; I was a hanger-on who joined the excursion in order to see the Russian provinces—an old theme thoroughly familiar in all Russian belletristic variations. The whole day long we inspected sawmills and dressed timber, and, according to the plan, the day was to end with a formal dinner at the apartment of Mr. Alexeyev, the chief accountant of the Gosek subsidiary Red North.

Diefenbach moved from one batch of his lumber to the other like a winded walrus in a fish market, confused as to what to nab and devour first. You could not say he was overscrupulous. An old hand, he would assess the assortment in a whole stack with one glance, and only from time to time, with an offhand, good humored, and witty remark, he would point to this or that defected plank here or there, or "not sawn perfectly," but given the pharaonically vast mass of Russian pinewood, that did not look like faultfinding but more a kind of simple statement for the records.

The day had been long and tiring, and a hard and strenuous night was ahead of us: we had to cover a distance of approximately fifty kilometers in a sleigh, through forests and over frozen lakes, to visit a new complex of sawmills that were also processing a mass of timber for Mr. Diefenbach—several tens of thousands of tons. The dinner at the house of the Gosek subsidiary's chief accountant, Mr. Alexeyev, seemed a wonderful diversion, promising good things in plenty: there would be a warm room, as well as tea and caviar. But a combination of circumstances saw it turn into a right little drama. In order to explain the very involved scene at the home of chief accountant Alexeyev, it will be necessary to present the overall situation, which is important for understanding relations between the Hamburg gentleman and Mr. Alexeyev.

Before the October Revolution, the whole complex of sawmills in the Red North district (which today is named after one of the revolutionaries of the 1880s, Stepan Khalturin, who was hung in Odessa) was property of old Nikolai Alexeyev, an industrial magnate and timber merchant—one of the most powerful moneybags not only in that governorate but in the entire north between Petrograd and Vyatka. The Alexeyevs lived in Petrograd in their hôtel particulier, and when they came to these distant parts on the Finnish border, where old Alexeyev had begun to saw wood in the 1890s, the children would drop by from time to time, like on a kind of excursion to the centennial taiga. When the firestorm of the October days swept away the Alexeyev's forests, the eldest son, Pavel Nikolayevich, a modest and decent man, reconciled himself with fate. As a specialist who mastered his field, he was able to work his way up to the relatively high position of chief accountant in his former enterprise.

Until the beginning of the war in 1914, the Hamburg gentleman was one of the best clients of the Alexeyevs' firm. Old Alexeyev stood godfather to Mr. Diefenbach's eldest daughter, Alisa—today a student of the Laban Dance School—and Mr. Diefenbach personally attended the christening of Pavel Nikolayevich's little boy, Alyosha Pavlovich Alexeyev, who died of typhus during the Revolution.

So, more than simply through business, Mr. Diefenbach was also connected to the Alexeyev family in a much more intimate way, and some time shortly before the war began in 1914 he toured all of the Alexeyevs' huge forest complex, when one lived without a care; life seemed just one big picnic in the sunny glades of the Finnish virgin forests, between a round of golf and a ballet premiere at the Petrograd Royal Opera. Mr. Diefenbach hunted in these tens of thousands of acres of forests and lakes, and he was a recognized guest at the sawmills, forest lodges, and rangers' cabins. Twelve full years had passed since that last excursion to these parts, and the trip to this distant province, which he connected a whole mass of personal reminiscences with, was to be a kind of perverse surprise for him. Until we left Moscow the day before, the gentleman from Hamburg had no idea that he would be carrying out an inspection of his ready-cut merchandise in the Alexeyev-owned forests, but that evening invitation with us all to visit the sole authentic and legitimate representative of the Alexeyev firm completely bewildered him. Above all, he was going to a friend's house without presents and flowers, and later he would be trading with the Alexeyevs' timber as if nothing had happened, because "business is business"; that is a fundamental rule in war, to be sure, because war is war, and if it was the other way round—if by chance Diefenbach had lost the war—the Alexeyevs would also not have had any scruples in that respect. Revolution is revolution.

The apartment of the Gosek chief accountant, Pavel Nikolayevich Alexeyev, was on a muddy lane in the city center, on the second floor of a large and dilapidated structure. One could even call it a dirty old ruin—a sort of public building with store-rooms on the first floor and wide, brick-paved corridors beneath arches and vaults dating back to the time of Ivan the Terrible. The Alexeyevs' summer house with a terrace and swans, in the middle of a enormous park beneath centennial Swedish firs, is today a children's home, while their current apartment in that odious building represents the dramatic final phase in a protract-ed struggle for a roof over their heads, which Pavel Nikolayevich wrangled from the housing authority through particular inter-cession for the re-establishment of the Alexeyev firm's former international connections. One of the addresses that Pavel Ni-kolayevich played, his best card, was that of Karl Diefenbach, the gentleman from Hamburg.

We found ourselves on a remarkable stage, with traces of a wealthy, Makart-style interior: lavish carpets, divans, cop-per armor, empty metal parrot cages. Everything was lit up by a sooty oil lamp and candles that smoked ominously like torch-es at some fateful, whirlwind funeral. The entire room, all the walls and the backs of the cupboards, were covered with fabrics and carpets, and photographs of various sizes: tiny squares with nine-inch ebony frames, painted miniatures on ivory, vertical and horizontal parallelograms, gold-framed ellipses with garlands and ornate laurels, Saint Petersburg-style family ensembles of ladies and gentlemen in dolmans, top hats, ballroom dresses, an aristocratic Russian dress suit, marabou silk, jewels. The lovely days in Crimea and Tsarskoye Selo—farewell to all that, goodbye till kingdom come.

I glanced over all those photographs of Saint Peters-burg-style interiors: rich, luxurious, and parvenu. Chande-liers, mass-produced Louis Quinze, stuffed bears with huge silver dishes in their paws, and Russian boyars' massive Lou-is-Philippe. And now the thirteen of us squeezed together to fit in that tiny, narrow space partitioned off with cupboards.

Here sat Mr. Diefenbach, and next to him Alexey Niko-layevich—also called Alyosha—the younger brother of the head of the house, whose wife was due to give birth at any time and who attended in order to show his respect and attachment to the Hamburg gentleman, an old acquaintance and friend of the family. Beside Alyosha Nikolayevich sat the Director of Gosek,

Pyotr Konstantinovich Andreyevsky, next to him Yevgeny Georgiyevich Bertenson, Chief Engineer of the Red North complex,
and to the left of Bertenson, the head of the Stepan Khalturin
Sawmill, Comrade Vasilyev, to whose sawmill we were to travel
later that evening.

The lady of the house, Anna Ignatyevna, gave a peerless
performance at the head of the table, and at the other end, vis-à-vis
his wife, sat the master of the house, Pavel Nikolayevich. Next to
him were three Party members, delegates of the trust Red North,
as well as the man they called "Comrade Bookkeeper," who did not
speak a single word until the end. The thirteenth guest, in the far
corner, between Comrade Vasilyev and "Comrade Bookkeeper,"
was Kuzma, busboy and valet, for whom the table had not been
set and who directed the servant girl Shura. He ran to get mineral
water, topped up our vodka glasses, gnawed at the occasional leg of
hazel-grouse; almost a holy fool at the end of the table, a twit, part
clown, part cousin and idiot. Dementia praecox; what can you do
if the Lord will not call him to Heaven? It was a wry twist of fate
that so many had fallen to the Grim Reaper, but this albino with
pastel blue, watery eyes, remained alive like this, a burden to the
family in its dire need.

Pavel Nikolayevich's wife, Anna Ignatyevna, a dignified
young lady of around thirty, with a deep, husky alto and costly
old-fashioned jewelry, was a beautiful woman, and ever so slightly pockmarked; those little spots covered with cream and pow-
der on her cheeks bestowed particular emphasis and charm to
that uncommonly mercurial figure. Anna Ignatyevna's discreetly hoarse voice and lively, temperamental movements betrayed
her arbitrary and unrestrained nature; her brightly rouged lips,
which black coffee seemed to have yellowed like the fingers of a
chain-smoker, her muffled voice fraught with tears, large, dark,
eyes, radiant yet red-rimmed—all of that shimmered harmoni-
ously about Anna Ignatyevna, and at the same time arrogantly, as
charming, unscrupulous, rich young women are, as luxurious as
stately borzois. At first, Anna Ignatyevna's elegance, or rather the
shadow of her former elegance at this spiritualist session, where
it would come to a dramatic summoning of spirits, hovered about
with the manifest scorn and spite that rise up in great actress-
es when they have to act to secondary audiences, and beneath

that tired and skillfully embellished mask of a half-dead goddess, beneath the nails lacquered with glistening and pale rosy pearl, there perceptibly smoldered a mass of hidden feline urges that revealed themselves in the violent clenching of her fingers and the nervous biting of her lower lip. In character terms, that woman was incomparably stronger than her husband, Pavel Nikolayevich: that pale, anemic, redheaded neurasthenic on the other side of the table would rivet his big, round, timid eyes on her, full of tenderness, panic, and a kind of helpless, indecisive smile; that gaze was clouded by a hidden inner tremor full of dread, like when an acrobat walks the tightrope, aware that one wrong step could mean catastrophe.

We were waited on by sixteen-year-old Shura. There was an unconcealed, haughty irony in the tone and the way Anna Ignatyevna ordered around the poor, stupid girl. Shura blundered about with the sauces, and everything was always the wrong way round, right instead of left. Etiquette, form, courtesy, servants' drill, service along good old traditional lines: What sense did all that have today in such a devilish requiem, when these barbarians were here mumbling "may her memory never fade" at her grave, and she had to serve dinner to her own gravediggers? What was the point of all that today—the damask to sit twenty-four with the enormous monograms symbolizing Anna Ignatyevna's name, the silver, crystal, porcelain, and everything else—when it stood in this wax museum, this repulsive panopticon with these gorillas, between these ridiculous cupboards, in this store of downfall and misfortune, in front of this band of vandals that had gathered at her table?

She thought: *And then there's that unknown, unpleasant foreign journalist with the beard (i.e. me), Pyotr Konstantinovich Andreyevsky, and the shady gentleman from Hamburg who trades with these burglars with criminal impudence, although those two Westerners are not the worst thing in the world that could befall a person. And that manager of the state export firm, that man from the central authorities in Moscow, is admittedly a Communist, but an intellectual, a Saint Petersburg lawyer, and ultimately a Communist general and renowned historical personality. But these wretches here on the right side of the table who lick their knives, mince their meat into a pulp, and eat it with spoons like beggars—how did they come to sit at my table absolutely uninvited? Like Tatar invaders from the east, tyrants who have perversely humiliated and tormented us for years.*

The fact that the Party delegates were present at that dinner in addition to us foreigners seemed to have been against her express will, and also against the will of her husband. But while he, of a passive nature, was presented with a kind of fait accompli and acquiesced helplessly, Anna Ignatyevna staged a violent scene in front of her husband in the kitchen. Her tirade could be heard clearly through the thin door, and when she appeared in front of us in the role of the amiable hostess, you could feel her grimacing in her elevated temper, with aversion, like an experienced madame who, if she dared, would raise her skirt like some dishwashing slattern and show us her hidden thoughts—au naturel. Despite her self-control, her irony and excessively sarcastic treatment of poor Shura contained malicious intent, and she obviously aimed to do her best to belittle the guests. She did not deign to look at the Party delegates and did not offer them a single bite of food. To the right of Anna Ignatyevna gaped a vacuum.

She was not particularly polite toward Mr. Diefenbach either, though at first she put on a show of civility with the stereotyped smile of a lady who sits at the head of the table as the hostess, playing a precisely defined role according to the rules of the ceremony. More cold and reserved, she replied to the Hamburg gentleman's questions with short staccato sentences, hardly more than "yes" and "no," and obviously had to make an effort to restrain herself under that torture. The gentleman from Hamburg was feeling awkward and perplexed just like Anna Ignatyevna, but instead of going along with the game in the conventional way, he virtually interrogated the woman about various acquaintances from their common Saint Petersburg circles, and in that way only intensified her growing discomfort.

"What about Yekaterina Georgiyevna's husband?" Diefenbach asked.

"He died, ha ha. How did he die? A normal death, ha ha, no, no, no, the gentleman from Hamburg thinks people here die a normal death, ha ha, yes, yes, yes, he died of hunger, and Nikolai Pavlovich, he disappeared. No, no, I didn't mean it literally, he didn't 'disappear,' but he 'dis-ap-peared,' at least we know how he disappeared. And lovely Katya—she was born a Golenishchev, you know—she was shot, but her sister is an admiral's wife and in Paris, yes, yes, yes, she's an admiral's wife in Paris, her brother-in-law is a prince, the ambassador is in Paris too, yes, yes, he's a taxi driver, but they're happy, free, they're doing fine. And poor Sasha is no more either. His only child, a daughter, Duchess Alya, is singing in Riga in an operetta ensemble."

The Hamburg gentleman went on asking his foolish questions (o sancta simplicitas!), and Anna Ignatyevna answered in her macabre telegraphic style—"yes-yes," "no-no"—as if an endlessly long Morse tape flowed from her lips—"yes, yes, yes," "no, no, no"—and that ribbon grew like a never-ending spiral of death and despair, with an enormous accumulation of stops: "Sasha"—stop—"Admiral's wife"—stop—"Kutuzov-Golenishcheva"—stop—"adieu pour toujours," and so on, accompanied by the nervous knocking back of one vodka after another. Anna Ignatyevna with loud, sarcastic interjections stultified the good-natured naïveté of her guest, who had no idea what this was all about.

Everything started off rather quietly, and if it had not been for Diefenbach's naïveté everything probably would have ended in a relatively boring and conventional way too. We ate savory pie with eggs and mince, sauces of pickled mushrooms, a chowder, and venison; we drank quite a lot of vodka, first as an aperitif, and then like water; the one or two bottles of wine from the Caucasus, with thirteen of us, were not enough to quench our thirst.

We spoke about unimportant things, as one does in feigned conversation at banquets. We wondered if there would be a good path for the sledge and if the wolves would attack us. The winter was relatively mild that year, the bears had moved back into the north, there were not many wolves, and they were largely satiated after having killed quite a few cattle in neighboring villages. Though it is true that two or three weeks ago, one night at around eleven, a pack of wolves made its way to the cathedral in the city center and mauled seven people to death. That was an exceptionally violent incursion of the ferocious wolves. But we would have a whole caravan of sleighs behind us, so there would be no danger at all. We had good fur coats, and the frost was mild, just minus five, so we would be able to sleep well in the straw, and moreover, the convoy also had rifles. Everything had been provided for.

There was discussion about frame saws, the most practical way of cutting wood, and the need to combine sawmills with cellulose factories. We talked about whether India needed timber, and of what quality, and the state of the markets in Algeria and Morocco because, as the gentleman from Hamburg put it, German trade had been torpedoed by the war but today was competing with the great powers again—not only in Africa and South America, but also in the heart of Britain itself.

The faltering conversation in German wound around our banquet like smoke around a hearth where damp wood will simply not catch fire, despite all efforts, and as moods warmed with the vodka, Mr. Diefenbach became ever louder in his German interpretation of the potential not only of German capital, but of German industry as such.

When the second roast came out on a huge silver dish, an enormous thigh of veal that no one now touched, Pavel Nikolayevich as host held his glass and proposed a toast to his dear guest, friend, and godfather of his late son: Mr. Karl Diefenbach. Pavel Nikolayevich was an acquiescent, fair-skinned northerner (his mother had been an ethnic German from Latvia), with a thin moustache and a finely trimmed Swedish beard; now he cast his dreamy, imbecilic gaze over the oil lamp to the ceiling and spoke like a chicken when it drinks water, and his beard wiggled queerly, as if it was an actor's fake held on with resin. His soft, warm tenor, which sweaty-handed neurasthenics speak with, rang out pleasantly; he stammered like an archimandrite standing before the Holy Doors, all jittery, and whenever he could not think of a word he would tap his forefinger against his thumb, interpolating the "er" sound in the course of his speech. That little word "er" seemed to particularly disturb Anna Ignatyevna because, as she listened to her husband, she tapped the quivering fingers of her left hand on the table like pressing the keys of a piano and would nervously draw at her cigarette and forcefully blow the smoke away over the dishes with the meat and salads to the other end of the table, while nervously biting her lips with a hysterical grimace.

Pavel Nikolayevich spoke mainly in retrospect: he mentioned Herr Generaldirektor Diefenbach's last visit here to the Alexeyevs' estate. Oh, weren't those times that today seemed... er... like a long forgotten novel. Pavel Nikolayevich spoke of a

beautiful moonlit night by the Finnish lakes, with champagne...
er... that they drank out in the forest by the campfire, and about
Anna Ignatyevna then still being his ideal... er... that is, his fian-
cée. And afterward, returning from Spain, from their honeymoon,
he and Anna Ignatyevna were guests of Mr. Diefenbach and his
dear wife at their property near Hamburg, but all that had vapor-
ized like a dream and none of it... er... existed anymore. Now Mr.
Diefenbach had arrived at this graveyard of the Alexeyevs, and
that was a happy event, and on the other hand also instructive
for Mr. General Director, because it showed—because practice
on the basis of experience showed beyond doubt—that that was
how life was, and no one was indispensible, and moreover, to be
sure, there also existed natural laws, without any doubt, and so
on, and so forth, and everything made sense, to be sure, but sailing against the wind was hard...

"Flettner proved with his rotor that that's possible too,
you know," the Hamburg gentleman interrupted Pavel Nikolayevich, thus throwing him an unexpected life ring in the nick of time,
and Pavel Nikolayevich, perplexed by this intermezzo, raised his
glass, and ended his oration. He stepped up to Diefenbach, and
they kissed each other affectionately.

"That's all... er... that I... er... can... er... say at the moment.
Et campos ubi Troia fuit...'"

After the host, Pavel Nikolayevich's younger brother
Alyosha stood up. He was a degenerate with an unpleasantly
protruding lower jaw, who had spent a whole year as an intern
at Diefenbach's commercial office in Hamburg, and as such
had been a frequent guest of "Herr Karl Ludwigovich Diefenbach." Alyosha toasted charming Mrs. Diefenbach, Henriette
Hansovna, a great tennis player and automotive enthusiast;
Karl Ludwigovich's children, his beautiful daughters; and his
personal and family happiness. Alyosha recalled their sunny
Hamburg terrace, where they used to drink coffee, and where
old, deceased Papa Alexeyev once burst into tears like a child
when Henriette Hansovna played "Volga, Volga, Mother Volga,
wide and deep beneath the sun" on the piano, tra-la-la, tra-la-la...
They all then toasted the Volga, went on long excursions with

* And the fields on which Troy once stood...

motorboats—it was all so idyllic. Papa was still alive then, and he would turn in his grave if he saw the shambles in this room today, with the broken old cupboards...

Karl Ludwigovich Diefenbach started to feel ever more uncomfortable. He perceived the chasm between the Alexeyevs and their Communist escorts, but he had come in order to conclude a good, fair, and profitable deal with today's traders in the USSR in keeping with all the rules and terms governing the exchange of commodities and money, not in order to philosophize and hold speeches beside fresh graves.

He thought: *Honor when honor's due, but the profits of my Hamburg firm are dependent on today's business conditions, and they are in the hands of my trading partners—those taciturn fellows in Russian workers' shirts, not these ruined souls and sentimental romantics. Let bygones be bygones, and if something has foundered, such a catastrophe must, strictly speaking, have had deeper reasons... Why was there no collapse in Germany?*

Mr. Diefenbach gathered his wits and began to say how immeasurably sorry he was that he had not found his little godchild Alyosha alive. "But, as I see, the Lord has granted the parents another son, a wonderful boy, who will bring joy to his father and mother, perhaps more than they themselves hope for. He will grow up to be a cavalryman, a revolutionary officer, a little Bonaparte, who will bring grandeur and renown to his magnificent fatherland..."

"I would rather strangle him with my own hands than see him turn out like that," Anna Ignatyevna interrupted, with demonstrative harshness.

She sprang to the coffeemaker, turned her back to us all, and nervously poured so much methylated spirit under the coffee pot that the bluish, sulfurous flame licked high and illuminated her outlines, as if she had burst into flame herself.

"Anna Ignatyevna, please, you'll catch fire!" Pavel Nikolayevich warily addressed his wife, glancing in alarm now at us, now at her furious form that clashed plates together and shouted profanities at Shura.

"Ooh, what a loss if I caught fire, pshaw, maybe it would be best if I caught fire, ha, ha, ha..."

A pause ensued.

The director of Gosek, Pyotr Konstantinovich Andreyevsky, was sitting there completely blasé, nipping at his vodka, between puff after puff of cigarette smoke, as if this absurd theater did not concern him in the slightest.

He thought: *It's so stupid to be wasting our time here with this half-wit from Hamburg. It's stupid that this dinner was organized here with these blockheads. It's stupid that they behave so inanely in front of these foreign numskulls. It's stupid that my half-wits here were unable to anticipate this. And finally it's so stupid that we can't leave this ridiculous mess straightaway because the horses haven't been harnessed and because a man is constantly constrained by follies. It was stupid of me to leave Moscow, my limousine, my game of chemin de fer. Now I will have to sit in an open sleigh all night long with some witless Kraut moneybags. It won't exactly be good for my rheumatism, dammit, but a man can say goodbye to an easy life when he becomes a timber merchant and is allocated to escort millionaire gangsters. It would be better to command a cavalry division than to saw wood!*

Comrade Vasilyev, the head of the Stepan Khalturin Sawmill, a pale autodidact with a long scar running from his left temple, past his jowls, to the cicatrized end under the scrofula on his neck, was silent on the left side of the table, watching Anna Ignatyevna with a gruesomely empty gaze such as one might ignore different insects in nature. In the man's lively, intelligent eyes I failed to detect a single, tiny spark of interest in the magnetism and charm that the woman exercised on everyone else present, from "Comrade Bookkeeper" to her feeble-minded cousin Kuzma at the end of the table. "Brigade commander" Vasilyev had spent thirteen years feeding the frame saws at the Alexeyevs' sawmills, and then in 1917, as a soldier in the tsarist army, he was badly wounded on the approaches to Lvov. Carried along by the wave of events, he was already commanding a red cavalry brigade in the revolutionary wars in 1918. As pale as death, he ate very little, spoke not a word, and did not drink a single drop of vodka. He did not smoke, and from time to time he would just take his knife and gently tap the blade on his porcelain plate, only then to stare again at the meat in aspic or the caviar in the crystal dishes decorated with sprigs of pine.

Most upset of all was the engineer of the Red North trust, Yevgeny Georgiyevich Bertenson, a shortsighted man whose eyes were lost behind the finger-thick glass of his pince-nez. A neurotic, likeable scatterbrain in the Russian fin-de-siècle sense, confused by superficial, so-called belletristic culture, he understood "going to the people" formally, like so many other Russian intellectuals—it was more show than substance. Generations of those beautiful minds headed off into socialism without seriously considering the consequences of their dangerous adventure, which later revealed itself to be more a barrage of cannon fire than the printing of clever articles for liberal newspapers. Engineer Bertenson's age group got over the first injections of Marx with a high temperature, in literary belletristic mode, closer to Maxim Gorky than to the Party, and when it came to the consequences, the Bertensons sided with the Slavs in the defensive war of 1914–18 and intervened, largely on the tsarist side: *Stepan, Dmitry, Russian brothers, please sacrifice an arm or a leg for Western democracy! Rise up, do your duty, join the fray!*

But when the Stepans and Dmitrys did join in the fray (in a Marxist sense) and turned their rifles around at the tsarist "interventionists," liberals like Bertenson did not know where was up and where was down, and in the universal rack and ruin of European values they lost their compass. The Bertensons—and their name is legion—were in favor of the Socialist Revolutionary Party's agrarian reform, but for compensating the landowners, in favor of revolution, but for a Herzen-style romantic revolution illuminated with bright flares, a revolution of the Constitutional Democratic Party sort, for formal democracy, for a normal bourgeois revolution with banks, profits, and parliamentarianism, not for "wild banditry and pogroms like Pugachev's."

The descendent of a Nordic Jewish family, Yevgeny Georgiyevich was almost killed in a pogrom as a schoolboy; he was rescued from their burning house with life-threatening burns, and as a consequence he was edgy and neurotic forever after, and, as if his whole body was still a fresh burn, he quailed at every abrupt movement, nervous voice, or provocative glance. So it was that he was unable to overcome his panic-stricken fear of the Revolution, and did not understand its catastrophic power. He saw the justification for structural change in society and recognized the social perturbations; he was in favor of electrification on the scale Leninist had proposed, but he simply could not understand why the entire Russian intelligentsia had been spurned and was being systematically boycotted.

"You're barking up the wrong tree, dear fellow," the Gosek director, Pyotr Konstantinovich, said to him with irony. "Those are just windmills in your head. Who spurned the 'Russian intelligentsia'? When was it ever spurned? Am I a member of the Russian intelligentsia or am I not, and who spurned me? Are you a Russian intellectual, and who spurned you? And how can you say you were spurned, when you're sitting here in front of a Kremlin ace and unfamiliar foreigners and saying whatever enters your mind, although it's quite nonsensical?"

"My God, not everyone comes into the world blessed with Bonapartist abilities, Pyotr Konstantinovich! The great majority of the Russian intelligentsia, a good ninety percent, has been spurned. It's good you're being told this, so you can let others know."

"You, Yevgeny Georgiyevich—you haven't been spurned! Let's get to the point and speak logically, please. You, for instance, are not a Party man, but you have a purview like never before, and a monthly pay thrice that of mine! Why ever do you think you've been spurned'? Please enlighten us!"

"It's not about rubles! It's not about the material side of the issue! It's to do with us having been morally trampled underfoot. We are subjects, and are treated as such."

"Quite right, bravo! That's the word—we've been morally spurned. We were masters in our own house, and today we're rags," assented the visibly agitated Alyosha, the younger brother of Pavel Nikolayevich.

"To an extent their treatment of you is your own fault, dear fellow! If the Russian intelligentsia wasn't so fatally incompetent it would be able to play a totally different role than it does now."

"When were we ever asked? No one ever asked us at all!" Alyosha Nikolayevich began to shout, almost livid, as his drunken, trembling hand took a whole little bunch of matches out of their box, and in his nervousness he spilled them over the table. "They simply took us and broke us in two—here, like I'm breaking these matches. They simply broke us and threw us onto the street. They ruined us. They've ruined the whole country, not just us!"

Alyosha Nikolayevich broke one match after another with his long, thin fingers, and in an ever lower voice repeated over and over: "They've wrecked all of Russia, two million Russians are starving and begging all over Europe, the whole Russian intelligentsia…"

"Oh, come on, you mean the whole Russian intelligentsia of swindlers and smugglers who ought to have been machine-gunned!" roared Pyotr Konstantinovich. "Russia has proved that it can do without that so-called intelligentsia, because whoever felt himself to be a true Russian intellectual didn't follow the tsarist generals, but the people! Ultimately, yes, the people have resolved the matter with machine-guns."

"Yes, that's the sum of your wisdom: the machine-gun. Machine-guns don't resolve anything!"

"No, Alyosha Nikolayevich. Rather, I should allow you and these foreign gentlemen to make mincemeat of us. Isn't that right? And now finally: to your health! Why all these words in vain? You are a splendid fellow, Alyosha Nikolayevich, only full of petty bourgeois prejudices! I raise my glass to our host, Pavel Nikolayevich, the most likeable petty bourgeois in all the governorate! Long live Pavel Nikolayevich! Cheers, let's drink. Down the hatch! Once more: down the hatch! Once more: down she goes! Hurrah!"

We drank three more toasts like that to Pavel Nikolayevich with three swift movements of our hands, and twice more we toasted Mr. Diefenbach from Hamburg—who thus had the opportunity to assure himself on location that people here were not evil cannibals and that the "You Es Es Are" sawed wood and delivered first-class wares like all the world's trading and industrial nations.

"Things are improving with every passing day!" Pyotr Konstantinovich explained. "Today Mr. Diefenbach had the opportunity to see that the peasant is becoming a consumer. Peasants buy timber at the sawmills, which means that the peasants have money! Meaning there's money in circulation, meaning an internal market really exists, meaning we're not up in the air!"

"That doesn't mean the peasants have money," Yevgeny Georgiyevich Bertenson protested.

"What? They have no money but were still buying timber?"

"It means that the peasants this morning were lading timber for the railroads. It wasn't timber for the peasants themselves, but for the state…"

"For what then really, Pavel Nikolayevich?" Pyotr Konstantinovich asked in an almost plaintive tone.

"It was timber for a new maintenance shop for locomotives."

"My point exactly: a new maintenance shop! A new maintenance shop for locomotives is being built. And who is building that new maintenance shop? Russia's spurned intelligentsia perhaps? Does that unhappy intelligentsia give a hoot whether new maintenance shops for locomotives are built in this country or not? That intelligentsia doesn't build anything and never has, because it has never had any idea what it means to build. One of the least intelligent intelligentsias in the world, which babbled on about God for decades and is still blabbing about God today—that's our intelligentsia. When we say the peasant is becoming a consumer, the Russian intelligentsia claims that's not true. When a clinic is set up, the intelligentsia claims that amounts to expropriating someone's apartment. When a Party club is organized, the intelligentsia protests that there's no freedom of conscience. And so on, and so forth. But, it makes no difference. Let's drink to the health of the ingenious spurned intelligentsia that always speaks the truth! Down the hatch! Three times! Cheers to Mr. Diefenbach, who tomorrow will see 300,000 tons of sawed and sorted first-class goods, as yellow as butter!"

"When the Alexeyevs were in charge of the concern, 1.3 million planks traveled down the river annually. That was the normal amount!" Yevgeny Georgiyevich Bertenson protested.

"Yes, but back then the 1.3 million of them went straight into the Alexeyevs' pockets! In 1927, the river will transport two million planks, without the Alexeyevs, straight into the pockets of the USSR, dear fellow, and you have to admit that's a slight difference."

"Who said it was all for the benefit of the Alexeyevs? Was it really our exclusive property? No, it was shared—it was both ours and the workers'. We all prospered back then!"

"Hear! Hear!" Karl Ludwigovich from Hamburg called approvingly to Alyosha Nikolayevich. "We who conduct national affairs in Germany also consider ourselves just interim managers of people's property. Quite right! We are registered as owners de jure, but we are only de facto administrators, and everything that exists belongs to the nation, and that's wise."

"So I raise this glass to the health of Mr. Diefenbach and hope that as interim manager of people's property' he will very soon be able to welcome us at his de facto socialist sawmills in Hamburg. Long live the Russian-German USSR!"

"Hear! Hear! I would have no objections, and all this is merely a question of formalities, as I've already said. I'd like you to know, gentlemen, that I'm prepared to sign a long-term contract the day after tomorrow in Moscow, to last from today for five years, under the same conditions.""Anna Ignatyevna, won't you clink glasses with us?" Pyotr Konstantinovich asked. "Don't you also wish Mr. Diefenbach to see the realization of his ideals sooner rather than later? As we've heard, he considers himself to be only an interim manager of people's property, and you heard him when he wished to bind himself to us for a whole five years, meaning that he assumes we will still sign agreements with him in five years time..."

"The gentleman is no business of mine! I just hope he doesn't go through what we did. If I wished him that, that means I would hate him like my worst enemy."

"Anna Ignatyevna, please," Pavel Nikolayevich pleaded, and the way he stood up with the glass of vodka in his hand, his gestures, and his bloodshot eyes showed that he was drunk.

Pyotr Konstantinovich repelled Anna Ignatyevna's invective with irony, but no longer with the same benevolence as if the conceited woman's tactlessness did not annoy him. "Subjectively, my good woman, you have the least cause to be upset! You live in a well-heated room, waited on by servants—you've got it good."

"I've got it good? Oh, how witty you are," Anna Ignatyevna said and burst out laughing, her forced guffaws sharp and explosive like the sound of breaking glass. "We're like the *Titanic*, so what else can happen to me? I can't sink deeper than the bottom. Kindly have a look at this 'got it good' of mine, this pigsty where I live. Come on, please have the moral courage to admit it: Is this criminal system in any way sane and humane? Here, let Mr. Diefenbach speak, let him testify what life was like before the war and just what it meant to live before the war."

"How did the millions live before the war who aren't alive now because they were slaughtered in the war? How you lived then and how you live today is an important question perhaps, but how do I live, and how do all of us live? Does anyone live better than you? My good woman, don't be unfair," Pyotr Konstantinovich said, openly distancing himself from this woman's nonsense with surprisingly harsh and distinct words.

"I don't care how others live, that's none of my concern! Let everyone take care of themselves! I'm finished, we're done for, we've sunk as low as this menagerie…"

"Because Kuzma isn't in livery, is that it, and sits with you at the same table, is that why you've fallen to this level you call a menagerie? There are several thousand women living alongside you in this city, my dear woman, who'd think they were dreaming if they could but live in this menagerie of yours, and enjoy what you do, for just twenty-four hours. Don't you see? Just once in their lifetime, in their entire life just for twenty-four hours. If you had to stand in the open at a frame saw every day, all your life…"

"I don't care about frame saws or trade unions. I don't go on about them. Unions this, unions that, always unions… that's all you talk about. But it's all a lie, you know, all you say is a lie. You drove the prostitutes from the streets and instead you've turned the whole of Russia into a bordello! All women are at your disposition like you were Tatar invaders, and you bloviate about unions, women, and humanity, as if I didn't know what humanity was. And your women at the frame saws, I know it all by heart, so please spare me the diatribe!"

"Anna Ignatyevna!" Pyotr Konstantinovich exclaimed, getting up and moving back a step or two from the table, so it seemed he was about to leave the house and this crazy woman. "I don't understand you: What are you getting at?"

We all stared in silence with wide-open eyes; the right hand of Pavel Nikolayevich Alexeyev, Anna Ignatyevna's husband, was stretched out over the damask between the napkins, flowerpots, and silver dishes full of red-currant-colored jelly; Pavel Nikolayevich's blue hand quivered as if galvanized, and his gaze followed his wife with the deeply unhappy look of a squashed frog.

Anna Ignatyevna also got up, as if about to make a fateful announcement, when Shura appeared at the door to call Alyosha, i.e. Pavel Nikolayevich, to come immediately because his wife was unwell.

Shura's running in with that alarming news; Alexey Nikolayevich's abrupt departure and his discomposed voice from the door; the Hamburg gentleman nervously offering him two German cigars as he was leaving; all the rest of us; Engineer Bertenson trying to persuade us that Russian midwives were a class of their own and that the birth would certainly be without complications—all of that dispelled the dramatic scene at the table, as if the aces had been laid and the cards were now being shuffled for a new hand. A different set of relations came about, and the picture turned into a new perspective.

Pyotr Konstantinovich returned to his chair. Kuzma was ruffled and now poured everyone more vodka. The Party delegates sat immobile, like supernumeraries, for whom not even a one-liner was anticipated in the play, so the conversation was slow to start again, bogged down in convention.

Mr. Diefenbach, like a real donkey in a china shop, who could simply not comprehend what had been going on, showed his good intentions to dispel the awkwardness of the situation and change the topic by taking a whole bundle of cardboard-backed photographs out of his travel bag. They showed his property in Hamburg, which he owned as an "interim manager." There were shots of his lakeside two-story marble villa; a rich, park-like garden with white statues; a fishpond with a fountain; Mr. Diefenbach's naked, sun-bronzed children; interiors of the parlor; arbors with pergolas and a winter garden; a tennis court; and all the other details of a villa built according to contemporary principles of comfort: fireplaces, Indian fabrics, carpets and rugs, Dutch paintings, marble bathrooms, etc. The gentleman from Hamburg passed round the photographs and explained that his summer house functioned in the most modern way, but that it was not particularly expensive because, despite everything, thrift was one of the fundamental principles of national prosperity.

"Bones aren't thrown away but are used to feed the poultry, and the wind, with the aid of a generator, provides light, cleans the house, pumps water, sweeps the courtyard, waters the garden, and does all the household chores. The wind-powered generator replaces a few domestics, and the harnessing of the wind on a national scale in Germany saves several million marks annually. A good businessman can make impressive profits from everything: wind, water, the warmth of the sun."

The Hamburg gentleman's greenhouses, for example, with citruses of every kind, were heated exclusively by a wind-powered dynamo, and the significance of wind in general was explained to us ingeniously by Flettner and his rotor. Russia, for instance, which has wind like no other country, showed no intention whatsoever of using this unique possibility.

"Sell me your wind, gentlemen, and I'll make this country a paradise on earth."

"It would be better if we sold you our production for the next season, Mr. Diefenbach!"

"Alright, I don't mind, I've already spoken about that with your minister in Moscow. I'm prepared to sign an agreement for five full years under the same conditions, with a seven percent discount on today's agreed prices."

Pyotr Konstantinovich waved at these words of the Hamburg gentleman as if he was shooing away flies, and his gesture basically meant that it was all nonsense. And so we settled back down to looking at the photographs of Diefenbach's country villa, built, so to speak, of the breath of the subtlest zephyr.

Anna Ignatyevna also took those cardboard-backed photographs out of conventionality, but her face was contorted by intense pain that seemed to clench her diaphragm. The Hamburg gentleman still lived there, with that same terrace, where eleven years earlier they had drunk coffee, in those same rooms with the heavy curtains and bronze statues, as if nothing had happened (and truly nothing had happened there). Her gaze was glassy and in the corner of her left eye and on the lashes there gathered and grew a thick tear, which slowly, as heavy as glycerine, slid over her cheek and onto the photograph. Anna Ignatyevna closed her eyes, threw down the photographs, and, twisting her face into a grimace, swallowed the tears that burned in her throat. She tried to get hold of herself, bit now her upper, now her lower lip, crumpled up her napkin, and it was clear that she desperately wanted to avoid succumbing to the horror that would drag her screaming into the depths of her reality in the here and now. Photographs of a life that still existed somewhere, a life that was not fiction but the everyday humdrum of Mr. Diefenbach, a man from her own circle, who still traded today with their forests—everything that was once true and had so perversely evaporated now brought Anna Ignatyevna to her knees, and she sobbed loudly like a child.

"Anna Ignatyevna, I beg you, calm yourself," her husband whined, headed toward her, and began to kiss her hands as humbly and self-effacingly as a beggar in an attempt to bring her to her senses, bring her back to consciousness, and make her realize how childish and scandalous this stupid scene was in front of foreigners and guests who were under their roof for the first time.

"Just leave me alone. Please!" Anna Ignatyevna rebuffed her husband. "A person isn't even allowed to cry anymore. They took everything from us, threw us onto the street, spat at us, and a person isn't even allowed to cry anymore! You're not allowed to cry anymore at your own table, under your own roof—my tears are politics too! They spit on my plate at my own table, they've taken away my children, they killed Alyosha and took Pierre into the Pioneers, into politics... How can there be politics for children? How can they fill a child's head with the idea that there's no God? And on top of it all they keep on telling you that you're actually happy, that you're being unfair, that you have no heart for humanity... O Lord, o Lord, o Lord..."

It was pained weeping full of grief. The whole of Anna Ignatyevna's upper body shuddered from an inner convulsion, and she tried in vain to smother her wailing with her handkerchief and dry her tears with her fingers. The smell of food, of the tiny, narrow, smoke-filled room, the smoke of heavy cigars, the smell of vodka and sooty tallow candles, the stinky yellow oil lamp above the black cupboards like the black timbers of a coffin—all of that coated the air like thick tar.

We all stood up, distraught and helpless. Pyotr Konstantinovich immediately went up to Anna Ignatyevna with a cup of tea, Shura dashed off to get some snow, and Pavel Nikolayevich poured a glass of wine from the Caucasus. But Anna Ignatyevna choked on her tears like a girl who wants to live capriciously, who does not want to die, but cannot breathe because a vile wound is constraining her chest and she has no air.

"Air, give me air!"

One of the delegates opened a fortochka, and a cold cascade of the winter night flooded into the room through that small ventilation window. We drew at that wave of serenity amid the clouds of smoke like a glass of water, and the night air foamed refreshingly like an ice-cold drink in that hazy, headachey space.

Song echoed out in the street: cheerful children's voices were singing a march.

"The Young Communist League!" one of the delegates exclaimed joyfully and stepped up to the window to see the young people returning home from their evening course, singing.

But Anna Ignatyevna kept moaning, broken, completely childlike, and wailed that she could not go on like this. She hysterically held her ears shut with a napkin so as not to hear the children's singing because it would drive her crazy—that deluding of the children, and the fact that her son was singing. She would go mad, she couldn't go on anymore.

Comrade Vasilyev, who had been silent the whole time, let out a muffled sigh and said, "It's late, we ought to get going."

It was a calm, northern night. Millions of fiery stars, from Alpha in the Little Bear to Hercules and Orion, glittered in the deep blue of the stellar cataract that fell in beams of astral cascades above the wolf-infested blackness that our sleigh was sailing through toward the North Star, a tiny boat on the endless sea of the sky. Wrapped in a thick fur coat, I lay almost flat on my back in the straw. My beard was turning to ever sharper glass from hoarfrost and ice, and I inhaled that stellar elixir with all my lungs. The castanets of 300 billion stars tinkled above my head like the jingle of the bells around the necks of our horses, which constantly shook their heads and whinnied from the hoarfrost in their nostrils and the smell of wolves that followed us like a shadow.

On warm seas there are starry nights in complete silence, when a gentle breeze as moist as glycerine flows down from the coast to the sea. There are dolphins in the silver cascade of the Milky Way that exhale and leap in the phosphorus silence, as if the sea was sighing from dark, plutonic depths. The stellar silence on warm summer seas is wreathed in silken veils of tropical smells, but this northern night was like Euclidean glass; you could sense the polar emptiness, where strong lights shine, and everything has its hidden logic: that that is the way it all must be, with everything smelling of Russia leather and pitch, of straw and mares, of the lupine dread that directs the movement of the stars and the wretched milling of our poor caravan in the snow and ice; the mercury shrank far below zero, and the smells in our nostrils vanished beneath the piercing, astral purity of nothingness.

The deep blue was infinite: around the sharp needle of the northern pole, around the Great Bear and Hercules, and toward the east the pale Pleiades lay scattered like translucent dust. Every root in the way and every outline of a bush was etched on the ground in contrast with the glass sky so black, massive, and heavy. The path was winding and worn, and we were tossed to and fro like a ship on the waves, slipping into ruts at the bottom of the track or banging against the icy crust of the snowdrifts, where trails of wolves menaced to both our left and right; the horses whinnied from the frost and effused a gentle tinkling with the movements of their thick, fleshy necks. The little bells on their harnesses rattled, their hooves thudded, the drivers called out to each other when they cracked their whips; nameless villages twinkled far away on the horizon and there came the sound of bell towers striking the late nightly hours.

The paths became livelier around the villages and monasteries. By windmills, birches, and lone pines we left behind us whole caravans of heavily laden sleighs moving in all directions of the compass. Masses of sleighs crawl over the endless plains of Mother Russia on clear nights, carrying loads of grain, soap, and petroleum over hundreds and hundreds of *versts* to different destinations, and only here and there blinks the occasional hand-rolled cigarette and resounds the raucous call of a driver: "Oho, oho, woah! Giddyup!"

And then the jingle of bells again, the shaking from the ruts in the path, the scraping of the wooden runners over the ground, the thudding of hooves, and the shimmering of celestial lights in the deep blue emptiness, strewn with the sparkling dust of starfrost that threatens human warmth with the icy breath of death.

A huge black figure loomed to the right in the snow; it was not an apparition but a solitary tree that stood twisted at the wayside; or it was a snow-covered fence that peered out through the tall wave of the snowdrift. Ghostly shadows grew far ahead of us on the path, and the hunched backs of the drivers could be made out, and the motion of the horses' mighty thighs, and there someone's face was lit up rosily in the glow of a rustic cigarette;

those were the locals from Akulovo, who got up at midnight to take grain to the windmill.

"Oho, oho, woah, giddyup, is that you, Dmitry?"

"We're going to Khalturin's factory! How is it on the lake?"

"Good! Oho, woah, oho, oho! Just you keep to the left! Oho, woah, giddyup!"

I was sitting in the sleigh next to the head of the Stepan Khalturin Complex, Vasilyev. He had recently come back from a three-month trip to Britain.

"There used to be quite a lot of Anglomaniacs in the Russian bourgeoisie and working class, but when we met the British face to face near Arkhangelsk it turned out that Russians also have some grit. We gave the British a good thrashing! Their canned meat is better than the Russian stuff, true, but that's all. They work with machines that metalworkers in Tula would laugh at, and their coal mines have fallen behind the Germans' by at least fifty percent. If they don't bring their mining facilities up to date and modernize the machinery, nothing will save them from unemployment. But today's economic system cannot do that, so there's no prospect for an improvement in the position of the British working class. In Russia today, average production is about seventy-eight percent of what it was before the war. In two year's time it will be one-hundred percent, and in four or five years, in 1930—one-hundred-fifty percent. Meaning that the life of the average Russian worker in 1930 will be seventy percent better than it is now. But in Britain, conservative Britain, that's impossible. It wouldn't be possible for the wages to be reduced by ten or fifteen percent in Britain, or for the level of the base wage to be raised in proportion to production because their system isn't sufficiently elastic. Profit is the only factor regulating production there. In Russia it's a different question because the worker is both producer and owner, so he runs his affairs himself. If it doesn't work, it doesn't work... He only has himself to blame if it doesn't work—it's his own fault! Today it's no longer someone else who's responsible! Today it's you, you yourself, so work as best you can. And that's hard, often very hard, because how do you explain to people that things can't go faster? We don't have the money, and there's the blockade, civil wars, new investments that don't bring returns, the development of metallurgy, the low living standard of the masses, ever greater investments for projects that produce no profit, for munitions, and so on, and so forth.

"I haven't been a member of the Party for long, just since April '17. Only when Vladimir Ilyich returned from Switzerland did I see the light. But we have old comrades, underground activists, who worked illegally for fifteen to twenty years or more in the shadow of the knout and the gallows! Their nerves are at an end now. All of them are tired, elderly people and they're dropping off one after another, like flies. They become exhausted and vanish. It was easier to work underground than today in offices, but that's absolutely essential. People are witless, and laws become more dangerous than the counterrevolution. Everything is set in paragraphs, everything is recorded, and everywhere it's books, regulations, accountancy, officialdom, careerism... Bureaucrats, careerists, they lie and bribe, they steal wherever they can. How do you explain that to an ordinary Party comrade at the factory who goes hungry, freezes, and suffers? The man has sacrificed fifteen or twenty years of his life in prison, in struggles and strikes, in Siberia, exile, and deportation. He's sacrificed his own life, and let's face it: What is there more than that? That man who fought from Vladivostok to Riga, who had wound after wound—how do you now explain to him that his wages need to be reduced, while some official, a tsarist idiot, sits and lazes in the office because no one is better equipped for the job? The man wants to rebel, to protest, but he can't do anything! Minds are clouded, ignorance reigns, backwardness—we're a peasant country and don't have an intelligentsia. If only we had a few thousand intellectuals like Engineer Bertenson today, Russia would rise up like an eagle, it would soar so high, in one flight... Bertenson has no idea about politics, he's politically illiterate, he keeps blathering about loving one's neighbor, and maybe he even believes in God, who knows. He reads poets, poetry, the Lord created poetry, that's what he says, so in a word, in effect, Bertenson is as innocent as a sparrow, but he is a specialist and a conscientious fellow. So why should we now worry what he thinks about philosophy or God, for example? Let him think what he wants, if only he does his job, and Bertenson works like a horse, you know, and he doesn't steal. If we had two or three thousand Bertensons we would grease our chins in a borsch like the world has never seen. But what can you do when the Russian intelligentsia is like those Alexeyevs? She was quite an amazing woman, to put it kindly, wasn't she?"

That simple phrase about Anna Ignatyevna ("quite an amazing woman") evoked for me the theatricality of the scene in that smoke-filled room among the Alexeyevs' broken cupboards: I could still hear the moaning voice of Anna Ignatyevna. To the monotonous song of the bells, in the red-orange and emerald icon lamps of the firmament, a misty apparition of those mad characters at the Alexeyevs' giggled raucously in the shadow of our sleigh like a pack of witches. I wanted to explain to Vasilyev, in my own way, that the very presence of the gentleman from Hamburg inflamed all the woman's pent-up passions, and the entire scene had in fact been provoked by Diefenbach, by his tactlessness when he began to rankle the woman with his constant, stupid questions about the countesses and admirals' wives. "'There is no greater pain than to recall happy days in time of misfortune,' a poet once said, and that's a profound human truth..."

"Yes, yes, maybe that poet is not far wrong," Vasilyev dissociated himself from my corrosive poetic propaedeutics, and so I wouldn't think he did not appreciate poetry, he stressed with particular emphasis, "Forget the poetics for now, I know those 'gentlefolk' better than you and any poet do. There can be no compromise between us and them. Nowhere! Nowhere in the world! You just need to have survived twenty-four hours on the Kolchak front, when they overran our positions, to see what someone like Anna Ignatyevna is capable of doing. Now she is free to savor her happier days, but who in their right mind believes they can make a river flow back to its source? Those blockheads are convinced that, if they spill enough blood, they can stop the wheels of the Revolution. They only have themselves to blame that the tables turned against them. Their crimes and the rivers of innocent blood they spilled were propaganda for us among people who had no notion who we are and what we want. They themselves agitated for us! In Siberia, too: Who would otherwise have known that we want what we want? I don't understand that upper crust. I never hated them, but they hated us with a blind fury. Real idiots! I was born here in this region, and as a boy I worked for old Alexeyev, and later at the frame saw. The old man was just as much a jerk as his sons. Zeroes, all of them. I was surprised Pyotr Konstantinovich wanted to talk to that damn woman at all. The way she pathetically declared that she didn't give a damn about the fate of others. That's what she said, and it's the truth—when did that lady ever care for anything that wasn't hers? Quite incredible. And what surprises me most is that those folk still live like they're in a different world. They don't see anything of what happens around them. Inwardly they've been convinced for eight years that all this will go down the plughole tomorrow—they just can't come to their senses. Talk about blockheads—thick as bricks!"

We passed through a small village with black, sleepy huts, the chalk-white wall of a small church with five onion domes, and tall fences; everything was silent and stock-still, as if dead. No movement anywhere, not even a barking dog, only the faint jingle of a chain around the neck of a cow somewhere behind wooden fencing. Three small windows shone at the end of that village, and many sleighs were gathered there in front of an inn, lit up like at a fair. We too stopped to feed and water the horses and to stretch our legs. The warm, steaming reek of the equine urine, their chomping on straw, the dull, bony friction of their teeth, the movements of the drivers with harness and armfuls of straw, in heavy fur coats, spectrally quiet, in rolled felt boots, like those worn by peasants in the mountains in our country—everything seemed suggestive.

The inn had two partitioned spaces, and an enormous, glowing Russian stove heated this huge room so warmly that everyone's cheeks were soon glowing red, and sweat flowed freely like in a bathhouse. Men were lying everywhere—on all the benches, around the stove, at the tables, and in the corner on the high peasant's bed. We had to walk over bodies, like in a dressing station during a battle. A silver icon stood in the corner above a large table, where a tall, yellow samovar steamed, and in front of it a lively little icon lamp flickered its tongue. A black Byzantine Christ with a prominent lower jaw, like one of El Greco's Spanish knights, and next to Christ a poster of Lenin in powerful oratorical motion; the call for an internal loan in the USSR; another poster for cooperatives, with a red slogan: "The power of cooperatives is not in money, but in the people who understand the purpose of cooperation"; a poster about the newly introduced decimal system; a placard from the All-Russian Agricultural Exhibition, and many papers of different colors with bold slogans—everything already yellowed by the smoke under the wooden beams of the loft.

When the men found out that we were foreigners traveling from Germany to Khalturin's factory, there was inquisitive movement among the barefooted figures in white shirts: countless radiant eyes shone around us in the yellow smoke, and it turned out that all those paupers and drivers knew our Vasilyev and were on very cordial terms with him. They asked how people in Germany live and what the land situation was like there.

While the gentleman from Hamburg explained to the men that land in Germany was divided into six categories according to its quality, that farmers in Germany plowed with tractors and used artificial fertilizers, and that the land produced so and so much grain per acre, I observed the men, their quiet way of interacting, in a constant low, soft tone, listened to the sonorous, open "o" sounds of their Kostroma dialect, and marveled at all the beautiful pale arms and hands, waxily translucent and lyrical. In southern Europe you come across tough, furrowed, hardened fists covered in scars, marks, and calluses, with stony palms and nails flat and ingrown. In industrial regions, the work-worn, toughened, rough hands and arms with strong sinews seem belligerent and cruel, and life is dark and gloomy in the factories and on the decks of ships, where arms are pinpricked all over, cured by saltwater, tattooed with anchors, coats of arms, and naked women. After those sunburned European fists, heavy and swollen from the flow of blood, in this inn I saw the strange and bizarre apparition of northerners' arms and hands: all of the arms on the tables, tucked in the straps and belts of their shirts, arms that braced themselves against doorframes or hung down vertically, were subtly articulated, seemingly bloodless, intelligent, with tender hands with long fingers.

In the half-light of the oil lamp, those sensitive, compassionate, martyr's arms glistened with a putrid hue like meat that hides from the sunlight, arms that decompose in the chiaroscuro of centuries. One young man with dense, shoulder-long blonde hair, a straight Greek nose, and eyes afire as if with a fever, folded his arms under his chin and watched the foreigners from Germany, effused with ecstatic Slavic spirit. The young man's face was cherubically fair above his white linen shirt; with straw yellow hair, he resembled a girl dreaming of a faraway fantastic, unseen Spain in the clouds.

The complex, named after Stepan Khalturin, stood overlooking a frozen lake, and the sylvan horizon on the far shore was of an intense blue in gently undulating perspectives. The basin of the frozen lake looked like a snowy valley crisscrossed by the long, diagonal paths of sledges, and the glass-clear air with colossal spruces made it very reminiscent of a clearing in an alpine plateau. Windmills, frozen steamers in the harbor, white-painted bridges and red life rings, the tall masts of sailing ships, dry docks with the snowy skeletons of boats, all discreetly surrounded by the ever-present trails of wolves—the combination of seaport vessels and the Wild North was quite unreal. Above the cottages, where samovars boiled and little lamps flickered in front of icons, a breath of deep blue light shimmered, although steam still rose from nostrils and hoarfrost spread over beards and moustaches, the cheerful cries of birds told that spring was coming. Breaking ice on the waters would begin to resound like the thunder of cannons. The yellow trumpets of sunlight would blare, the lake would go green and turn choppy in the spring breeze, and thousands and thousands of tons of graded merchandise from the Stepan Khalturin Sawmill would depart for the open sea. Spring comes, saw blades ring, sirens wail, and white clouds of smoke rise, as if the whole factory is traveling along brightly lit roads.

This settlement on the shore of the lake is borne by the verve of this region, where colonizers fight their way into the north, winning the taiga with rifle and ax. Shaggy Siberian horses neigh, thudding axes and droning saws resound, the snow is covered with woodchips and sawdust, and a new fortress can be seen growing in the forests. Pleasant residential buildings rise, drills buzz, clamps creak, fires crackle beneath sooty pitch cauldrons. Civilization grows in the icy wilds. Where just the other day she-bears raised their cubs in forest dens, today there stretches the red building of the workers' club with 500 seats, a cinema, and a stage. Streets are opened with canteens, stores, a doctor's practice, a school, a hospital, and workers' apartments—all Nordically neat and tidy.

Some 2,000 kilometers from Moscow and 100km from the last railroad station, in the vast forests that reach to the Arctic Ocean, dynamotors thunder, lights shine, children sing, and a balalaika band strikes up. There is a good, rich library with a collection of socio-economic literature that university libraries in Western Europe would envy. A reading and writing course for illiterates operates at the Party club as well as a university-level technical and political seminar, where they speak about a range of current topics in a more settled and disciplined manner than at any political rallies at home.

On the way back from the excursion to that settlement, I walked alongside Karl Ludwigovich Diefenbach and waited for him to speak. He trod the whole way in silence, with his head bowed, and at dinner he was pensive and serious. When we went to bed that evening (we slept in the same room, at his request, so he would not have to sleep alone), Diefenbach spoke resolutely and deliberately, like a soliloquy: "You have to admit, those Russians sure know what they're doing!"

We visited a small hut lined with bearskins, the home of the sawmill's manager, Comrade Vasilyev. A copy of a British illustrated magazine from the 1880s stood out above his desk. It depicted the assassination of Alexander II in front of the Winter Palace: horses rearing and tearing away from the shaft in panic, the bomb bursting in a bright flame, a scattered herd of passersby and mounted police, all rendered with rough strokes of the pen, obviously the work of an autodidact who traced even the finest detail with much naïve attention. One of the moral-intellectual architects of Alexander II's assassination was Stepan Khalturin, a worker and autodidact, a native of Vyatka, where a monument stands to him in the main square, raised in gratitude by a later generation that captured the positions Khalturin had so bravely assailed—a solitary standard-bearer who died before his time. Khalturin was one of the organizers of the North-Russian Workers' Union and was hung in Odessa for the assassination of the military commander of Odessa, an infamous butcher. The countenance of Stepan Khalturin, the patron of the new industrial settlement, dominated Vasilyev's study in a black, stylized frame like a photograph redrawn with charcoal. A pale, gaunt-faced, tubercular young man with a downy beard and red, feverish eyes.[*]

The millions of avengers who rose up to continue Stepan Khalturin's cause also set off into these distant northern forests to bring the light of civilization into the darkness of centuries, and one of them was sitting right here at this desk, inspired by the heroism of Khalturin's generation, and himself prepared for the great cause, when Man frees himself from outmoded medieval ideas and practices to live a life deserving of his consciousness and experience. Today Vasilyev develops the sawmill and is raising a settlement in the far north, and on his desk stands Lenin's plaster head, mutely staring at *Teach Yourself Higher Mathematics*, which the sawmill manager stays up studying for nights on end like a devoted young autodidact so he can sit the entrance examination for a high-level course for senior technical staff. On the wall a photograph of the same man, in the grey greatcoat of the tsarist Russian infantry with a peaked service cap, standing beside his girlfriend, in front of a canvas backdrop with a painted old-fashioned convertible with spoked wheels. What a gulf it was between that conscripted, uneducated Russian soldier in his greatcoat, who as a candidate for death in service of the tsar was saying goodbye to his girlfriend, and this manager of an entire settlement, studying a course in higher mathematics. Today he is a revolutionary general who has fought his way through fire and gunpowder smoke to his office with an enormous Swedish stove, to a large glass verandah full of luxuriant ficuses, and to a library of books scattered all about the house. If the guns of the cruiser *Aurora* had not convulsed the world, Vasenka, as he is affectionately known, would have returned to this hungry village in his bullet-riddled greatcoat, a hero of battles for the tsar, and would

---

[*] In a film I later watched in Moscow depicting the life of Stepan Khalturin, that young man, in his last act at the gallows, puts the noose around his neck himself to console his friend who is waiting to be hanged under the next gallows. "We are dying for a just cause. Millions will avenge us." At the same second, a vista opens up over their heads with the fulfillment of Khalturin's vision: Red Square in front of the Kremlin with hundreds and hundreds of thousands of heads, hands, and flags: a mass meeting in the tempestuous agitation of a storm that threatens the whole tainted world built on crime and murder.

have toiled for the rest of life at the frame saws of the Alexeyevs, for Anna Ignatyevna and Mr. Diefenbach from Hamburg, and perhaps only his grandchildren would have lived to see the Alexeyevs' grandchildren curse them as liquidators of their happiness.

This New Man is not sentimental. He reads *Soviet Culture* and other literary journals, he cites John Reed, Romain Rolland, Henri Barbusse, and passages from the works of Soviet writers from Boris Pilnyak to Ilya Ehrenburg and Mayakovsky. His hardcover series of Lenin's works is not just a decoration above the divan. The books are underlined in many places with red and blue pencil, and every word of Lenin's has biblical significance for this brigadier. Every day, at lunch and dinner, he looks at a large map of Russia, on which electric power stations, new transformers, and new sources of energy in millions of kilowatts are marked with red circles, and the map shows that the space from Arkhangelsk to Odessa and from Tobolsk to the Baltic is turning red from those circles, foundries, and that thousand-ton rhythm of iron and steel. Great plans for electrification, industrialization, cooperatives, and all the political slogans that these people use to motivate the masses for the winning of the people's rights thunder through our general's mind like the newest model of Trans-Siberian locomotives.

This is a new type of Russian man here in the bleak forest region, among Siberian bears. He resembles Jack London's gold diggers more than Anton Pavlovich Chekhov's Russian intellectuals from the turn of the century. And while Russia's Chekhovian intellectuals today are really in emigration (like all those Izabela Georgiyevnas, generals' and admirals' wives, who Anna Ignatyevna dreams about) or are émigré yearners at heart (like all the Alexeyevs), Vasilyev is a fighter who dealt blows because he was right, and who even in his wildest dreams cannot imagine Anna Ignatyevna getting into her coach again or traveling to Hamburg or Biarritz on a honeymoon. What does he care about Anna Ignatyevna and her tears? He builds bathrooms, screens films, plays a phonograph with Lenin's speeches, and all the drivers, lumberjacks, and workers at the frame saws call him Vasenka and believe Vasenka works wisely because he follows a plan that did not come like a windfall but grows according to the law of the Russian land. And when Vasenka calls them one day, they will take their rifles and helmets and follow after him, in his brigade, to the Urals, Vladivostok, or Peking, wherever he orders, because Vasenka is their man.

As I looked at Vasenka, I remembered Cromwell's Round-heads and felt terra firma beneath my feet once more in this apocalyptic time.

LENINISM ON THE STREETS OF MOSCOW

Tolstoy says of Moscow that every Russian feels its maternal significance; foreigners, even without knowing that Moscow is the "Mother of all Russia," sense the feminine character of the city. According to Tolstoy, Napoleon too felt the womanliness of Moscow: "This Asiatic city with its countless churches, sacred Moscow! Here it is at last, this famous city! It was high time!"

Looking at Moscow in the distance on September 2, 1812, at ten o'clock in the morning, he called his translator, Lelorme d'Ideville, and said to him: "A city occupied by the enemy is like a girl who has been dishonored." Then, turning to his entourage, he ordered that the boyars be brought before him: "Bring the boyars to me!" Two full hours passed after Bonaparte's command, and still there were no boyars. They had fled the city, which, owing to an optical illusion, seemed to Bonaparte a "dishonored girl," but actually it was a mine that would reduce his grand career to dust and ash.

When bourgeois-minded travelers from Western countries arrive in Moscow today, they expect to see boyars, but the boyars have fled the city and there is not a single trace of them. And if Moscow today, owing to a Western European optical illusion, may seem like a girl "dishonored" (by the Communards), it is, as in Bonaparte's case, a mine, whose mighty blast will reverberate for generations to come.

There is nothing womanish about this city, whose flags and slogans symbolize a synthesis of contemporary political activism, both European and international, on the ruins caused by the world war, which shook the foundations of bourgeois civilization in 1914.

Moscow today is the smithy of Leninism and has been Leninized with innumerable decorative means. Monuments to Lenin stand in the vestibules of the stations, and the traveler sees countless variants of Lenin's figure from the first moment he sets foot in Moscow. Lenin in a dynamic pose, rearing up with a temperamental gesture, as a standard bearer and storm petrel, as an admiral at the bow of a galley, as a leader of mesmerized masses that follow his every word; there, from a cornucopia, he pours a rain of golden chervontsy from the internal loan for the modernization of the economy, and there his bald head with its Tatar features looks at us from a red-framed locket, with two shrewd, dark eyes, and a sensual lower lip. In shop windows, on posters and flags, on cinema screens and advertising banners, in streetcars and on the walls of churches and palaces, he appears as Moscow's spokesman, as the teacher and preacher of Moscow's political primer, aiming to make Moscow the "Third and last Rome," as the West writes.

Lenin is engraved into Moscow's walls like a foundation of granite, he floats in a tympanum above facades, and Moscow's buildings are covered with Lenin's quotes like mosques are with words from the Quran. You drink a beer in a restaurant, and by chance your gaze falls on the round paper coaster under the mug, and in the mug you see Lenin's analysis on the colonial question: "Five sixths of the globe are slaves of capital. The only free sixth of the world is the Union of Soviet Socialist Republics!"

You wander the streets, and there engraved on a multistory building in stylized, early Cyrillic letters you read: "The Revolution is a whirlwind that breaks all its opponents." At the Church of the Iveron Mother of God, where Enlightenment figures Bogoslav Šulek and Ljudevit Gaj prayed to God, and Canon Rački was struck by the devoutness of the Russian people, Lenin's paraphrase of Marx's declaration "religion is the opium of the plebs" is engraved in the stone. That slogan of Marx's, which destroyed all the charm of that metaphysical narcosis, became the motto of the review *Bezbozhnik*, the organ of Russian atheists, which is delivered all over Moscow in thousands and thousands of copies by large trucks adorned with the same slogan.

You stop at the intersection of two wide boulevards in the city center, and your gaze is drawn to the stone relief of a furious lion: "Every great idea causes fear, just like the lion's roar." From one wall a gigantic fist threatens you with its pronounced force and the slogan: "If you're right, strike hard"; and a red length of fabric fluttering over the street like a colorful Chinese advertising banner reads: "Ilyich spoke: Don't forget the children," and there on the poster Lenin explains to servant girls that they too are called to direct the fate of Russia.

You see Vladimir Ilyich in confectioneries, made of chocolate or cream, and tarts and cakes are decorated with passages from his works. In florist shops he is made up of red and white flowers, in bookstores he is the title page of a book, and in bazaars a toy. Children do a jigsaw puzzle with scenes from his life, from his high school days, when his brother was hung, to the historical revolutionary rallies on Moscow's Theater Square. In kiosks and newsstands Lenin is made up of stamps, and on the calendars in banks and the price lists of coffeehouses and stores he threatens capital with a raised right arm or speaks to huge mass meetings about state capitalism and the transitional New Economic Policy (NEP). In fabric stores he is made up of different colors of material, in restaurants he is a label on a bottle, and in barbershops a medallion of hair. Lenin is made of horseshoes and nails, lard and wax, he is a postcard and a bill of exchange, a government bond, an advertisement, and a Party program. His name begins lead articles in the press, introduces political rallies and lectures, and when you go to see a play, your Moscow acquaintance will not tell you about the theater or the actors and their artistic significance in the city or on an overall Russian scale, but about Lenin once having spoken from that stage—Here he drove down the street, that's where he stood that historical day when Kolchak advanced, there he lay ill, and that is where we saw him for the last time...

"Lenin is dead, Leninism lives on," you read a hundred times or more every day at tram stops; it flutters on red flags and glows at night on facades and roofs. In shop windows, in the urbanized city center as well as on the outskirts, where there are long yellow barracks and cows walk the streets, Lenin stands between the bathroom soap and perfume, ersatz coffee and white sugarloaves. His white, plaster bust sits in a marble display window between hams and sausages, illuminated by a lantern wrapped in red, and in a store selling devotional objects he is a gold-haired child alongside relics of saints and icons. Lenin today is a tricolored oleograph in a golden frame, payable in monthly installments, which hangs in offices and above conjugal beds, he is a transparent watermark on love letters and the topic of doctoral dissertations. His mausoleum is an alabaster inkpot or a case carved of walnut wood, a chest for letters or a cigarette box; he is a traveler's souvenir in the form of a vase or glass; he is engraved on plates, ashtrays, brushes, pocket watches, menus, banners, and agitation posters.

A large building in the center of Moscow houses the Lenin Institute, where a legion of professionals is occupied with researching his personality, the books he read, the letters he wrote, and the people he knew. A special Lenin anthology is published, and it prints every trivial reminiscence of that legendary man who took Moscow by storm. His funeral was a historical event of international proportions, and the fact that today Petrograd is named after him, and that not a single city from Moscow to China is without a Lenin street or square, and that some Russian children are named Lenin just as French children were once called Napoleon—these are signs that the avalanche that is Ilyich has not yet stopped its acceleration. Ilyich was, Ilyich said, Ilyich wrote...

So Ilyich is not just a photo on the wall in police stations, a motto of lyrical poems, or a voice on the phonograph. He is not just an army flag or a toast at a banquet, where plenty is drunk and said, though not much thinking is done. He is certainly anchored deep in the consciousness of the Russian man, and his figure is becoming an ever more magic formula of Russian life with every passing day. The Russian people went through so much suffering in the shadow of Leninism, they made it through the bloody period of imperialist interventions and civil wars, and however much bitter and negative experience accumulated in the struggle against harsh and inhumane reality under the idea of Leninism, Lenin's name nevertheless has a warm, conciliatory sound—almost soft. That is not the sentimental gentleness of lyrics but a catharsis, when a higher sense of tragedy is spiritualized over generations.

"Oh yes, yes, Ilyich, yes—that was a man... yes, yes, he was a genius of a man... and if death hadn't taken him away so soon..."

You hear cursing and swearing about everyone. The great figures and the small supernumeraries of the Revolution often appear ludicrous in the eyes of contemporaries, and bitter jokes circulate about all the personalities in the Kremlin, but when people speak about Ilyich you can sense genuine restraint and respect, simple and honest. He is a master and a rabbi, a symbolic initial and a light in the darkness. He is Ilyich, who at that time said to his disciples: "Verily, I say to you, not even the gates of hell will restrain me..."

Today Leninism has spread all over the globe, like a shadow of the large intimidating continent that stretches from the Caucasus to Alaska, and from Vladivostok and Mongolia to the

Baltic, and the forge of Leninism of both Russian and international magnitude is Moscow. Here the sets of his twenty-six volumes are printed, and from Moscow those books are churned out in millions of copies throughout the world in all the languages of the continents, like holy scriptures. The former tsarist Officers' Club in Moscow is today a large commercial house of seven floors, which drones like a beehive with its forests of typewriters, with the clamor of clients and the giant enterprise's staff, who are busy organizing the delivery of Lenin's opus. Several hundred shipping clerks work eight hours a day to distribute those yellow-packaged volumes, which travel in freight elevators, are loaded onto trucks, and are delivered to all corners of the world, from Shanghai to Tierra del Fuego.

In Varvarka Street, in the Kitay-gorod part of Moscow, there are several huge palaces with entire departments dealing with the newest branch of industry: the "Lenin Corner." Every Russian school, public enterprise, Party and army unit, every literacy circle, and professional association had its "Lenin Corner." Images from Lenin's life are tacked onto the wall in the corner of the room together with diagrams of the plan for electrifying all of Russia, the historical victories of Soviet armies, coking works, blast furnaces, hydroelectric power plants, and flags; Lenin's books are on display too, along with photographs of his manuscripts, a plaster cast of his death mask, a phonograph with records of his speeches, and documents from Lenin's life from his earliest childhood days to his apotheosis on Red Square. All that material is forced into the market in great quantities, so it is not surprising that the industrialized cult of Lenin is reflected at every step in Moscow's streets, dominating the capital and the countless other cities across the breadth of Russia.

Lenin's Mausoleum is today the center of Moscow. A temporary model of the Mausoleum designed by architect and academician A. V. Shchusev stands on Red Square in front of the Kremlin's Senate tower. The Assyrian cube is a symbol of eternity, with a sign in five simple, uppercase letters: LENIN. The model is made of wood, but the intended tomb is to be more enduring than bronze or the poetic word.

Pilgrims come together in front of the model mausoleum every day to bow to the deceased. The Siberian gold digger and bear hunter stands alongside a yellow-skinned Chinese coolie, the muzhik from the Tula governorate next to an asthmatic Dutch petit bourgeois or a farmer from Westphalia. Women and children, old men and soldiers, beggars and deacons with tall caps and long, wet beards—all of them stand and get drenched in the snow and wind, waiting to enter and pay homage to the shade of the man who believed in the victory of human reason. Every day since January 21, 1924, crowds have mutely filed past his embalmed body in the glass coffin.

Napoleon's sarcophagus beneath the dome of the Hôtel des Invalides in Paris, with banners and trophies of victories from Wagram to Moscow, makes an architecturally solemn impression, with imperial pathos, and indeed those Boneapartist days were full of pathos when the destiny of Europe was drawn up in Tuileries. Bonaparte's sarcophagus is positioned with such sophistication that everyone who wants to see it has to bow their head (whether they want to or not) before the general who liquidated the Revolution, leading Beethoven to erase his dedication of the *Eroica*, indignant over this megalomaniac comedian.

Embalmed, yellow in the glass coffin, Lenin with his reddish goatee in an ordinary Russian proletarian shirt, a clenched fist and a concealed ironic smirk on his lips—that Lenin, waxen, motionless, completely and Pascalesquely alone in the most banal rosy lightdark. On the one hand, it seems rudely barbaric, like out of a wax museum, and yet that wax doll, illuminated by the magic of the mysterious East, speaks in the secret, unintelligible voice of Russian-Asiatic mystery that smokes in the sooty, damp Moscow churches and is scarcely comprehensible to the materialist people of the twentieth century. Lenin sleeps beneath the glass of the transparent coffin, and on either side of the body a Red Guard stands watch; the ruddy reflection of the one bare blade flickers on the razor-sharp cavalry saber of the other, just as reflections glittered ominously on the knives of the guards of honor who went as stiff as wax at God's tomb in the night from Good Friday to Easter Saturday.

In that wooden mausoleum four meters below the ground, where bareheaded, quiet processions pass inaudibly along the red carpet in the tepid, stuffy air with a sense of unearthly dread, their gazes trained toward the bald, yellow skull of the corpse, whose nostrils shine from the whiff of death—a miracle is occurring there. There a man continues to agitate obstinately in the interests of his Party, from the distance, from another, unknown shore, present among us here through his corpse, but actually he has departed and is only a shadow, but a shadow that—to spite all gods—lives on in the slogan that only the unity of the proletariat can save the world from future catastrophes.

All the Persians and Indians, and people of dark complexion from central Africa and the American South, who have filed past that waxen body with its clenched fist take with them the indelible imprint of their posthumous audience with that white man, who spoke and wrote for twenty-five years that the question of the colonies is exactly as important for the European working class as the question of the eight-hour working day or social welfare. Bonaparte lies in his tomb in the Hôtel des Invalides like an emperor before whom, according to court etiquette, one has to bow one's head, but Lenin still agitates in the middle of Moscow like he did during his lifetime, when the squares of this city resounded with his voice, and thousands and thousands hearkened to his words like the voice of a whirlwind.

Lenin's final resting place is today the center of Moscow, and just as Muscovites used to ask if you had seen the Ivan the Great Bell Tower or Saint Basil's Cathedral, today they ask if you have been to see Ilyich.

When the city is festively lit up, all the buildings and factory chimneys are illuminated with Lenin's name; an innumerable mass of his photographs and reproductions can be seen in shop windows, displays, private houses, and albums. He is the topic of a monograph, a Biedermeier silhouette, and a futuristic drawing; he hangs in the foyers of theaters, Louis Quinze parlors, and sleeping cars. In the former English Club (so well-known from *War and Peace*), in today's Museum of the Revolution, Lenin now moves at the head of the Russian masses, who sensed a reflection of their own character and will in Yemelian Pugachev and Stepan "Stenka" Razin, and who wanted to take their fate into their own hands. Pugachev and Stenka Razin boldly crossed the Volga, each commanding a host of thousands, and a fear of burning cities went out before them and announced a new dawn that could not yet come. The boyars in Tsarskoye Selo trembled before

115

Stenka Razin when those legendary muzhiks lit fiery beacons on the Russian horizon; but all the halls of the English Club, where the laughter of courtiers rang and general's liveries gleamed in tsarist dress not long ago, are built up around Lenin today, and focus on him.

Lenin is not only a historical anecdote in school text-books; he is a malediction in the souls of all those pale figures who today wander the streets of Moscow like straw-clutchers and human flotsam, cursing the day and hour of the proletarian victory. In the streets, Lenin is sold as cufflinks and as a brooch for servant girls; he is the red Party star in the buttonhole of a worker's tunic, cheap toothpaste, advertisements for the machines of metallurgical trusts, the name of a locomotive, or a freshly painted red electric tram. Masses throng through Moscow's streets selling tiny white rubber cockades with Lenin's likeness; peddlers, long-bearded adventurers in dirty caftans, sell Lenin on drinking glasses, flower vases, plaster bas-reliefs, coffee cups, and cigar holders. When a foreigner arrives in Moscow today, his first and most unusual impression is that the entire city, in its dynamism and the movement of the masses, bears the imprint of an unreal shadow that appears again, symbolically, after death, just as Christ returned. Lenin speaks from the top of trains, marble plaques, the facades of large and majestic Moscow buildings, and from the Kremlin walls. Lenin watches you from storefronts, flutters on flags, and hangs in boredom above your bed in an empty hotel room; he is a lamp and a signpost, an everyday conversation, a newspaper article, and state power.

THE ADMIRAL'S MASK

Admiral Sergey Mikhailovich Vrubel was not a stupid man and, on top of that not overly flattering phrase, it could be said that he perceived things and events with a lot of imagination. Already as a young frigate officer, Sergey Mikhailovich went to war on the Tiger Peninsula, in Port Arthur, with a battery of 15cm guns, and he was there at Stessel's capitulation, where he surrendered his *espada* into the hands of the Japanese admiral.

The battle cruiser on which Sergey Mikhailovich steamed into Port Arthur ran aground at the beginning of the siege in the narrow channel between the mainland and Tiger Peninsula, in that damned strait full of dangerous reefs, which sealed off Port Arthur Bay like an impenetrable barrier. In the Port Arthur basin, full of terra rossa, where there was not a single tree far and wide on the bloodstained mud, and the wind wept sad and lonely over the juniper scrub, in that borderland constantly lapped by the yellow-green, muddy Chinese sea, in the middle of that marshy, malarial landscape, Sergey Mikhailovich fell prey to melancholy. He had been considered a good pianist on the *Zhemchug* (Pearl), but that poetically named cruiser sank most prosaically when entering the harbor, together with his Chopin and Rachmaninoff études. He had two or three quite decent friends at the battery, excellent chess players, but they gave up the ghost during the siege, due to Japanese bullets or scurvy. There was no shade, no water, and food ran low; the sun beat down ever more unbearably, and the Japanese artillery bombarded them with greater and greater precision, twenty-four hours a day.

Admiral Sergey Mikhailovich spoke about those long-past Port Arthur days with sarcasm and pronounced disdain, as is the wont of tired old soldiers who in retrospect have nothing but scorn for complex military issues.

"All of Port Arthur, the monumental tsarist disgrace in Port Arthur, was in fact one of the most shameless confidence games the world has seen. The concrete of the bastions and artillery casemates was all just rubbish and dust, the cheapest English junk! Material was miscalculated and major components built badly, and even the most essential corrections would have required at least three years of systematic reconstruction by fortifiers who knew what they were doing, not by the swindlers from Shanghai. They were Japanese agents and the whole fraudulent scheme was in their hands from the beginning. The woodwork all rotten, the girders, cables, dynamite, heavy guns—all of it English rubbish of the worst sort. Why the Russian general staff bought that old Chinese fortress for so many millions, God only knows! It was rumored in Saint Petersburg that circles of the court were interested in the forest industries on the Yalu River and the Manchurian mines, but those were just parlor intrigues in the capital. At the end of the ballad, someone has to take the blame for all the disgraces of history."

It has become customary in Russia today for all scandals to be blamed on Nicholas, that idiot of a tsar, and lady-in-waiting Anna Vyrubova, but as far as Port Arthur is concerned, Sergey Mikhailovich could be an objective historical witness that Rasputin did not have his fingers in that sanguinary affair. Port Arthur was an entirely different thing—a clear case of so-called strategic madness, but not sabotage. The whole fortification system was based on manifestly imbecilic, yes, even clinically insane assumptions.

"Every general staff in the world is made up of paranoiacs, paralytics, maniacs, and schizophrenics of every kind, it's true, but the perspective of the tsarist general staff was uniquely cretinous: they assumed that the Japanese would be unable to put ashore at all and that the 15cm batteries would be more than adequate to prevent any such attempt. It turned out, however, that the Japanese disembarked elegantly, so to speak, with absolutely no hindrance from the Russians, and began to strike at Port Arthur's fortification ring with the most modern 30cm batteries, based on their own calculations, which, unlike the Russian ones, were exact. 'One ring of fortifications will suffice,' they blathered, but in reality even three rings would have been too weak to ensure any kind of meaningful defense. The gentlemen, of course, did not fortify the Laotiehshan Promontory because they stubbornly believed the Japanese would not be able to fire indirectly over the top of Laotiehshan. But it turned out that the Japanese gunners fired from a range of 12,000 meters with pinpoint accuracy. It was all one imbecilic folly after another, one seriously false hypothesis after another, nothing but corruption, prostitutes, champagne, espionage—that was the madhouse of the tsarist general staff. Besides, what is modern European warfare in this day and age?

Twenty kilometers away even today's biggest dreadnoughts look like tubercules under a microscope. It's all a molehill being dug two or three kilometers away."

When Sergey Mikhailovich today thinks back to those distant Port Arthur days, all the horrors have gone and the only thing he remembers in his panic is the motor of the Port Arthur icehouse. All night he had to listen to that accursed icehouse motor chugging and reverberating from the wall of the magazine, tuff-tuff, tuff-tuff, tuff-tuff, tuff-tuff...

That was the music that the melancholic Sergey Mikhailovich made, scorning his career as an admiral, and at the end of the ballad during the world war, which Russian poets went so far as to title "Madam War," he commanded a division of the Baltic Fleet and ultimately surrendered it to a social democratic delegate of the Baltic Soviets, without having fired a single round from one of his cruisers during the entire war. His flagship, on which he signed the capitulation, was the *Slava*, meaning "glory"—sic transit gloria. Things took their normal course. He lost all interest in politics, and when they shot his wife in 1920 (a blondee Courlandic baroness), he was already rather aloof and above all our banal, everyday trifles.

It was in the winter of 1920 when the GPU shot his missus. Moscow was waist-deep in snow and one single path led along the middle of Petrovka Street between towering drifts. Sergey Mikhailovich took his wife a spoonful or two of hot soup every day, and when they told him he did not need to come any more, he knew what that meant. His first thought was that it would be best to eat the soup straight away so it would not get cold. He immediately downed the hot soup and then returned home, sat on the divan, and reflected on having lapped up his wife's soup like a dog. Yes, that's how it was, and that was all. Now he works as a correspondent in an industrial enterprise, writes in English, and is doing well. He paints, tries to forget, and plays music. Chopin, Rachmaninoff, Skryabin—there are a few interesting names among the young Russian composers, but none of them write so well for piano.

That monstrous Admiral Sergey Mikhailovich was a man of his kind, and a good actor, with the allures of an artist: his apartment looked like a wax museum. He lived in a two-story wooden cabin from the middle of the last century, and through the window of the rear room white birches could be seen in the snow of the garden, and a high wall of rough red brick stood at the far end. Vapor rose from a steam duct in the house on the other side of the yard, and the sound traveled inside and constantly reverberated in monotonous, Port Arthuresque intervals: tuff-tuff, tuff-tuff, tuff-tuff...

Perhaps when he fantasized there at the grand piano over ivory keys as a young frigate officer in his dolman with gold braid, medals, and dainty epaulettes, playing romances, when the candles' brightness spilled over the porcelain and gleaming polished surfaces, and when the spider-webbed mirrors shone with the shoulders of beautiful young ladies, busts of luscious marzipan white, discreetly bordered with black velvet and silk—perhaps there was personal warmth and laughter in the Admiral's apartment that frothed like champagne from witty aperçus, and perhaps the mise-en-scène of those days gave the moldy, grey space a different, more charming note, but today it all smelled of that fine, scarcely noticeable mold that spreads like a silver breath over the now dull surfaces, mirrors, and heavy fabric upholstery of the armchairs. Candlesticks, a shabby tiger skin, Makart lamps, a samovar—all of that was steeped in dense reminiscences of the dead baroness, a tall, svelte lady painted in plein air with a parasol, and now veiled in black. Immediately next to the low stove of ordinary, simple rough brick, with a red-hot iron slab where the Admiral cooked his food, was a pile of wet fir, two or three armfuls of gnarled wood, an ax, and a small handsaw. Everything stank of the baroness's cats, three corpulent, old scabby beasts that meowed around the Admiral—a gap-toothed, stooping gentleman with molting tufts of hempen hair.

Those damn cats also filled his life with bitterness, but what could he do? They were all he had left of his late wife.

I first met Admiral Sergey Mikhailovich in a circle of enthusiasts for eighteenth-century copperplate engravings, and in connection with that conversation about old Russian panoramic etchings he invited me to visit him because he owned a whole collection of old Russian etchings from the eighteenth century, and he saw he was dealing with a "connoisseur" (a very complimentary expression, coming from him).

And indeed! The Admiral had a whole series of interesting etchings from the pre-Napoleonic period, various old weapons from Peter the Great's times, porcelain, and furniture (Russian Louis-Philippe), and he was at pains to assure me that these were just the last remains of the trove that had once been considered the Vrubels' family fortune. The whole collection of porcelain and the Vrubels' family silver went to hell in a hand basket. In 1919 and 1920, before the death of his wife, the two of them had lived on that family silver and porcelain, so everything one could see there in the hutches today was just the last of the rubbish, compared with the riches the house had once been overflowing with when his departed grandfather of blessed memory, Admiral Vrubel, still lived there.

Those were days when people died a little every day: in driblets. Every morning Sergey Mikhailovich would take some silver icon or miniature and leave for the Sukharevka market, where he stood around in the biting cold and returned in the evening with a dried fish and a crust of moldy bread in exchange for a piece of Peter's silver. The stupidest thing about that trade was that all those historico-culturally unique pieces ended up in the hands of foreign agents, abroad, for a ridiculously low price. In 1919 and 1920, through until the death of his poor wife, whom they shot as innocent as a lamb, living was like being in agony at death's door.

"Why did they shoot Madam Vrubel?"

"Why? For perverse pleasure. For no reason at all. Why did they shoot her? Just like that... On a whim one morning. They were bored. They found out she was preparing to emigrate, and that's why they shot her."

"Surely they didn't shoot her because of that? People aren't shot just for pleasure, Sergey Mikhailovich, for God's sake!"

"You are young and naïve, dear fellow! What do you know about why people shoot each other? For perverse pleasure, to be sure, and why else would they shoot her? Why didn't they shoot me then? It would have been logical for them to shoot me, and not her. Because if she was preparing to emigrate, then I, logically, should know something about it. But they didn't shoot me, as you can see... You don't know what the GPU is. They've shot hundreds of thousands of people, for absolutely no reason. I call that perverse pleasure!"

"You told me yourself that you ate up the hot soup made for your wife immediately after they informed you of her death. Was that perverse pleasure too?"

"Of course it was. Perverse pleasure, exactly! It was all perverse, mad, wayward... It was all perverse, but nota bene: to crush a human life because someone decided to emigrate..."

"So you confirm that you wife was preparing to emigrate?"

"Yes, she was, naturally."

"And you?"

"Yes, of course, I wanted to emigrate too! But what can a dog do without a tag and without a roof, other than to go down the road with its tail between its legs, wherever luck takes it? We were all at the end of our tether and no one was quite sane anymore."

"Why did you resign in the end?"

"I didn't have the strength to shoot myself. I can't really say why. It wasn't cowardice as much as a question of taste. One of my good officers shot himself in Riga on board our ship, in his cabin. He stuck his carbine in his mouth and his skull burst to smithereens onto the roof of his cabin. So I didn't shoot myself. After Alice Petrovna's death, I fell into total abulia and became a kind of cretin. If we had been lucky enough to save ourselves, we'd be safe and sound today."

"Sergey Mikhailovich, do you really imagine things would be better for you today if you had emigrated? You don't know how émigrés live. What would you be abroad? A piano man in cafés, if you were lucky. You'd probably be playing the balalaika in Cossack costume. Or you'd be dancing the trepak like a hetman in red pantaloons, in provincial cabaret-bars in the Balkans or in Turkey."

"Why should I object? I'd be a free man! Apropos, is it true that there are quite a few Russians in your country? Wrangel's staff is also there, if I'm not mistaken."

Admiral Sergey Mikhailovich took an unusually lively interest in the fate of Russian émigrés in Yugoslavia: the generals and other such gentlefolk, as well as the bishops and high dignitaries in Sremski Karlovci, and I had to tell him in detail about the sufferings of those poor Don Quixotes. I explained that they opened cabarets and bordellos, were tax-collectors and gendarmes, fought as mercenaries in the army of Ahmed Bey Zogu in Albania, sold newspapers on the streets, hired on as police informants, and generally lived futile lives without any prospects at all.

"What do you mean there are no prospects? The Wrangels, Kutuzovs, Golenishchevs, and Denikins know why they are suffering! These gentlemen are gamblers playing *va banque*! Who knows if the tables can still be turned. And if they are turned one day, these gentlemen will return to Russia like the French nobility did with the king, twenty-three years later. And so the émigrés will gain moral and material satisfaction after all, but the rest of us, those of us who stayed behind, we will still be rubbish like we are today. For us, everything is lost, but it's all we deserve."

So as to console Sergey Mikhailovich and comfort him a little in his illusions, I told him about a sad and squalid scene I'd experienced with a tsarist Russian emigrant, a renowned ambassador to European capitals, Baron von X, in the drawing room of one of the counts of Dubrovnik, the bearer of a famous historical name. I had been told in Dubrovnik that Count G. owned a whole set of fine old Dutch cupboards from the first half of the seventeenth century, and since the Count had some plans with those cupboards I found myself in conversation with the naïvely senile Count, a snotty little old man. I was entangled in hopeless chitchat about those damn things and how I ought to persuade Dubrovnik's chief conservationist, Professor M., to purchase them for the prince's court. The situation became completely forlorn when a scrawny hinterland "goat" (ostensibly a chambermaid) burst into the salon and informed the Count of a visit from Baron von X. That illustrious tsarist Russian ambassador in Constantinople, one of Wrangel's émigrés, who had been known to travel in a coach drawn by twelve thoroughbred Arabians, guzzle champagne with Turkish pashas, and detonate mines from Madrid to the Quirinal Hill, now turned up as obsequious and meek as a beggar at the church gate.

This man was now housed in Count G.'s loft in the unenviable role of a subtenant, together with the mice, rats, and pigeons under the roof of the Count's palace. Miserable, wretched, wet, in a filthy, knee-length frock coat with worn-out greenish lapels, as thin as a rake, with the small, reddish, twirled beard of a Spanish grandee, Baron von X came to see his amiable host, the Count, in order to lodge an energetic protest in a no doubt delicate affair.

Baron von X: "Our dear Count has made the attic of his palace freely available to us—a loft with broken furniture and much old clutter—and that is undisputedly a very kind gesture by the esteemed Count, and Baron von X is thus able to enjoy the wind and the song of the rain weeping all night long, and to observe to his heart's content the frolicsome mice, whose games are a cheerful affair, and rather loud, and know no end. But the ambassador's spouse, Baroness von X, is a seriously ill lady, and anyone with a sense of objectivity will admit that to descend from the loft to the first floor, to the toilet, to go down all those four flights, and then to climb back up— to the attic, the mice's parlor, Hotel Draft—all that would not be particularly enviable even under the most normal circumstances, if a man were surrounded by truly charming and well-bred fellow citizens who did not think they had a monopoly over the one and only available toilet. The truth is that the Count has given the Baron his loft to use under the condition that he not disturb him anymore, which is very generous of the Count. But since the Count lives all by himself in an eleven-room apartment, he cannot possibly have arrived at the bizarre thought that the universe is such a masterpiece that it actually abounds with flaws, particularly our paltry human body, which Gautama Buddha described long ago as a worn-out sack with nine holes, ha ha ha. Our paltry body is a misfortune, and there exist perverse natural laws regarding our worn-out Buddha sack, especially with ailing elderly ladies, which some barbarians will take no note of..."

Count G. (interrupting Baron von X diplomatically, manifestly disgruntled by his carping and complaining): "Who is the cause of this problem?"

Baron von X: "It is Mr. Majdić, the shoemaker on the first floor, a tradesman of undoubtedly good reputation—and in possession of the sole key to that one and only miserable toilet. And that tradesman, Mr. Majdić, has been so 'kind' as to impound that strategic key, and thus he practically holds the loft's tenants hostage. He has condemned them to death, so to speak, and if intervention by the competent figure of authority does not occur soon, by the esteemed Count, who ultimately, one must admit, is the sole arbiter in this affair, an authority with the undoubted right of final adjudication under the law—if the Count does not challenge Master Majdić's monopoly over the key for the toilet, which that sansculotte considers his vested right—the Baron and Baroness will have no choice but to commit suicide..."

Count G.: "Why did the Baron not resolve this trifle with that vandal down on the first floor directly?"

(The Count's evasive question in resistance to the ambassador's verbal note admittedly did not make much sense in the moment it was uttered.)

Baron von X: "My words mean nothing to that mad Mr. Shoemaker. He despises us like the most detestable creatures, your Excellency. He even spat at my wife's feet. For that man we are just dregs, wretches who bother him because of that accursed key. Each of us despises all the others, that is understood, but it would still be necessary for the esteemed Count to speak to Mr. Shoemaker—directly, to assert his authority so as to attain some modus vivendi in these impossible relations, because is very difficult to be ill in such dismal circumstances, when a man is forced to trouble his fellow citizens and molest them for the simple discharging of a more or less acknowledged civil right. And when unfortunately he no longer has any social attributes because he now belongs to the lowest in society, he is a zero, so to speak."

The manner and tone of the old diplomat, a virtuoso of verbal prowess when it came to avoiding the direct expression "toilet"—all of that was spoken in a dignified, diplomatically couched way, as if he were negotiating to demarcate an international border, with the decisive threat of a possible double suicide, but at the same time with complete respect for the sacrosanct right of the Count to live in aristocratic seclusion, all by himself in his eleven-room apartment, and for it not to occur to him to help his blue-blooded friend in need.

Our doddery Count remained serenely enigmatic to the end. With a pose of false innocence, he twisted his sclerotic pink mask of a face, like a rubber grimace, and flushed like a little rooster, and thus he offered von X a golden armchair by the fireplace, which was crowned by a gold-embroidered Empire-style lampshade; he served us plum brandy and offered us cigarettes with the obvious intention of returning to the interrupted conversation about his old Dutch cupboards, simply so he would not have to lose time on the open issue of Shoemaker Majdić, the Russian ambassador, and the famous key that had become an existential problem for that shadow of an émigré squatting in his loft.

The scene turned out incomparably weirder than I was able to sketch in words for Admiral Sergey Mikhailovich, in my attempt to convince him that the situation of Russian émigrés was not exactly so brilliant that he should yearn for the ideal Russian life abroad, where boyars became concierges and, as he thought, lived "in freedom" as taxi drivers.

"'Freedom,' like everything in the world, is a relative notion."

"Yes, yes, I agree, 'freedom' is a relative notion," said the Admiral. "A free man who doesn't feel free compared to other free men who do feel free isn't relatively free, now is he? And that's relatively logical. Everything in the world is relative, of course, and even this makeshift here, for all it's worth, cannot but be relatively temporary."

"You're mistaken, Sergey Mikhailovich, if you think this is makeshift. What you call makeshift is now into its eighth year and isn't makeshift at all, but life as such, life taking its most correct course. Your poor understanding of reality, your false explanations of events and circumstances, and the clinical lack of order you are foundering in lead you to believe that the life all around you is makeshift, and you hope that 'something' will happen as metaphysical intervention from above. A force majeure in the form of a world war, perhaps? Those are all fictions, Sergey Mikhailovich. You have to logically and realistically come to terms with a whole range of facts, reconcile yourself with reality, accept..."

"I don't care. There's nothing for me to realize, I'm at the end of my road, and I will, I hope, soon close my eyes forever. So what point is there in making an effort to come to terms with things, and why, and for whom? All of us here already have one foot in the grave, they just need to cover us with soil and everything will be over."

Indeed. In the grey half-light of that snowy March afternoon the man, in his admiral's dolman, from which time had worn off all the gold, looked like some otherworldly apparition. Pale and gap-toothed, with a single tuft of ash-grey hair on the top of his head, and faded, parchment-like, pastel blue, quivering eyelids like a half-dead chicken that flies into a flurry when it sees the ax, the Admiral sat with his back to the light like the corpse of a haggard morphine addict. He spoke and his lips moved, his feeble, neurasthenic fingers leafed through the eighteenth-century etchings as if they were touching rotten veils, but the frightened gaze that emanated from the membranes of the swollen, jaundiced whites in his eye sockets as dark as if they had been shaded with black Chinese lacquer—that gaze skimmed the objects in tangents that dwindled somewhere above that conversation, that apartment, and that time, like asymptotes far away outside in endless, unknown spaces.

Yes, maybe I was right! He seemed to be burdened by the prejudices of his upbringing and his social circles. Perhaps he was one those screwballs (unfortunately so abundant in Russian life) incapable of seeing things as they really are, but see them as they wish them to look. Maybe he also suffered from political color blindness, or false perspective, because of an optical illusion. He did not realize that he no longer saw anything. He was bewildered by events, and the dynamism of Russian life carried him along like debris. Maybe he had become truly confused in his assessment of reality. I was a foreigner and had come to Russia for the first time, so what impression did Russia make on me? How did this Russian life today compare with Europe? What was Europe doing?

"One thing struck me immediately after crossing the Russian border, and since then I've devoted particular attention to it: nowhere did I notice a single person with poor footwear! Everyone had more or less good boots."

"It only *seems* to you like good footwear, from your coach, en passant. But ultimately, even if all the boots in Russia are well-soled today, was it really worth shedding so much blood for those unhappy boots?"

"It's not just about boots and galoshes! A middling simplicity rules the streets, there's no luxury, but nowhere have I seen any of the visible poverty that abounds in big cities in the West. I didn't notice any conspicuous pauperism."

"Then you didn't look very closely, dear fellow. Our Russian poverty doesn't sit in a shop window. It's not shown to foreigners. It's buried deep, and you have no idea what Russian poverty looks like. If only you had the opportunity to see a Russian village!"

"I've been to villages. I've seen electric lighting in villages, and I've listened to the radio there!"

"How strangely gullible you are!" Sergey Mikhailovich laughed bitterly. "I assure you, it was a Potemkin village if you heard the radio there. On my word of honor, dear fellow. If only you had seen Saint Petersburg. What a city! The whole of Saint Petersburg around the Admiralty was a treasure-trove of history and culture. All of Empire-style Saint Petersburg could have been put in a museum. But today it's ruins and rubbish."

"Rubbish" was the Admiral's favorite word and he used it with special emphasis.

"My God," I said, "the class that slaved away when Saint Petersburg was an Empire-style showcase had absolutely no benefit from that, and neither does it today! Consequently, that class has neither gained nor lost anything from that broken urban experiment. I've been to collections and museums, and I found them in good condition. So the treasures of rich Russian history are probably not as ruined as all that... In general, there's too much bile about. Everything is tainted with animosity. No one hates as much as a class that has been declassed."

"What a bizarre attitude! Do you really believe in 'class'? Do you really think classes exist? Once, long ago, a man wanted to convince me that class existed and was a factor in history. He gave me the *Communist Manifesto*. I read that cruddy pamphlet up to page seven, but it was all so naïve that I tossed it. What class, I ask you? The Vrubels have been around for over 400 years, the records say, and one old Vrubel, my grandfather's brother, fell in July 1830 at the barricades in Paris. What does class have to do with it? What does the death of my paternal great-great-uncle have to do with class? Eighteen years before your *Communist Manifesto*, that old Vrubel fell for the cause of the Revolution! But I get beaten blue today because of that very same Revolution! Come on, tell me, what logic is there in that?"

And so we talked about the Baltic Fleet: about the horrid, inhuman, distorted life on board the ships, about the warship being the pinnacle of technical organization on the one hand, but life on a warship being dehumanizing; we talked about half the officers of all the world's fleets being confirmed nutcases, and about the Revolution only having been able to succeed thanks to the mutiny in the Baltic Fleet.

"There was a time when a little piece of fetid herring was considered a first-class delicacy, and then the hungry stood up and overthrew state power. It seems to me that a time will come when rotten fish will become a delicacy once more. Then the hungry will stand up again and topple state power! Russia today is ruled by the triumvirate of Bronstein, Dzhugashvili, and Dzerzhinsky. After the triumvirate it will not be long till the time of the First Consul, ha ha! And everyone knows what comes after the *Eighteenth Brumaire*! Ha ha! Step aside so I can take your place! That's all!"

Night was falling when I took my leave. Admiral Sergey Mikhailovich was so discomposed at my impending departure, in his convivial-conventional way, that I could not refuse his offer to accompany me, and so we went out onto the street together.

It was snowing in the yellow March evening. Wet, heavy flakes clung to sweaty nostrils and eyelids, and Moscow's streets hummed with an unusual briskness, rolling like a sinking river that never stands still and roars away behind mighty walls. On Lubyanskaya Square, around the Vitaly Fountain, trams rang their harsh, reverberating bells, sirens and horns wailed, newsboys shouted "Evening Moscow," as they wildly played some kind of game in the muddy snow for a fifty-kopeck silver coin. That was exactly the day when the Soviet president Dr. Narimanov lay on a catafalque in the Trade Union Palace, in the great hall of marble columns, and black flags were draped from all of them.

The first lights went on in the department stores, a black human wave bobbed and swelled in the yellow evening light, massive black domes of the city with bell towers and antennae, the deep blue misty perspective showed wet black banners amid the hubbub of the street—an unsettled image full of movement. Endless processions of union and political organizations paced along Moscow's streets to pay their last respects to the President of the Soviet, and above the crowds on the squares and streets countless red flags waved, unfurled high on poles with black veils, as if moving all by themselves above that human mass, that torrent in the street. Lines of red banners of the eastern nationalities with Turkish and Arabic letters and slogans in English, a mass of banners with slogans of individual factories and neighborhoods, a vast sea of banners from Moscow and Leningrad, in Georgian, Tatar, Lapp, and Finnish. People with slanting eyes, bronze, dark brown, lacquered complexions, a throng of Latvians, Ukrainians, and Byelorussians, a Russian and Soviet mass, a revolutionary magnitude that flowed like a great river, flooding the sidewalks. Mongols, from distant parts of Asia, wrapped in light-yellow reindeer fur, waved poles with an enormous sign: "Comrades, let us prepare the Universal October." Schoolchildren marched with drums and trumpets, trucks rumbled past packed with delegations of workers from the furthest factories on the city's outskirts, and that whole mass of hundreds and hundreds of thousands of heads flowed together in front of the Trade Union Palace where the Soviet president Narimanov lay in state on a catafalque.

"Please look, Sergey Mikhailovich," I said, unable to restrain myself from sharing my impression with him. "You probably won't deny that this movement of the masses is spontaneous, that it's an active sign of affection for the dead president. It would be technically impossible to drive hundreds and hundreds of thousands out into the snow and wind like this with an order."

"It seems you haven't read the history of a single revolution. Take the French Revolution, for example. Don't you know that the Paris mob cheered Robespierre only two weeks before his death? What do you know about the mob? No, look instead at the lights on the building over there. That's the GPU!"

Admiral Sergey Mikhailovich Vrubel uttered those three letters—G, P, U—with such mysterious emphasis that I inadvertently cast a glance at the pale yellow illuminated windows of that tall, dark building on Lubyanskaya Square, on whose tympanum shines a transparent globe of glass, in the glow of its red equator, meridians, and the symbols of the proletarian dictatorship: the hammer and sickle. GPU! Those three letters are pronounced with great earnestness in all of Russia; the significance of the notion GPU is truly momentous, and it is used in drama and film as a tragic effect in the final act. The role of the real or imagined GPU in contemporary Russian drama coincides with the role of Fate in the classical tragedy, and when the GPU appears on the scene all the antagonists are doomed.

"Yes, but I don't understand the connection between that building and this demonstration."

"A causal connection, Sir! It's a causal connection. If you don't mind me telling you, it's a specific case of Russian causality. If it were not for those illuminated windows, there would not be this parade. There would be none of these things in Russia today if it were not for that building with the glowing globe. That's the bloodiest building in the world! You haven't experienced what it means when someone near and dear to you disappears behind those doors. You go with them up to that sentry, and never again... You don't know what that means."

Sergey Mikhailovich stared at the illuminated building on the far side of Lubyanskaya Square and I noticed that his eyes had filled with tears. He bit his lower lip nervously, nodded slowly and importantly, and then took off his hat and crossed himself three times piously, and stood there bareheaded like that: mournful, quiet, and bent.

"*The Collected Works of Alexander Herzen*, one and a half rubles!" a hoarse secondhand-book dealer yelled behind our backs in the snowstorm. Life kept rolling on, ponderous and heavy, according to its own deep and irrefutable laws. Vendors shouted "Crimean apples!", spit out the husks of sunflower seeds, sold dried fish and little tin toy frogs that scooted here and there on tiny wheels, and over the wall of Kitay-gorod from Nikolskaya Gate palls of dense, black impenetrable, smoke came billowing, wreathing the whole street in soot and the thick smell of fire.

I looked at the bareheaded Admiral, balding, pale, and with tears in his eyes as he gaped feeble-mindedly at the intensely illuminated windows there at Lubyanka, and I felt the man become more unpleasant to me with every passing second. I thought: *Why the hell is he tormenting me with his story? Is there some system to it? It's plain pathological. I can't help him.*

I wanted to say goodbye to that jerk of an Admiral and board a tram for Arbat, but he suddenly declared that he had a matter to attend to in Arbat, so we rode together. It was crammed with passengers, and we barely managed to squeeze into the sweaty press of bodies, creased textiles, and muddy gum boots.

"Just look," the Admiral said, drawing my attention to that mass of human meat, coats, boots, and slush. "See how miserable and mournful all these faces are! There's not a single person here who you could say is happy."

"People are returning home after work; they're tired and have their worries. My God, who doesn't have worries today?"

"And that widow lady—doesn't she look like she's spent the whole afternoon fathoming the depth of Moscow River?"

True enough, a bourgeois widow with a doleful face sat huddled on a bench of the streetcar, in a black veil of mourning, in line with all the decorative sepulchral norms, just as widows look in genre compositions of the 1880s, on canvases that are meant to seem sad and sentimental because they have no other purpose than to appeal to unhappy widows. With her red-rimmed eyes, thick fluffy eyelashes, in bourgeois mourning garb, engrossed in her sorrow and with arms folded on her lap, the lady looked solemnly aloof, above the throng of the masses, concentrating on her own personal despair, and in regular intervals, accompanied by a deep sigh, she would dry tear after tear with her black-trimmed handkerchief. Apart from that doubtlessly unhappy widow, there was a man with his right arm in a sling, who grimaced and changed color with the tram's every shudder, as if pierced by pain from his recently dislocated arm. Those were the only two faces that an objective observer would affirm were sad. The other faces in the streetcar were banal, dirty, grey masks beneath greasy fur hats wet from the snow, and in that odor of wet clothes and skin, in the melted snow that trickled in a little stream down through the tram, behind the fogged-up windows, and in the weak illumination, we were sardined together, breathing into one another's cheeks and nervously waiting to alight as soon as possible.

Facing the unhappy widow in black, on the opposite bench, sat two very young women, Party members with red Jacobin scarves. They were both cheerful and seemed happy to be riding through the city. The one at the window was putting stickers on the wet pane. She peeled off the backing with her forefinger very carefully. The stickers were no larger than the advertising labels commonly stuck in shop windows. A voice from the throng told the girl to be careful: she was risking a fine of five rubles because putting stickers on streetcar windows was prohibited. But, after the first few stickers, she applied more and more, heedless of the well-meaning warning from the fellow passenger.

"Didn't you hear, citizen? You're not allowed to stick things on the windows. They'll fine you ten rubles," came the voice of a passenger from another seat.

"It's a completely harmless label and doesn't hurt anyone! They won't fine me for that," the girl said and continued putting her stickers on the window.

"It's not only you who'll be fined, but also me, citizen," the conductor joined in. "Sticking any kind of paper on these windows is prohibited. Come on, please, would you kindly read what it says on the sign!"

"If I'm fined, I'll pay," the girl answered calmly and continued what she was doing.

"But I forbid you from sticking bits of paper in the car I'm responsible for! Citizen, did you hear me?"

"Why are you yelling at me? The times are past when men yelled at women!"

"I'm not yelling at all, citizen. I'm just calmly asking you to remove those stickers now!"

"I will not!"

"But I'm telling you to remove them at once, and if you don't I'll call the police!"

"Go ahead then, if you must. This is ridiculous! Why are you threatening me with the police, and why are you yelling at me?"

"So you really want me to call the police, do you? Alright, you asked for it!" The irritated conductor hysterically pulled the cord of the bell three times to signal the driver to stop. "Let's see if the police will help bring you to your senses."

Agitated and offended in his dignity, the conductor started to fight his way through the passengers toward the exit. The streetcar stopped.

Other passengers: "Why didn't you take off your silly labels like he asked? What sort of game is that?"

The second proletarian girl, who until then had sat in silence, in a lofty, neutral voice: "Why was he yelling, what gives him the right to yell? We know very well what we're allowed to, and what not!"

A man with an emotionless, Beethovenesque face: "Comrades, please, would you take down your silly little stickers, we're in a hurry and don't have time for this nonsense!"

A student with a bag full of books: "Exactly. We can't let the stupidity of others hold us up!"

The widow in her mourning veil, in a semblance of solemnity, above all earthly embroilments: "Is it worthy of a woman to play with things like this?"

The girl who until then had calmly busied herself with the stickers, in an agitated and slightly trembling voice: "What are you trying to say? What do you mean: 'play with things like this'? With what things, and what do you mean by 'play'? Sorry, citizen, I'm not in the least curious to know your opinion, seeing as it's less than intelligent!"

A citizen with a pointy little beard and pince-nez got up and squeezed his way through to one of the freshly applied stickers on the streetcar's window, removed his pince-nez, leaned toward the glass, and read: "MOPR."

Several passengers left their seats after that shortsighted citizen, and all of them pushed and shoved their way to the little sticker on the window to try to decipher the mysterious significance of those hieroglyphs: MOPR.

The other girl: "Come on, citizens, please just keep out of this. It's is absolutely none of your business!"

A man in a black shirt: "Those are labels of the International Workers Aid Society, MOPR, an organization to help revolutionaries. Our comrades are rotting in prisons in Europe and need help. International Red Aid is a good thing. It can't be banned!"

The tram had stopped on one of the busiest streets leading from Theater Square toward Mokhovaya Street, and around twenty trams were already queuing behind us, all of them nervously ringing their bells. Angry voices and shouting. The streetcars signaled again and again, and our own driver rang nervously for us to get moving. There was cursing and swearing. Pause.

When the conductor brought up a policeman, the tension in our car grew considerably and all the passengers, like a gaggle of penguins, respectfully made way for the representative of authority. The policeman, a blonde, smooth-faced boy with a good natured look, visibly indifferent to the whole entanglement, was quite out of his depth with this veritable quandary. Yes, applying stickers to the windows was prohibited in the spirit of positive legislation, there could be no doubt about that. But to campaign for aid to revolutionaries languishing in capitalist jails was not prohibited; on the contrary, class-conscious revolutionaries should consider such assistance their outright duty.

Despite the commotion and raised voices, the proletarian girl who had caused the scene gesticulated defiantly—she was fighting for the revolutionaries out of solidarity—and kept on putting her stickers on the windows ever faster, as if nothing had happened. All of this confused the policeman and he did not know what to do: To enforce the law or not?

"I warned her. Citizen, would you be so kind! The regulations are such and such. I'm responsible for the streetcar, not you. Sticking any kind of slogans on the windows, and paper in general, is prohibited, and you can read that on the sign," the conductor grumbled, expecting help from the policeman.

"Come on, come on, we don't have all day, it's getting late. Chuck her off the car and sort out the problem on the street!"

Someone pulled the cord to signal the driver, and that made our conductor bellow at the top of his voice: "Citizens, I simply can't do my job like this! I'll leave the streetcar!"

A voice: "Good riddance then!"

A gaggle of voices: "He thinks he's still an officer!" "Those times are over, comrade, there are no more epaulettes today!" "Please show me your identity card." "What? We are Party members and have been given permission to glue these labels. You don't read the papers, you don't follow our press! The papers have printed as clear as day that MOPR has been excepted from the ban! You illiterates! This is the cause of the International. It's our revolutionary duty to show solidarity and help our revolutionary comrades in the capitalist dungeons! What backwoods do you live in, comrades? Are you going to arrest two MOPR girls?"

Voices in disagreement: "Comrade policeman, you're here to enforce the letter of the law. Come on then! How can it be that the rules apply for some but not for others?" "What kind of equality is that?" "Who are you?" "And who are you?" "I'm a proletarian!" "We're all proletarians, and I'm a proletarian just like you!"

A nearsighted intellectual, with a bag full of paper and writings: "Citizens, please, citizens, please: Can we get going? They're waiting for me at the workers' university."

And so the commotion grew. The other streetcars honked and rang in the traffic jam behind us, and their conductors and drivers gathered around our car and beat their fists on the windows: "Get a move on!" "What are you waiting for?" "Are you crazy?"

Sergey Mikhailovich Vrubel passively observed this wrangle about a little MOPR sticker, with ironic disdain, but at one point he exploded with a flash of hidden zeal. Like an old warhorse that hears the sound of sabers being drawn, the man flung himself into the fray. In the altercation with the policeman, in the threats and the din, an avalanche of sinister passions started to roil; a fury that begins with an insignificant detail like a sticker on a tram's window, and spreads like wildfire to overturned and smashed streetcars, ruined cities, twisted rails, cannons and catastrophe. Sergey Mikhailovich had clearly made an effort to control himself—visible in restrained spasms of his whole body—but then he launched into the chaos of that scene and started to shout at the policeman: "Do your job, comrade! We are all citizens, we are all equal! Citizens, we cannot allow the rules to apply for some but not for others! We have rights, not just obligations!"

I watched the Admiral in his tattered navy coat, his toothless mouth, his hoarse voice trembling, and I thought that two conceptions of life existed in that idiotic tumult for and against, two mentalities incompatibly separated by the quite insignificant question of an ordinary little MOPR sticker, through to fundamental philosophical problems of capital and labor, God vs. the Devil, beauty and ugliness, good and evil... Gangs of Reds and Whites roared, rude and gruff, voices of gentry and slaves, boyars and serfs. And as I watched Admiral Sergey Mikhailovich Vrubel it was clear to me that the jerk was submitting to the inner voice of his destiny. My nerves were overwrought from the long, hard afternoon; I let the man fight for his fictions, and he protested and shrilled like a suicidal maniac. I squeezed my way out of the throng without being noticed and found myself out in the snowstorm, all squashed and sweaty.

Thick rags of snow flew like slanting streaks in the wind. In the melting snow on the ground, when galoshes are covered with wet mud and when slush sprays from under automobile tires like water beneath motor boats in the grey, turbid light of violet boulevard lamps, the commotion of the draymen, butchers, newsboys, and passersby took on the ghostly forms of an unsettled dance of shimmering apparitions. People were out selling bloody meat in wet newspaper, waving huge, fat fish, running across the street and vanishing in clouds of fog and snow, and at the end of the boulevard, as if borne on the wind, there came a huge procession with red flags: bearded old men with walking sticks, and women holding the hands of children singing sad and obscure melodies. That human river moved like a host of pilgrims, piously and solemnly, and all those people paced with their heads held high, gazing up into the hazy, windy sky. At the head of the procession, on long poles horizontally bent in the wind, went a banner with shining golden letters: "Long live the labor of the blind!"

The wind blew, wet snow fell, and above the heads of the blind there thundered the deep bass of bells, seriously and theatrically like in Mussorgsky and Rimsky-Korsakov at the coronation of the Russian tsar Boris Godunov. The blind marched, singing through that snowstorm, and the red flag slowly moved forward to vanish in the distance, in the grey turbulence of the streets.

I thought of the late Yakov Sverdlov, who spoke on his deathbed to his friends about the great happiness of people who had the opportunity to experience such wonderful days when humanity began to wake from slumber. And on the tram a contemporary of Sverdlov's, Admiral Sergey Mikhailovich Vrubel, was rebelling against precisely the beauty of those Sverdlovish days, with no idea where he was living or of the days he cursed so resentfully.

I found out from a reliable source that Admiral Sergey Mikhailovich Vrubel had played a bloodthirsty role in crushing the sailors' rebellion of 1905–06 in Odessa, where he was one of the most ruthless executioners, and those Odessa events became the foundation of his career as an admiral. Secondly: I learned that in 1915, on his command ship, he had ordered the execution of three mutinous sailors. He later defended himself before a revolutionary tribunal by adducing proof that he had only been following orders from above. Thirdly: Sergey Mikhailovich Vrubel was never married, so the story about the murder of his wife, the Courlandic baroness, was a complete fabrication. Finally, and most importantly: Sergey Mikhailovich submitted a report about me to the police. He had thoroughly questioned me concerning my perception of Russian émigré circles and my impressions of Russia, he wrote. I had a negative opinion of the émigrés and related to Russian circumstances critically, but overall favorably.

THEATRICAL MOSCOW

I think it was August Strindberg who wrote that theater ought to be a Bible for beggars. Indeed! In the last 300 to 400 years theater has been nothing but a sort of picture book for the poor in spirit, and in order that illiterates be able to follow the happenings on the boards, dramatic texts are explained in pictures.

The stage and painting have been inseparably linked ever since Molière's days, and separating the problems of the stage from those of visual art is a futile endeavor. There is a continuity in the development of theaters' mise-en-scène in painting, which can also be neatly traced in Moscow's galleries. If you go through the halls of the Tretyakov Gallery, from the eighteenth century via Romanticism and genre painting to the Russian symbolist decorators and so-called artistic revolutionaries of the last fifteen or twenty years, you will notice on canvases dating back to the end of the nineteenth century that the painter tries to evoke for us full agreement between the form (expressed through color) and the forms and phenomena in nature, but later, from the first decade of this century, the pictures ever more strongly accentuate the "abstract" and the "spiritual," from Kandinsky to the Suprematists and the painters of nonobjective motifs. From Saint Petersburg's Empire-style vistas to rich genre painting with clear and precise scenes like in Canaletto's works; from princely interiors, curtains, coats of arms and gold-embroidered uniforms, from the shiny, lacquered canvases, on which the skin of the ladies is rosy and the furniture massive and regal, to the miniscule worlds that reveal themselves to the inquisitive eye under the microscope, where all things turn to apparitions, like the world of a fly's leg is ghostly beneath a magnifying glass, to the abstract band of dreamers and adventurers that move in the shadow of Kandinsky (proof of the evident decay of academic taste and the cultural anarchy of our time); from the paintings in the eighteenth-century hall of the Tretyakov Gallery to the Museum of Painting on Rozhdestvenka Street—herein lies the entire span of the contemporary schism in painting. From the objective to the nonobjective, here new formulae of consciousness and cognition are being cultivated, technology subordinates all new possibilities of artistic expression to its imperatives, and the moral and intellectual span of contemporary poetry becomes the sole force of creativity and the sole source of inspiration, in the shadow of the vacuum.

And precisely because theater has really become a kind of mass, folk plebeian picture book, it is hardly surprising that a shift in taste has occurred on the stage and frontally challenged the boring academic and Postimpressionist blueprint, not so much in the texts themselves as in the visual fields of screenplay. A doubly paradoxical and illogical tangle unfolds before our eyes: the drama of our days is simple in its contrasts, and the elements of contemporary tragedy are well known; they occur because of the understandable collision of logic and interests, and so poetic expression in contemporary dramatics, which aims for an Aeschylean reflection of reality, should likewise be loud and trenchant—clear, simple, and plastic. Instead, the scenic illustration of theoretically unambiguous dramaturgical collisions is decadent and abstract because it lags behind the artistic taste of our time, and it is in disarray, doubtlessly as a symptom of the slow death of a civilization that is disintegrating, not only in artistic fields but equally in almost all intellectual disciplines. Although today's contemporary social drama ought to be modeled sculpturally, its expression on the stage is abstract and experimental, and it lyrically submits to the abstract adventure of contemporary painters' excursions into nothingness. This gives rise to anxiety, chaos, and confusion in the programs and plans of theatrical life on the stage, and all forty of Moscow's theaters are today just a reflection of the hazy uncertainty and unsettledness that surrounds modern drama like smoke around an improvised fire site where, as far as twentieth-century stage realizations are concerned, there was never much of a blaze. Petty bourgeois events are performed with a nod to tragedy, full of classical analysis and subtle detail; the first attempts at on-stage synthesis with futuristic and Dadaistic scenographic absurdity have been shown, and apart from a handful of successful attempts at experimental theater, the ancient régime flowers on prominent Moscow stages like nowhere else in Russian life!

In theater lobbies decorated with gold-framed portraits of renowned old actors, and in foyers where the milky globes of gas lamps from the 1870s gleam, the aristocratic mood of Empire still prevails, and everything seems as if we were living behind the set of a fantastic status quo ante. Here Maeterlinck and Griboyedov are played, Ostrovsky and Saltykov, Schiller and Shakespeare, and when you return home after a show, where you attended an old-fashioned game of intrigues, played on prospect scenes with three layers of backdrops, out on the street you forget for a moment that you are in a city where all the tsarist monuments have been toppled, a city where the victorious Revolution has politically implemented the dictatorship of the proletariat, a concept so denigrated and slurred in the West. Let us leave aside the golden rococo theaters, in whose boxes one increasingly sees ladies' bare shoulders and décolletés trimmed with a discreet twinkling of diamonds; far away on the city's outskirts there are theaters of the masses, theaters with tendentious revolutionary slogans, where the stage is not a cultural-historical museum but a popular forum for articulating the current problems of the Revolution. The decor and scenery in those theaters are Futuristic, Dadaistic, and Expressionist (in a word, abstract), but the auditoriums are crammed with men in workers' outfits, women with red Jacobin scarves, proletarian masses in boots and work shirts. The seats in those theaters on the periphery are simple, the walls are not papered, samovars steam, the plaster peels, and it smells of phosphorus, damp dust, and disinfectant tinctures. But when the hangman on the stage executes a revolutionary and the orchestra weeps "You fell victim," the wooden seats in the whole auditorium boom spontaneously (like pews in churches), and everyone present sings the death march devoutly and with their head bowed. Those souls' attitude to the beauty of the stage is chaste and religious, and when the guns fire at the barricades and heroes fall in the explosion of dynamite, they stamp their feet on the floor, and shout and applaud with absolute fervor. As in politics, religion, and commerce, as on the street and in the trains, Russian theaters also reveal a differentiation of the two divergent streams in class politics. The agony of bourgeois society today is a symbolic nuance on the stage, a sterile, pessimistic sigh and decorative gimmick, but the masses rising from the depths, that proletarian population whose class consciousness has been woken, want to see its heroes on the boards—those who fall by their own tragic will, but whose idea is victorious.

Theatrical life in Moscow is still largely dominated by the Moscow Academic Art Theater (MAT), whose prime movers are Konstantin Stanislavsky and Vladimir Nemirovich-Danchenko.

Many great names perform here, of whom perhaps only Ivan Moskvin, Olga Knipper-Chekhov, the young Chekhov, and Vasily Kachalov are familiar in the Balkans. The Moscow Academic Art Theater represents the academic past in Russian theatrical life, as its *epitheton ornans* "academic" says; it is a kind of distinguished eminence, about which complex studies are written, and which one speaks of in a monotonous tone, indeed dignified and academic. All of the more eminent names of that "academic" theater bear academic titles, are protectors of newly established studios, and are invited on prestigious tours from New York to Constantinople as representatives of Russian stagemanship; in a word, those ladies and gentlemen are genuine immortals who are assured a sound existence in this world and the next, and who are proud of their new revolutionary honorific title: People's Artist of the Republic.

The sentimental white gull (*The Seagull*, the first dramatic work by A. P. Chekhov, which MAT staged despite the failure of the first performance in Petrograd) did not fall from the sky, shot and bloody, like in Anton Pavlovich's lachrymose drama, but flew high and settled like a fat duck on the rock of theatrical success, glory, and tradition. Today that old duck is fed academic laurels and still sings its same old song full of yearning for dear old prewar Moscow, a symbol of good old days that have gone. From the grey Sturm und Drang of the Secessionist theater in what was formerly Kamerger Lane, with Chekhov's white gull as a symbolic emblem on the grey curtain—that theater has become an international sensation, with its own building on a street that today proudly bears the name of the famous company. Despite strong and fairly vocal opposition on the Russian theatrical left wing, MAT still represents the highest, most exalted level of Russian theatrical life. The gull, a bold storm petrel, a bird of tempest and revolution, a herald of squalls and thunder, took off in Moscow's boyar-bourgeois environment and flew through to its twenty-fifth anniversary, and then stopped, just as Anton Pavlovich's guitar wept on the wall and fell mute. The Moscow Art Theater has none of Meyerhold's rumbling, crane-maneuvered constructions nor rousing banners with slogans linking Shakespeare's stage to the revolutionary scene of the twentieth century. Here virtually no attention, hardly the slightest, is devoted to the revolutionary tendentiousness of the Party slogans that are used on stage to turn theaters into mass meetings. The Moscow Art Theater performs Griboyedov, Maeterlinck, Gorky, and again and again, for the thousandth time or more, *The Lower Depths*, *The Blue Bird*, *Tsar Fyodor*, and *Woe from Wit*. And again *The Blue Bird*, *Tsar Fyodor*, *Woe from Wit*, *The Three Sisters*... And so on, for all eternity.

The rhymes of Griboyedov's romantic world propagated by old Stanislavsky from his boards certainly do mark the beginning of a deep, socio-political engagement with open questions of the boyars' milieu; they are not a boring and uninspired exaltation of socially narrow, inane, lordly "ideals" that are pushed in Yugoslavia almost professionally through the cult of the free city of Dubrovnik and its aristocratism, for example. Griboyedov's heroes feel Byronesquely alone, like recluses, like pioneers of new and revolutionary ideas; in the provincial, backward atmosphere of Moscow in his time, Griboyedov was not only a negative critic of reality but also a poet who moved at the fore of his age. In the period of liberal ferment at the beginning of this century, Griboyedov told the Russian liberal intelligentsia things that perplexingly coincided with the freethinking of the nascent bourgeois class. Patrons of theater and poetry, wealthy men who bought Cézannes, Gauguins, and Van Goghs for their private galleries, founders of museums, protectors of ballet and music, financers of the liberal democratic press, bourgeois like Morozov and Shchukin—that was the element of society that really took to Stanislavsky's stage concepts, discovering in them a deep affinity with its own spiritual aspirations. Back when Gorky protested in Milyukov's paper *Russkoye slovo* against nihilistic self-denigration à la Dostoyevsky on Nemirovich-Danchenko's stage, a time that has vanished like prehistory, Russian liberal audiences listened to Griboyedov on the stage with pathetic fixation as if his words were those of a clairvoyant. To have a Cézanne, a Van Gogh, or a Gauguin in one's parlor, to supervise several thousand miners in the pits of the Don Basin, to attend premieres at the Moscow Art Theater, to enjoy Griboyedov, Maeterlinck, and Chekhov, to read Milyukov's constitutional-democratic homilies—that was the bonton of Moscow's liberal bourgeois society. Griboyedov's heroes were perhaps speakers on the eve of the Revolution, but from a Moscow perspective today MAT's repertoire is doubtlessly rather démodé, with a whiff of expensive ballroom fans. The mechanism of that MAT stage world moves with perfection. Here every movement, even the most insignificant, is mathematically pedantic—a directorial skeleton so exact and structurally calculated that the texts are played on stage with the precision of a chamber music score. Today every MAT performance is a classical concert under the hand of a virtuoso, but the whole repertoire, as a programmatic stance of the theater, is out of line not only with the open questions of Russian theater, but also with Russian reality.

A vague Chekhovian disposition reigned in the souls of the Russian bourgeois intelligéntsia in the pre-revolutionary period, the mood of a sentimental cantilena, where one fantasizes in an ongoing future of illusions: that Man will one day overcome all the negative facets not only of human society, but also of the universe. The Moscow Art Theater found and presented just the right expression for that petty Weltschmerz: thus the fundamentally positive reaction and unprecedented success of its performances, of that "philosophical cult," one could almost say, of the sweet and bewildered yearning of Uncle Vanya and the whole gallery of Chekhovian wailers for what Giambattista Vico long ago called "non so che."

Russian literary life is developing today in the context and spirit of surmounting great resistance, both internationally and in Russia. Never has Russian literature believed in anything as wildly and fervently as the Moscow book today believes in political victories. Novels, novellas, and the belletristic prose of fictionalized chronicles and eyewitness accounts take us through galleries where life in Russia's revolutionary present is still being depicted more in the simple technique of black-and-white contrasts than with a broad range of monumental frescoes. The heroes of the contemporary Russian book are more rhetoric than fiction. Russian literature today is more a medley of events borne by the dynamism of the Revolution, more decorative illumination than analysis, more a propaganda poster than testimony to these turbulent days, more literary material than a reflection on that political reality that is not just a mirror image of a moment but a method and a key to an entire epoch. The Russian book today is still dominated by the chaos of the first biblical days, where the light before our eyes separates from the darkness. It is a struggle for the most fundamental elements of socialist existence, when individuals spiritualized by the great enthusiasm of social awareness, yet isolated in their social environment, make superhuman efforts to struggle against outmoded ideas and practices, not only from the period of Tolstoy's *Power of Darkness*, but going back to the days of Denis Fonvizin and his satirical comedies mocking the Russian gentry. In Ivanov's Siberian and Trans-Baikalian chaos, in the cult of calm farmers and their energy by a writer like Pilnyak, in Tarasov-Rodionov's puritanical earnestness, in the dynamism of Ehrenburg or the wild revolutionary animosity and sarcasm of Mayakovsky, who began his literary trailblazing as "A Cloud in Trousers" and managed to find his poetic vein as an apologist of Leninism, and in the overall bewildering and agonizing turmoil of Russian reality today there exist a mass of issues, and a host of ideological and artistic problems, which Stanislavsky constantly relates to with passivity.

The wheels of time have run over his liberal conception, so the man in his mill just keeps on churning out *The Blue Bird*, *Tsar Fyodor*, and Griboyedov. Stanislavsky goes on lamenting over the catastrophe of *The Cherry Orchard*, he cries for Moscow, playing his old song on Chekhov's guitar tirelessly and unperturbed, in such a way that his defiance appears flagrantly out of kilter with all the issues in Russia's literary and political life today.

In addition to its home on Kamerger Lane, the Moscow Art Theater operates today at four other studios: the Moscow Art Theater–2, the MAT Studio, the Fourth Studio, and the Stanislavsky Opera Studio. Every evening, those studios put on a largely old-fashioned and bare-bones repertoire: Dickens's *Cricket on the Hearth*, Ostrovsky's *Forest*, and Saltykov-Shchedrin's *Hamlet* and *Death of Pazukhin*.

Yevgeny Zamyatin's *Flea*, a "lighthearted piece with dance" in four acts, was a big success at MAT 2 last season. The main hero of that cheerful piece, the smith Levsha ("Lefty") from Tula, shod the tsar's flea. In this adaptation of an old story by Nikolai Leskov, the tsar received a walnut of diamonds containing a gift from England: a toy flea with such a precise mechanism that it hopped like a real little flea. The tsar's illustrious relative Platov took the flea to Tula, escorted by a regiment of Cossacks as if it were a princess, and ordered the Tula master smiths to shoe it. The smith Levsha lit a lamp in front of the icon of Saint Nicholas, and thus the Tula smiths worked day and night, night and day, for thirty days and thirty nights, and finally shod the English flea, ruining the fine English mechanism in the process, of course.

Zamyatin's "lighthearted piece with dance" contained quite a lot of visible, as well as invisible but perceptible, symbolism of contemporary Russian life, e.g. the wish to put the finishing touches on an English invention, and, naturally, if smiths from Tula were able to shoe the English flea, the comedy logically had to end in the destruction of everything the precise English mechanism represents. The emphasis of this farce, which Zamyatin made very compelling for us all, lay on the positively connoted pre-revolutionary notion of "Olde Mother Russia" and a lot of openly counterrevolutionary content was allowed to strut the stage, along with the many equivocal turns of speech in that humorous piece, which official criticism condemned for "standing far from the Soviet social ethos."

"The MAT crew either Hamletize the past or cover it in confetti," is a formula that could be taken as correct in terms of the group's orientation in the space and time of the October Revolution.

Of the theaters on Theater Square (now named in honor of Sverdlov), the largest is the Bolshoi Theater, a monumental opera house built by the architect Bové in 1824, with eight enormous Ionian columns at the front, above which, on a tympanum, a bronze Phoebus/Apollo steers a quadriga, with torch in hand. The Bolshoi presents classical Russian ballet, still with Vasily Geltser at the head, and the company plays *Aida*, *The Fair at Sorochyntsi*, *The Snow Maiden*, *Carmen*, and the other works of its operatic repertoire all over the world.

Apart from the Bolshoi, Theater Square is also home to the Maly Theater, which is small but still historically significant. It was built in 1830 by the merchant Vargin, a counterpart of the Zagreb theater patron Stanković. Griboyedov, Gogol, and Ostrovsky staged their classical pieces there and also attended the performances in person. Today, too, the Maly Theater plays those three classics. In addition to these theaters that were already famous in the prewar period, Moscow also has the Hermitage, Aquarium, and the Lenin Theater—three stages under the management of Moscow's trade unions.

Komisarzhevska Theater, the Theater of the Revolution, Meyerhold Theater, Vakhtangov Theater, Kamerny Theater are all under the management of Tairov, and the Korsh Comedy Theater are all first-class theaters under the direction of their heads, theoreticians, critics, and directors; Meyerhold, the late Vakhtangov, and Tairov are considered directors of great scope in Russia and the West today.

The Empress Plot, a historical chronicle by A. Tolstoy and P. Shchogolyev, caused a sensation at the Comedy Theater. The piece was written based on the hypothesis that the tsarina had intended to usurp Nicholas II and take power herself in the name of her son and Rasputin. All the archpriests and princess Vyrubovas, ministers and generals, great princes and duchesses, are excellently played in the imbecilic atmosphere of court intrigues; despite the actors being excellent and the performance as a whole, including the script, first rate, and despite the tsar and tsarina and Rasputin and Vyrubova being unforgettable theatrical realizations, the piece is shallow and weak, and thus it demonstrates that the presentation of current chronicles on the stage is always an equally dangerous game. *The Empress Plot* is played as a propaganda piece, and whoever wishes to assure himself that the tsarist idea has lost its cards can go to the Comedy Theater and watch how the Moscow audience reacts when yesterday's idols are represented on stage as straw dummies.

The anti-NEP piece *The Meringue Pie* at the Theater of the Revolution raised a lot of dust. It depicts the career of a NEPman and profiteer, Semyon Rak, who rises to join the stockbrokers and rich misers in the heyday of the New Economic Policy, only to ruin his life in the end and fall into the hands of the GPU, like in some American movie.

In addition to Vakhtangov, a huge, justified hope of Moscow's theater world who died young, who was able to raise the decadent symbolism of the MAT artists to his own, specific, individual, decorative overtone comparable only with Chagall's most excruciating, quintessentially Russian ghetto visions, and apart from Tairov, who is an anti-naturalistic stylist (*Giroflé-Girofla*), the name that really stands out in Moscow today is Vsevolod

147

Meyerhold—the manager of the theater of the same name on the corner of Tverskaya Street and Triumphal Square. It would be beyond the scope of this piece (more a sketchy travelogue than a theater critique) to specifically go into Meyerhold's experiment, not least because it is not his individual excursion into these fields; ever since Piscator and Brecht, new staging concepts are being sought today, both in the West and as in Russia, that will no longer be the Hamletesque symbolism of Gordon Craig. The sketch *Give us Europe!* in seventeen episodes by Ilya Ehrenburg depicts a titanic struggle between American capital and the USSR. Transatlantic liners sail the stage, billionaires buy grandiose armament schemes, parliaments squabble, streets and bordellos dance the foxtrot, the navy of the USSR goes on exercises, artillery fires, mines detonate, Europe founders, a tunnel is dug under the ocean, and Washington capitulates! In the mad shouting of the crowds, the shine of the spotlights, and the rapid changes of scene, in the illumination of halls and streets, and the turmoil and movement of surfaces and physiognomies, Meyerhold managed to resolve the problem of a huge stage that, in that sketch, in an enclosed space, is meant to represent the entire globe. A revolving stage with movable scenery, banners and signs to interpret and accelerate action, the collapse of capital and the victory of Russia—all of that has eliminated the distance between the audience and the stage. There is no fence, ramp, or curtain, rather the stage becomes part of the same body as the audience, the body of a party embroiled in the drama, and therefore it is no wonder at the end of the second act, when an aviator holds a speech about the need to develop Russian aviation, that none of the viewers knows whether it is an actor speaking the script of the drama or an actual aviator. But it certainly is a most authentic Soviet aviation officer, and when that trick was declaratively revealed, the great majority of viewers, glad to know it was an authentic aviator, generously let coins rattle in the donation boxes. The sketch *Give us Europe!* thus gave the Soviet air force several new aircraft.

At the Meyerhold Theatre I attended the premiere of a comedy in three acts, *The Warrant*, by a very young, unknown playwright, Nikolai Erdman—a comedy from the lives of a ruined and miserable monarchist official's family, which keeps all that remains of the old Russia in its one suitcase: the last skirt of Her Majesty, the Tsarina of Russia, was given to the poor official's widow for safekeeping by a former court general who has emigrated. But it dawns on those poor buffoons that this whole revolutionary jumble is going to remain for some time and that they should therefore take their bearings from reality. That widow's son, the comedy's main character, decides to join the Communist Party for transparent, opportunistic reasons. The young man is prepared to sacrifice himself for the good of his family and become a Bolshevik, but he cannot find anyone in his circles with any connection to the proletariat. The only person who comes close to having any link with proletarians and knows at least a single member of the working class is the small, anonymous, dim-witted servant girl in the kitchen of that declassed family. You should see that young gentleman and the way his standing grows (and to an extent his self-esteem) from the day the word gets around in the family that the snotty-nosed kid is going to become a Party member, the way those deplorable bow before the shabby rag of the tsarina's forgotten skirt, and the way they crawl on their knees in front of the phonograph that speaks with the deep bass of a priest, to realize that Meyerhold is a good director and Russian actors are good interpreters, even when they do not belong to MAT. Meyerhold's actors, with all their sincere enthusiasm for the "new modern style" (which in Dante's time was called the "sweet new style"), are scrupulous realists down to the finest detail, and analytical irony and derision at the cheerless characters of Russia's officialdom are the dominant themes all evening. As usual with Meyerhold, the intonation of the whole performance is consistently and calculatedly more a circus gesture than armchair refinement like Stanislavsky's. Meyerhold is more of a Wedekindish cabaret with a clownish grin like George Grosz, and devoted to revolutionary activity with extreme persistence; in this sad comedy, he manages with just a few appropriate gestures to demonically underline the absurdity of a life like that of birds in closed, stuffy, paltry officials' cages, in complete and maddening isolation from reality, the cretinism of a life spent sitting around in kitchens, the wax museum imbecility of the petty bourgeois mortal degeneration of impoverished officials' widows who scuffle in slippers over the parquet floor of their chambers and polish their polished closets with flannel rags, while worlds collapse outside and the giant foundations of the new Russian revolutionary life are poured. One could write an interesting parallel about Meyerhold's élan and the academic rigidity of a director like Stanislavsky.

The ellipse of Russian theatrical life today with its two most distinctive focuses does not represent the totality of Russian theatrics. Fundamental questions are being asked in open discussions in the press and in public opinion. What will ultimately be affirmed: the academism of MAT or the modernist formulae of Vakhtangov, Tairov, Meyerhold, and Korsh? That is a question that depends on an whole mass of factors of a more socio-political than aesthetic nature. One thing is beyond any doubt: theater in Russia, regardless of the stylistic problems and staging issues, is a mass phenomenon.

I once attended a Sunday matinee staging of Georg Kaiser's *Kolportage* (Hawking) in the Lessing Theater in Berlin. It was a hot June afternoon, flies could be heard buzzing in the dimly lit auditorium, and all around me, to the left and right, Berlin cooks and chambermaids chattered. They were bored, and one of the women started to snore; others complained that there was no music, and the great majority rustled the paper bags that held their rolls. I must be truthful, because "writing the truth is the only revolutionary act," and emphasize that those cooks not only snored in the Lessing Theater that Sunday afternoon, but it was also rather loud due to certain ruder sounds.

I remembered the Lessing Theater when I was at the Hermitage, when Moscow proletarian women, completely absorbed, listened to lectures about the significance of Zola for world literature, or again, when they sat without moving for five hours at a panoramic performance of the play, with a cycle of pictures painted for the occasion, interpreting the development of the group "People's Freedom" and its move toward terrorism, which ended with the death of all the movement's initiators.

Georg Kaiser and Zola, Berlin and Moscow! Proletarian women both here and there, but what a difference!

In addition to those sixteen Russian theaters, there is another large opera house, the Experimental Theater, with its renowned ballet company and an excellent orchestra. The GITIS Theater (State Institute of Theater Arts) under the direction of the "theatrical Octobrist" Meyerhold adopted the principles of "biomechanics" and *tefizkult* (i.e. theatricalization of physical culture). Foregger's and Ferdinand's theaters tread Meyerhold's path, and students of those schools play in nightclubs, cabarets, and on provincial stages.

Habima is a Jewish theater with plays in Hebrew, and drama in Hebrew is also performed at the State Jewish Theater with its repertoire based on Russian Jewish life and the Jewish Kamerny Theater with Yiddish motifs.

The Operetta, the Moscow Operetta, and the Theater of Satire perform banal operettas like in other European cities—from *Countess Marizta* to *The Yankee Princess*. The Reciter's Theater is an interesting institution, directed by Vasily Scryozhnikov, whom August Cesarec portrayed in detail in the journal *Književna republika*; the Theater for the Deaf and Dumb is certainly unique among Moscow's other theatrical curiosities, where deaf-mute actors play to deaf-mute viewers. The First State Children's Theater and the Moscow Children's Theater put on Kipling, Andersen, Hoffmann, and Russian folktales every day to grateful over-capacity audiences. There are a series of cabarets and so-called "miniature theaters," including the Bolshoi Tver Theater, Krivoy Dzhimmi, Petrovsky Theater, Shalyapin Studio, and the Theater of Old Farce. Several of the district workers' theaters also deserve special mention: those in Baumanovsky, Zamoskvorechky, Krasnopresensky, Rogoshko-Simonovsky, Sokolnichesky, and Sretensky.

Thousands of actors perform in all these theaters. Conferences are held about Fonvizin and Marcel Martinet. Ernst Toller is played, and Émile Verhaeren and Walt Whitman are recited by choirs. Theater education is taken to the masses because Moscow's theaters are overcrowded every day. Dramatics and drama are still lacking, but when a person somewhere in Zamoskvorechye sees a performance of Duncan's young students, who work at the machines in the factory, he feels a great liberation of talent. Those talents will continue to be set free in geometric progression, and that paints bright prospects.

EASTER EVE

Eight days before Easter, there is a perceptible anxiety in Russian churches. Padlocks are removed from iron-bound medieval gates, dust is wiped from ancient, Old-Testament golden candlesticks, brooms scratch at Byzantine mosaics; there is a rumbling of pews, and the theater of the church prepares for the great Easter gala.

Nervousness reigns in private apartments, too, as if people are expecting guests: savory pies and cakes are baked, paskhas made of honey and cheese, floors are washed, carpets beaten, and everything takes on the sour, damp smell of humble cleanliness and poverty. In that festive buildup to Easter, windows puttied up all winter are opened for the first time, and people air their rooms through the *fortochka*, a miniature rectangular window. The pungent smell of Russia leather, fish soup, parquet oil, wet galoshes and boots, stuffy cupboards, dim halls, and thick coats of winter dust—all those aromas of human habitation disperse in the icy draft for the first time since the fall. Adults inhale deeply the fresh spring cascades of the clime, children revel in their toys, voices grow on the street, and the pre-Easter restlessness hums in apartments and churches.

The beauty of Moscow's churches is gentle, as are the hymns from dead old times. The triumphal glory of the Russian churches and cathedrals is fading more and more, like a mellow reminiscence of long since withered flowers pressed in albums. That was a time full of suffering, chaos, and evil, when people lit lamps in dark spaces before aromatic mists of frankincense, tore their hair, and wailed on their knees to the music of bells and the chanting of indiscernible figures in sorcerers' black robes. The theatrics of Byzantine tsarist ceremony function through the obscurity and mysteriousness of Greek black magic, as do all sophisticated performances, with purple curtains, golden backdrops of iconostases, the eerie trembling of icon lamps and memorial candles on the wax masks of saints—beauty as sweet as the rind of celestial spices, as sweet as the violins of the Holy Grail in Wagner's *Parsifal*. The secret of the success of Russian operas is concealed in the ecclesiastical chanting, which exudes the mystery of ancient choirs, one of the most powerful propagandistic tools of Greek Orthodoxy.

A Gothic cathedral has something of Grünewald: God is a scholastic secret, the victim of a vile and despicable crime, and there God speaks in a Calvarian mystery play before the execution of the death sentence, when a man in extreme despair and loneliness realizes that he has been abandoned by everyone, including God himself: "Father, Father, why have you forsaken me?" In Italian, Mediterranean otherworldly rites, actually from classical antiquity, God is the tombstone of a duke and prince, with a crown, heraldic plumes, helmets, and coats of arms—symbols of victory, good fortune, and wealth. The great pageantry of the Bucentaur, the Ascension Day triumph of Doge Orseolo, who with his winged lion seized the Adriatic, or the ceremony for the Nativity of Mary, *Dies nativitatis Virginis* in Santa Maria Maggiore, when the Holy Father arrives with an escort of cavalry: that is the God, of whom Bossuet sarcastically said it was a decoration that people believed in "the Italian way." Cinquecento brocade and marble pagan sculptures were the God of the Renaissance, which even just as a word, *rinascimento*, speaks of the rebirth of ancient Olympus. In Russian churches, too, God is a tsarist iconostas, the sound of bells in two octaves, and an Old Church Slavic song droning in the nave about God, the Almighty and King, who rules over the Scythian, Sarmatian, and Hyperborean expanses, whose lion's roar resounds from the Arctic Ocean to Constantinople, which must sooner or later return to the fold of Mother Church, the one and only, Orthodox, as it was before the schism. The outstretched arms of saints and great dukes in dalmatics, and the abundance of lightdark with the flickering of icon lamps, are the decorative, imperial-Orthodox instruments of political and theocratic propaganda, whose standard-bearers are Dostoyevsky, Solovyov, Leskov, and Berdyayev.

The Russian churches and gods are dying away; the Orthodox Olympus is living out its final twilight. Just as the light of icon lamps is extinguished with a ruddy flash and the dying stage of fall is a burgeoning of bright colors, so too the Russian churches shimmer in dreary richness in the hour of their death.

In the grey-yellow, warm spring light, on the muddy brown background with melting snow, when the counterforts and walls of the churches and cathedrals stand out moldy and dirty against the light of day, the pale aquamarine blue, rain-washed, watercolor hue of the church walls shines like a magic lantern in the fiery colors and playful outlines of strange Oriental architecture. The patchy, faded frescoes with saints and tsars in coronation vestments spill over those pale, age-old church arches like the dead palettes of icon painters and ascetics, whose skeletons await us sardonically at the inevitable meeting under the ground in these houses of God where no one lives.

It is not just circumlocution, it is really so: those colors glow like grapes in the fall sun, golden like an aureola in the supernatural reflection of metallic plates, for which, like a posthumous triumph, one has paid a blood toll with one's own head. The sharply pointed Indian portals of Moscow's two-story churches, with century-worn steps, the decorative bars on the windows, red-brick arches, carmine– and sepia-colored brickwork, the stench of beer hall, soot, and frankincense—all of that is as putrid as an ossuary and as passionate as every deceased past, today still cultural history, but tomorrow a handful of ash in the wind of biblical ephemerality.

There are churches with walls coated in glowing oils and with cupolas bearing hundreds and hundreds of kilograms of gold, so that the Harun al-Rashidic souls of immensely wealthy boyars might be cleansed of the blood of vile and sordid killings; a few tinkling coins for an indulgence. Those bell towers are dark red like congealed blood, and the poppy seed-heads painted on the swirls arc like slices of melon, in succulent contrasts of red-green tints of emerald and ruby. Bright yellow-blue-and-red spiral swirls with golden crosses bore into the blue of the sky, and the wind hums in them like the copper strings of a celestial harp—the music of spheres of a man-eating age, when people devoured each other according to the law of big fish and little fish.

Silver-framed figures of the Black Mother of God gleam with hundreds of icon lamps and the vestments of the whole Company of Heaven and its Viziers, the Boyars, shine in pearl and jewel, silk and brocade. With the flickering of hot coals in silver braziers and thuribles, the sooty odor of candles, and the muttering of legendary beggars in colorful foot rags—everything seems hungry, like the tubercular voice of a psalm-reader praising the Passion of Christ in the time before Peter the Great, in the backward and archaic atmosphere of consciousness and feeling. Nameless churches cower silently in muddy little dead-end lanes, hidden in corners; green churches, churches yellow and blue, churches with white, Russian Empire-style colonnades, mice-eaten, rotten, and rain washed; they stand alone like remnants of romantic theater sets, painted pink and with slapdash peasant gilding. Amid the dirty brown monotony of Moscow's streets, when the thaw begins and the gutters sing, countless red-white-and-yellow-painted church towers jut forth in loud contrast with the surroundings. Amid the mud, melting snow, wooden huts on the outskirts, peasant carts, and draymen's sleighs, Moscow's churches seem like caskets of ancient relics utterly unrelated to today's life. Who built them here and when, and what was the purpose of these four-story, terraced towers that chime fantastically in the moonlight like huge, old-fashioned alabaster clocks from Catherine the Great's time? Sheer masses of churches and chapels stand secluded on Moscow's streets, and above their antiquated roofs and bell towers bulge the golden orbs of supernatural balloons, glistening with imperial ornamentation and tied down by shining wire so that they not drift off into the sky. Those golden aerostats with oval arches float airily above black, heavy reality like Montgolfier balloons, anchored only temporarily on the ground, like golden gondolas preparing for voyages to cosmic archipelagoes in the distant unknown.

In the sad, rainy evening, when green gas lamps and the orange squares of illuminated windows bathe in puddles of rainwater, bent old women traipse along the muddy avenues between black, wet trees to vespers. The bluish light of day fades, and the dark aquarelle smudges of the passersby disappear on the brown-grey, muddy curtain of the provincial wooden fences of Moscow the village. The golden gate of Bogoyavlensky Church is flung so hospitably wide, the lights inside the rosily illuminated church shine so intimately and warmly, the empty mahogany chairs with golden, Empire-style garlands amiably invite passersby to visit, and the voices of the choir so solemnly call the human soul hungry for rest and music to their concert, that poor human creatures passively submit to the gratuitous charm of transcendental poetic illusions in this quiet moment of twilight sorrow. Everyone who enters the church portal is Maeterlinck's lyrical dreamer, yearning for his blue bird...

At the gate to the undying, otherworldly Empire of saints, tsars, universal patriarchs, and counterrevolutionary generals there stand lines of beggars and the blind; children cry on the cross, corpses dream on the catafalque, and all bow to Christ on the pearly pink banner of the King's Gate. The gigantic figure of Christ observes that boat crammed with travelers for the other world, his devotees, and his face is good natured and marzipan sweet—the smile of a blonde young man reminiscent of D'Artagnan, Dumas's fourth musketeer, with a Louis Treize lace jabot. One such sad evening, when all waters are grey and the muddy snow, as thick as chewing gum, sticks to galoshes, and the church bell speaks in an ambiguous bass, children play cops and robbers in front of the church. But the world of ruined generals' wives who hope and pray all night that their solitaire will bring them salvation, that world of illiterate housekeepers and cats, beneath the grey, gloomy sky and black ravens—that world of Philistines and lumpens sees the rosy, baroque Christ as their cavalier and champion who will come and achieve his political pledge: to topple the Kremlin's Red Beelzebubs into hell.

There are also desperate, bloodstained, despondent Christs in Moscow's churches, Nazarenes who have lost all hope for a change of the international political situation and quietly stare into emptiness like those intent on suicide and gamblers who have lost their last chip. One such Calvarian desperado hangs with a care-worn, sooty face in a golden frame and gazes like an Indian hypnotist at a procession of children that passes by, laughing at the sooty specters from the time of Ivan the Terrible—innocent children's laughter, devilishly sublime. Today, Russian children giggle in churches like in museums of the weird and wonderful, looking at dead saints with the same distance with which we as children eyed African fetishes and idols. It is lovely to stand in a Moscow church and listen to the echoes of children giggling while the priest reads the Passion of Christ; the breath of the chanter coils through the fug in the dimly lit space like smoke, the beggars ply their singsong at the end of the nave, and an old woman in a voice hoarse from vodka sighs and rambles, with the flickering of a small green lamp. A deity that becomes laughable in children's eyes! The agony and twilight of an Olympus that departs the stage without inspiring a single tragedy.

Anxiety and rejoicing at the twilight of the gods are two basic dramatic motifs of bourgeois civilization on its deathbed. Jeremiah's psalm about Jerusalem razed to its foundations thunders in extremis over the carcass of the church, and like the Byzantine patriarch who once got up from his catafalque to warn the blasphemous sinners, Moscow's mummies come forth from their graves in a grandiose uprising on Easter Eve. In this fiery unrest of delirium, Holy Orthodoxy refuses to be embalmed by the barbarians, and it rises from its deathbed in its last, ritual spasms to face the last fight: *This is the final struggle, let us group together.* On that Easter Eve, Orthodoxy unfurls its last banners to combat the Antichrist and, with admiral's aplomb, to set sail into the fireworks of bright, new triumphal victories.

In that dramatic Easter Eve, Moscow's two-and three-story churches are lit up like houses preparing for a feast, and the light pours in rich cascades and broad shafts onto all the windows. Shadows of the Orthodox faithful sway in sharp profile in the illuminated squares of the window as they bow and cross themselves with a servile, ceremonial, and slavishly pronounced Oriental sweep of their arms from the right shoulder to the left. Wooden stairs creak in unsightly, humble houses of prayer on the outskirts, where it smells of fresh pinewood, men's sweat, and tallow candles. People's homes, too, are lit up and as boisterous as inns that constantly open and close in front of processions of guests and well-wishers; the voices of drunkards reverberate along with the sounds of an accordion and the squeak of the door. Greenish jars of gherkins and yogurt can be seen in the illuminated windows, together with thighs of veal, sausages wrapped in newspaper, and snowy white pyramids of paskhas with sultanas wrapped in white napkins and tied with three rabbit-ear knots.

Restless traffic rumbles, swelling and surging along streets bathed in the green light of gas lamps: all over Moscow black masses pour to midnight service, in different directions, from Yelokhovskaya Square past Basmannaya Street, and all the way to Arbat and Lubyanskaya Square in Kitay-gorod. Here and there the intensive, incandescent magnesium lighting of several thousand electric candles spills over the muddy street to reveal full galleries of halls overflowing with sweaty human figures. Those are Party clubs with anti-religious meetings in halls decked with scarlet garlands and slogans in golden letters, and laurel wreaths above Lenin's countenance. The door has been left open and the echoes of brass trombones resound in the dark like the clang of a soldier's bugle from an enemy camp.

All the churches shine like scenery lit for the stage. Green and red icon lamps blink, iconostases gleam, the blind grumble, and a host of womenfolk pushes and smiles with red Jacobin scarves and young women's white teeth. In the basements of underground churches, beneath smoke-stained, damp, sooty vaults in a green, drowning color, sinister, unearthly shadows creep over the icons, gems, and people's faces. The treasures in glass showcases with relics of saints, figures of God's warriors, faces of the Christians in the catacombs, frescoes of tsars and saints, in monumental figural disproportion, images of crucified Jesus that reach their bloodied and broken arms over dark domes, the shadow of a crippled hunchback contorted before the altar, and the ghostly, swaying projection of his earthly form looms over the golden mosaics—all of that melts and dissolves through the multitude of red, bloody masks into visionary turmoil with an agitated flickering of shadows and the cheerless light of mortuaries. Through a cracked golden slat in the King's Gate on the iconostasis bearded priests can be seen dressing up for the show, like actors putting on makeup backstage. People clear their throats and shake the mud from their shoes; hot steam rises from nostrils. People talk quietly, flow along the streets, fill the churches like a black flood, scale the wooden stairs of two-story houses of worship, and their faces are lit up in the glow of candles and red like scarlet fever. Whenever a person mechanically raises their hand in the throng at the small door of the tower, the icon lamp in their palm makes it look as if the hand is covered in blood. A dog yelps disagreeably somewhere in the dark; a squad of soldiers in greatcoats marches over the bridge singing, and their song sounds to me like Hungarian.

I found myself in a relatively new baroque church with a white-golden iconostasis illuminated like in a scene for *The Magic Flute*. As I watched the disturbed reflection of icon lamps and candles on the rubies of chalices and on huge silver-bound tomes—a full church of maids and officials, widows in black, and daughters of the petty bourgeoisie singing the Old Slavic Easter hymn "Khristos voskrese" (Christ is Risen)—my view rose to the top of the gold-framed iconostasis, a soapy, slimy thing as banal as the icing on a cheap punch cake, and there, amid white stuccowork renovated with barbaric bad taste, wreathed with garlands of artificial roses and costly Secessionist *lampade*, I saw a strange allegory of the tsar's crown on a skull.

Several moments before the mob swept me into this white-painted church, I had been to see the Communist Easter celebration of the Pioneer Club at the Western University. Children, members of the Pioneer Club, staged their own anti-religious demonstration in the form of a ballet, accompanied by a choir and an orchestra. Suspended from Meyerhold's crane, a hundred boys and girls in blue sailor suits rowed to the whistle of sirens and the ring of balalaikas, symbolizing a victorious admiral's galley. A large red banner on the bow of the galley bore the words "The Eighth Communist Easter"—the slogan of this rhythmic, choral sculling, accompanied by a children's choir.

> *Never,*
> *never,*
> *does a Pioneer*
> *fall before God.*

So sailed the admiral's galley crowded full of sailors and blondee, winsome Russian girls, serious Pioneers, and dark-skinned children from Azerbaijan and Bukhara. Alongside the blondee Moscow comrades rowed little Mongols, Tatars, Latvians, and Germans from the Volga, singing:

> *Never,*
> *never,*
> *does a Pioneer*
> *fall before God.*

On its atheist voyage on the Russian Easter Eve, the admiral's galley *The Eighth Communist Easter* encounters a procession of Orthodox patriarchs, corpulent abbots, monks, and nuns carrying relics of saints, frankincense, and icons—all the supernumeraries of tsarist Orthodoxy in the style of Demyan Bedny's anti-religious carmagnole dances. The ballet's action unfolds when the sailors on *The Eighth Communist Easter* drop anchor, disembark, and pursue anti-religious propaganda in the Orthodox procession. And, of course, there is a happy end: under the weight of anti-religious arguments little abbots rip off their grizzled beards, tear apart their archimandrite robes, and throw away the holy paintings and icons, and nuns become sailors; they all embark on *The Eighth Communist Easter*, and thus the children, united in the apotheosis of atheist victory, hoist their sails for new, victorious voyages, to the refrain:

> *Never,*
> *never,*
> *does a Pioneer*
> *fall before God.*

Then I stood in the white, renovated baroque church in front of the iconostasis, looking at the tsarist crown and decorations on the skull in the stucco and listening to the Easter hymn of the monks, but my ears still resounded with the Easter message of the Pioneer ballet, and I wandered off in thoughts about the relativity of people's convictions. How much subtle, inner energy European children have to expend in their struggle against religious apparitions to be able to save the white flag of naïve but candid "freedom of conscience" in their unpolluted minds—a freedom so often talked about in Europe but not guaranteed for children in any Western-European civilization! So as this young European Darwinist and Feuerbachian makes his way to his convictions based on his own observations, to the moral-intellectual, heroically high-minded level of consciousness where he can bravely resist the force of his church and school, i.e. crude religious propaganda, he can risk making his own, godless confession. How many slaps in the face, beatings, imbecilic counterarguments, and humiliations did he have to face before that, and how many troubled nights did the child lie awake, dreading the consequences of such a confession, which actually is nothing other than a naïve paraphrasing of boring old experience-tested facts?

A torrent of people flowed in the processions; all of Moscow was on its feet. So empty and mute at night, the Kitay-gorod center now came to life: the churches on Maroseyka Street smelled sooty and provincial, of simple candles, like a pauper's funeral, and underground in Saint Basil's Cathedral a woman stood with her back to the iconostasis and, as if absent-minded, leaned her head against the window pane despairingly and forlornly and let her tear-filled eyes wander the expanse of Red Square. Columns with red flags marched on the squares, quays, and bridges over the Moscow River to the thunder of drums, on the way back from a Party rally, and in the opposite direction columns with Easter candles in hand headed for the church. Toward Arbat, all the churches were overcrowded, black vespiaries droned on the two-story wooden stairs, and clusters of people hung there together, singing and lighting candles. On the square around the Cathedral of Christ the Savior, on the marble and granite slabs, the trampled flower beds and benches, the stone steps and the quay, black masses of Komsomol members milled in their red scarves, together with women, children, and loiterers.

Cigarettes were lit, there was a murmur of voices, young women giggled in folksy cheer, here and there you smelled a waft of vodka, and everyone listened for the sound of the midnight bell in expectation of the great moment of Easter triumph. When the flag-bearers with the church banners appeared on the terrace in front of Christ the Savior's portal, above the undulating sea of human heads, the crowd became unsettled before the arrival of the patriarch, and when the first rockets went off on the distant horizon and the first reverberations of the mortars were heard, the ringing of Moscow's bells came from out of the midnight darkness, like faraway, muffled thunder.

The monasteries in Moscow's old ring of fortifications were the first; long ago, with their towers and high walls, they were the defense against the Tatars and Poles, and now, in this Eighth Communist Easter, they gave the starting signal to the city that Christ had arisen. The sound came in waves from the Novodevichy and Donskoy monasteries in the southwest traveling to Novospassky Church in distant Zamoskvorechye, and so it grew in a circle in the darkness and was ignited as an alarm in the citadel. Like a prelude on the organ—that is how the ringing began, in great chords into the expanse of space, from the north from Strastnaya Square, from distant avenues and boulevards on the city's margins, and toward the center in Kitay-gorod and baroque Arbat. Humble churches with small bell towers far out in the suburban darkness began that eerie nighttime ringing, and those obscure yet distinct sounds from the marshy plain flew over the massif of the city center and started to swing the giant bells in the monumental basilicas and cathedrals there.

All the houses of worship of Bogoyavlensky and Blagoveshchensk, the churches of the Vladimir Icon of the Mother of God, and the Georgian Mother of God, as well as those of Iveron, Kazan, and the Don, and all the Saint Basils and Resurrections of Christ—they all started to boom one after another, ever louder and bolder. That thunder combined the voices of Saint George the Victorious, who heard the Holy Venerable Mother Paraskeva, and Saint Nicholas of the Great Cross, and Saint Nicholas of Khamovniki, and Saint Clement of Rome, and Saints Cosmas and Damian—all of them beat proudly, indomitably, and provocatively. In the first moment of that musical overture the ringing began as festive, joyous, and glorious Easter bells to celebrate Easter and the poetic, biblical moment on the Sunday morning when the women found the grave empty, and a white seraph atop the marble slab. But when the voice of Christ the Savior roared above its dominant, 316–pood-heavy gilded dome with a detonation that made one's eardrums bulge like the blast of an explosion, there was more artillery bellow than conciliatory Easter bells in those circular sound waves issuing from the booming of countless bell towers, making glasses, granite slabs, and human brains tremble. Slowly, imperceptibly, that peal grew from a lyrical Easter prelude into a patriarchal, inquisitional, cruel, and imperious cannonade, a paroxysm that fires at the clouds, the city, and Moscow's endless plain, and rises from a tumult of panicky, hysterical little bells into a vast, remonstrative rumble, a protest. They were all demonstrating in unison, in a chorus of the compact, democratic flock of the Lord. Old Tikhon the Miracle Worker at the Arbat gates, and Archdeacon Stefan, and the Nativity of Mary, and Saint Catherine, and Saint John the Baptist—all of them protested loudly and together with the militant motif of Christ the Savior, which thundered most awe inspiringly: a tocsin for fire, anathema, and counterrevolutionary uprising! Every wave of that ringing and the great, disturbing circles of midnight dread made all the crypts and tombs of the Russian Empire burst asunder; graves opened, and all the tsars, patriarchs, and martyrs arose in their vestments, with lamps and golden crosses, and spoke an anathema on the Antichrists, Jews, and Bolsheviks who had dishonored the Russian lands.

"Curse the Bronsteins and Apfelbaums, who tied up the Ivan the Great bell in the Kremlin on this holy night," thundered the 316–pood-heavy gold Christ the Savior, and beat at the heads of the Orthodox faithful with its forty bells as if pounding them with a millstone.

"Curse the Bronsteins and Apfelbaums, who have thrown God out of the schools!" echoed whole galleries of saints on the plain beyond Moscow River.

"The Apfelbaums have turned our churches into museums and Party clubs, they are making atheists of Orthodox children, they have nailed Orthodoxy to the cross, they have ravaged and dishonored dear Orthodox Mother Russia!"

Moscow's forty times forty churches with their 15,000 bells boomed and protested that night in the name of the Lord God, in the name of His Imperial Majesty the Russian Tsar, and in the name of Their Excellencies Kolchak, Denikin, and Wrangel. "We protest in the name of His Holiness the Russian Patriarch in Sremski Karlovci. Curse the Bronsteins and Apfelbaums!"

That was no longer the ringing of Easter bells, nor a lyrical cantilena of seraphic legend. A furious, bloodthirsty tirade, a toxic barrage of profanities, bile, and hatred, an anathema of crazy curses—that ringing shrilled like a requiem for the freedom of the human mind. Thousands of bells broke into a ghastly, epileptic exaltation of delirious passion, and when those choirs began to hum, when the theatrical thunder with flashes of lightning reached its paroxysm, at that moment there began a procession of archpriests, bishops, and deacons, in boyar vestments, with relics of saints, icon lamps, gold, smoke-stained candles, and trumpets around Christ the Savior. There could have been at least 20,000 people in the square in front of the cathedral just then, and over the longitudinal line of Moscow River, above bridges and palaces on distant elevations, rockets began to gush and flares to blaze. The river's mirror ruddied in the festive illumination of red-and-green rocket streaks as if from a great fire; grey facades and countless domes burned brightly in the glow of that blaze and the frenzied passion of the Whites' Easter triumph.

Whenever a rocket hissed high into the sky, the Kremlin shone in the darkness above that vulgar din; illustrious without illumination, sullen and serious, with its bells tied up, with ramparts, towers, and artillery like a proper fortress. The golden dome of Ivan the Great would shimmer in the reflection of a rocket, and that thunder thus made it look as if shrapnel was bursting in a wild bombardment above the Kremlin. High up above the Senate's tower, in the eastern wind, fluttered the Red Flag, made visible by powerful spotlights. Its red cloth streamed and trembled in the surrounding blackness, began to burn when blasted by the wind, flickered its fiery tongue above the whole city, tall and stark, on a staunch pole like the admiral's mast.

THE COMING OF SPRING

At dawn, while the walls still held the blue of night, someone plucked a mandolin in the courtyard: two or three notes and a long silence. Again, two or three notes of the mandolin and, as if from afar, the hushed voice of a singer, sorrowful and barely audible. Then a coach thundered past on the granite cobbles and its sounds receded in the direction of Lubyanskaya Square; solemn silence reigned again, like on a great holiday. Above Maroseyka Street and "B. Boulevard" (whose dilapidated houses date back to Peter's times), the sound of the early morning bells spread outward in a vast, quivering circle over the flat, stony vistas of the City to the faraway, deep-blue horizon, wooded and rippling. Above the golden domes of the churches and the open windows shining in the morning light, the gentle ringing hummed in the telephone wires like a zither; suddenly the wind swirled up in a spiral of dust and, like in a lively scherzo, dropped its gritty load onto a little, black, curly-haired dog, which started barking and ran along the fences.

Mornings are quiet in Moscow's parks, where the wind whirs in the tops of the pine trees; the grass is soft and lush, and the water in the mirroring lakes glistens in the grey half-light beneath the clouds—low, warm and heavy like wineskins. Through the reddish boles of the pines and the lyrically weeping birches peered the brutally hard wall of a factory. A woman dressed in black, somber in appearance, plodded along the avenue slowly and solemnly; carefully, with both hands, she carried a kerchief of consecrated Easter cakes like a holy object. The kerchief was tied, and a red paper rose peeped out at the top through a white serviette. The morning began very solemnly that day with the somber, gaunt woman in black, as if a roll of drums covered in black had opened the bright tracts of a spring song that began to drone above the city that morning, loudly and triumphantly.

The sound of piano scales came in through the open window. A sickly young woman, her face pale green and her head in a bandage, watered geraniums on the windowsill and water splashed down onto the sidewalk. A corpulent peasant girl with smoothed-down, straw-like hair and a red scarf beat the morning bell with monotonous swings in a stout, light blue bell tower beneath a stone dome: ding-dong, ding-dong... A tabby cat woke up, stretched and licked the fur of its soft paws in a shoemaker's

167

window, sitting between tools, strips of perforated leather, glue, and cord. In the display of an old-fashioned pharmacy, plaster figurines of Aesculapius and Lenin, white and dusty, stood among anti-worm candies and red and green glass balls, passively contemplating the goings-on through the dazzling glass, which separated them from the morning's ringing, the wind, and the barking dogs. Although decorated with red paper and garlands, that glazed space of the pharmacy's display was dusty and dreary, and the two plaster figures took on that same dirty dullness.

Spring arrived in Moscow that morning with a smile and a loud laugh, like the cheerful clashing of cymbals in martial parade music. Cascades of yellow sunlight and warmth spilled through the boulevards and wide streets of the city center. But it was still cold in the courtyards of the towering, red-brick apartment blocks, in the shade of their tall and cheerless walls, where men cut ice with axes; the thick slabs cracked beneath their blows and were loaded onto oxcarts.

A lively scene unfolds meanwhile in another part of the city, on Strastnaya Square, where golden domes shine and red balloons waver high in the air; women, babies in prams, monuments on the promenades, horses, cats, passersby—all of this seethes and swirls and shines in joy and excitement. Nickel samovars steam at Smolensk Market, where crowds of bareheaded women in colorful skirts buy flour, needles, vegetables, and meat; cobblers repair the shoes of passersby, pungent butchers' stalls creak beneath piles of red, bloody meat, and three blind men sing a Ukrainian folk song accompanied by an accordion. Between pyramids of large, white Kiev eggs there are tubs of butter from Vologda, ready-plucked hazel-grouse, huge fish from the Volga, lard and bacon, mimosas, the first flower of spring, and cigarettes. An ocarina weeps.

The grey-blue morning sun of April is the basic leitmotif as it spills over the slabs of asphalt, the faces of sooty icons, and the wet snouts of playful dogs barking and running around restlessly. The sun's rays stab the frozen hands of the pedestrians and raise the temperature in the soft fur of the first buds; the massive, Empire-style iron fences from the time of the boyars with their meanders, tsarist fasces and rusty rosettes, as well as doorknobs, gate handles, coins and all metal objects, which yesterday were still so icy to touch, have now all become friendlier and warmer from the sun's fire. Freshly painted barges rock on the waters of the Moskva River and smell of turpentine and tar. Trucks rumble by, overloaded with leather and wooden beams; old women kneel before the locked doors of churches. Clouds sail on the clear aquamarine sky, featherbeds and carpets are dusted in open houses, red flags in the easterly wind, migratory birds in triangle formations high above the city, the shouts of children and the babble of grey, turbid thaw water in the dazzle of spring light—all of this swells in a choral crescendo.

The easterly breeze plays on the streets of Moscow: from the deep-blue forests, across the ploughed fields to the telephone wires, everything hums in the restless wind. It flaps the red flags, rustles the Chinese and other advertizing banners strung out across the streets like sails, whirls the dark red scarves of the girls, lifts their skirts, whistles among the graves and antennae, and carries masses of little white clouds across the clear sky to cheerfully greet all "comrade folks," just as white handkerchiefs wave to ships leaving harbor. The wind rocks metal signboards and weather vanes, drives the flocks of sparrows, and plays with their chirping. It giggles to the children to let fly their kites, raises rubbish and scraps of paper above the grey and dusty roads as a sign of mirth and morning greeting. Everything is in motion, ever swifter and wilder: freshly lacquered red trams, red-green-and-yellow painted gingerbread houses on the walls of the fortress, airplanes in the grand blue above and carters in green Tatar caftans, factory sirens, chimneys, and train stations. People smell Crimean apples, and the warm aroma of chocolate from a confectioner's shop mixes with the sweetish odor of cars' gasoline and bitumen fuming on the footpath beneath the tools of the pavers.

Ivan the Great gleams above the Kremlin; endless wagons of hay ring idyllically at Smolensk Market with a primitive, pastoral ding-ding, ding-ding. Six bronze horses rear up at the end of Tverskaya Street atop the "Triumphal Arch of 1812" in the full glare of the sun's torch, and patients in striped hospital gowns suck in the breath of the dewy morning at open windows. A red-bearded tramp in dirty rags explains to a traveling cobbler how to hammer a nail into his shoes, and he seems not to be happy with the result. The cobbler searches through his pouch of heel– and toe-plates, comes out with a fistful of little nails that he sticks between his lips, and mutters something under his breath as he keeps poking around in the greasy, ragged bag. A blind man smoking a hand-rolled cigarette kneels in the mud, bows to the passersby and begs them to have pity on his unhappy Russian soul. A pregnant woman sticks her thumb and forefinger into a loin of beef and claws at the meat, while holding a chunk of bread coated with half an inch of caviar in her left hand; with her mouth full, she blathers to the butcher's assistant, a lad of Oriental physiognomy, that she would be crazy to buy flyblown meat. Buns, bread, hot pastries and pies, pumpkin seeds, chocolate, caviar, boiling samovars—all of this steams and smokes above the last patches of dirty snow, mingling with bags of flour, with the blind folk, photographers, booksellers, and calendar-peddlers, looking like Pugachev in a primitive, peasant-like way. The sun shines on this game of light and shade in a light blue jet of spring, and the horizontal outline of the city sinks amid the undulating Sparrow Hills and the banks of the Moskva River, as if in a basin. The plane of the city clings to the horizon like a long, uniform line, its monotony awkwardly emphasized by the gilded dome of the Cathedral of Christ the Savior, a tasteless, obtrusive pseudo-monumental highlight that has ruined the modest outline of old Moscow with the Kremlin's bell towers at its center.

I sat in the park of the Institute of Chemistry, fascinated by the coming of spring. Never had I yearned for it as deeply as this year, and never had I followed its approach, inch by inch. Longing for a rich, warm spring, in my mind's eye I departed at the beginning of February (when the fog hung thick and heavy here), seeking the Adriatic and the sun. I stayed up all night in the railroad coach in sleepless anticipation of the south and the spring light; it dawned when we arrived in Plase, near Rijeka. The stars went out above the rugged range of Istria, and the sea was dreaming, as white as milk, beneath the grey horizon of the Kvarner Gulf. The lighthouses of Sveti Marko and Malinska were still blinking, and the islands launched into the water like ponderous, black, antediluvian turtles. Out across the Kvarner Gulf, a light on a mast moved slowly and steadily: the ship's bow pointed toward Velika Vrata, with Brseč and Plomin ahead, beneath the tall Liburnian Hills, and a little farther out was the open sea.

All of us suffer from the illusion that we can depart our old, squalid harbors with their stagnant garbage water for a place far, far away, where bright horizons of space are open to us and where everything is crystal clear and sunny. All of us like to believe there exists such a serene land, where we might put ashore and cleanse ourselves of our life's fogs and burdens.

In our sad age fraught with political troubles, Europeans delude themselves with a romantic yearning for unknown tropical lands, as if India today were not a political penitentiary and industrialized prison like Europe. Or as if the streets of China were not aflow with blood, and as if Asian bankers and feudal lords did not puff on thick cigars while overseeing armies of living corpses—emaciated workers who sell their skin by the same laws as the wage slaves in the mills and foundries of Černomerec, Podsused, or Trbovlje. All this happens on one extremely small globe, and the time has come for people to take this shiny little planet into their hands and cleanse it of blood, suffering, and misery. All the yearning to put ashore on happier continents belongs to a prehistoric mental epoch, the pre-Leninist age before the discovery of the Sixth Continent, the USSR.

So it was that in my mind I basked in the February sun on Baross Quay in Rijeka, looking at sailors' dirty washing on a grey Italian warship and yearning for the Sixth Continent in that vision of the south. The bells of Rijeka's trams rang faintly in the distance and a dark orange sail slowly glided out from Brajdica Harbor in the spring silence beneath the green, copper dome of Rijeka's theatre; it was spring, but I longed for the northern Sixth Continent, the USSR. And here now in the land of wolves and samovars, having really put ashore on that Sixth Continent, I started to pine uncontrollably for the real, authentic, ideal, clean spring of the Kvarner Gulf. How very puerile, how preposterous and whimsical!

Here I sit in the garden of the Institute of Chemistry, watching Moscow in the sunlight with its gasholders, factory fences, chimneys, new buildings, and scaffolding. The sound of a brass band comes on the wind from afar, strains of the Rákóczi March, and in that instant the city strikes me as a metropolis, like all big cities on this civilized, poverty-stricken planet. People are tired after work, throw copper coins into orchestrions, snack on dry rolls, drink vodka, and the landscape is joyless, yellow, and sandy. But here, in the middle of the park, stands the Institute of Chemistry with its test tubes and bright, sunny, linoleum-clad corridors, all washed and shiny clean, as the scientific institutes of the twentieth century are. Large, engraved slabs of marble bear the gold-lettered names of Mendeleyev, Lomonosov, and Mechnikov, and everything is defined and clearly classified under its own number and formula in showcases or processed in tables.

Humans are extremely clever creatures, and just as they have ordered, listed, and classified everything in this Institute of Chemistry, so too they will order, list and classify everything else that calls for it all over the world. Export and import will be brought into balance, and all the statistical tables will be a thousand times richer and more impressive than today. There will no longer be wars or premature deaths, nor British pounds or American dollars, nor the ruinous, magnetic games of the great powers. But in the shadow of the most exact scientific insights there will still be confused and capricious folk who secretly listen to the wind buffeting the branches before the coming of spring. They will be the shame and disgrace of the institutes of chemistry, but, obliviously, they will listen to the grass growing in the garden beds and the wind whispering to the cherry blossom. Those crazy characters will contemplate the chirping of the sparrows and the flight of clouds with attentiveness worthy of respect. They will sense the sorrow of spring, conscious that people are enchanters of serenity, of deep blue perspectives in the noon of spring. Which means nothing other than an enchanting torrent of images and impressions, a cascade of colors, smells, and sounds, which plunge roaring into nothingness. People move like an avalanche of colors, smells, and sounds, and their yearning is just one of the innocent illusions that events have some semblance of meaning.

LENIN

The reality of war is odious to man, and long ago Homer began the *Iliad* by intoning Achilles's baleful rage:

> (...) *which put pains thousandfold upon the Achaians,*
> *hurled in their multitudes to the house of Hades*
> *strong souls of heroes, but gave their bodies to be*
> *the delicate feasting of dogs, of all birds.* [*]

Herodotus thought wars were incited by demons, and Socrates said of war and generals, with the irony of a contemporary pacifist: *We should do philosophy until we see generals as donkey drivers.*

Plato dreamed of a Republic and of philosopher kings, and David Hume thought about war with repugnance: *When I now see the nations engaged in war, it is as if I witnessed two drunken wretches bludgeoning each other in a china shop. For it is not just that the injuries they inflict on each other will be long in healing, they will also have to pay for all the damage they have caused.*

Hume's formulation about war was borrowed by Immanuel Kant, an intimate Jacobin, as the motto of his study "Perpetual Peace," an ironic title he chose based on the satirical signboard of a Dutch inn, which shows a cemetery as a symbol of "Perpetual Peace." Pascal wrote about war with the acuity of Goya's copperplate stylus

---

[*] This passage is cited here exclusively for informative purposes. In Yugoslavia, Lenin has been written about with myopic bias and animosity. But for millions upon millions, Lenin represents the portentous revelation of a political and moral-intellectual realization, and there is no harm in barking at the moon. I have used statistical data and quotations from various articles by Nicolai, Zinoviev, E. Varga, Gorky, Spengler, Korsch, Lukács, Sternberg, etc., without verifying the information or the dates, under the assumption that they are correct. Studies by Yaroslavsky, Gorky, Stalin, Guilbeaux, Edouard Bert, and Victor Serge, or pamphlets, of which I mention only those by Landau-Aldanov, Wells, etc., encompass the huge span of issues related to Lenin; I have not gone through all of these thoroughly, nor is it the purpose of this cursory presentation to go into detail. A particular shortcoming when undertaking this type of journalistic, nonfiction writing is the perceptible lack of any, even the most basic "required reading" in Yugoslavia, and especially literature about Lenin's works, which censorship here has rendered illegal.

("Los desastres de la guerra"), and from Bonaparte, who declared demagogically several times that he hated war, to Tolstoy and Stendhal, all Europeans gave their voice against war, condemning it as an antediluvian monster for its disastrous consequences, but not investigating the true causes of martial crime.

The First International (which no longer represented the foggy aspirations of isolated individuals but the first conscious exertion of cosmopolitical conceptions) issued its first antiwar resolution in Lausanne in 1867, demanding the abolition of compulsory military service. During the Austro-Prussian and Austro-Italian wars of 1866, the First International defined the dynamics of war as a very favorable opportunity for class liberation, "because labor is international and knows no fatherland."

A good twenty years later, in Paris in 1889, then in Brussels in 1891, and Zürich in 1893, unanimous resolutions of the Second International concluded that the internationally organized proletariat should consider it its primary class-conscious duty to vote against war budgets through its representatives in the bourgeois parliaments, and to struggle for international disarmament. These theses were reaffirmed in London in 1896, Stuttgart in 1907, Copenhagen and Paris in 1910, and finally Basel in 1912.

The stance in Basel was particularly resolute, adopted in November 1912 under the immediate impression of the First Balkan War. The Basel resolution warned the proletarian masses of Europe that, to paraphrase, *the Franco-Prussian War of 1870 was followed by the revolutionary outbreak of the Paris Commune, and the Russo-Japanese War of 1904 set in motion the revolutionary energies of the peoples of the Russian Empire. Proletarians consider it a crime to fire at each other for the profits of the capitalists and the glory of dynasties.*

In its organizational and ideological quintessence, Leninism is nothing other than the ten resolutions of the First and Second International applied in the context of the imperialist reality and the international conflagration of 1914–18, based on the Marxist theses in the *Communist Manifesto* of 1848. Leninism is inspired by the élan of the idealistic aspirations of Plato, Socrates, Kant, and Marx, and whoever wishes to think seriously about Leninism should imagine it on the fiery horizon of the world war, with which it is inseparably connected. We must not forget that twelve million died on European battlefields before Lenin could appear. When Lenin's first radio signal "To All" boomed forth from the Kronstadt antenna, it sparked off unrest in the trenches from Ypres and Verdun to Macedonia and Riga—turmoil full of hopes for a brighter future. Leninism spoke to the warring international masses as a symbol of peace, and that was its strength and the mystery of its magic. Men climbed out of their trenches, cut the barbed wire, threw down their weapons, embraced, kissed each other, and cried together like brothers; from the Baltic to the Carpathians, the air along the front lines, so often rent by the roar of cannons and the rattle of machine guns, began to fill with the sound of balalaikas and the voices of soldiers eating, drinking, and singing. In that instant, Socrates's words came true: certain "donkeys" mobilized for death at the front actually became Socratics, chased away their donkey-driver generals, and made off home with a song on their lips.

"Peace without annexations and plundering, land to the peasants, and the factories to the workers"—those were Lenin's demands for overcoming the chaos of the last imperialist war, and I do not think there was a single European citizen under arms (at least of those able to think and draw logical conclusions) who did not feel the suggestive veracity of Lenin's theses.

M. Panz from Greifswald in Germany wrote: *I was on the Eastern Front north of Baranovichi in November 1917 with the 2nd Battalion, 404th Infantry, 5th Company when the Russians started to signal to us with red flags. It came to an altercation between us and our sergeants, and, despite the strictest prohibition, we crossed over into the Russian trenches. The merriment was beyond words, and there I was first handed a German leaflet printed on red paper: Proletarians of the world, unite! Our whole regiment was considered mutinous and we were redeployed north of Pinsk.*

I, Dettless from Kiel in Germany, was on the Western Front with the 31st Infantry Regiment near Ypres: *One day, at four in the afternoon, when our meal was brought from the rear, they told us that the Revolution had broken out in Russia. The Ivans showed the stupid Germans how it needed to be done! All of us were immediately full of hope and began discussing: How? and if so, When? We constantly expected a general strike, and we were ready to go over to the British and reach out our hands. That day was the beginning of the unrest and turmoil.*

These are just two out of a mass of German documents written by soldiers without rank, and now they make up a whole body of literature; they clearly show how Lenin's ideas affected the international masses, on different fronts, in different armies and nations. Massive rebellions broke out in French units and were repressed with brute force. One ought to compare the indemnity debate in the Croatian parliament in 1917–18 and the position of the opposition speakers toward the Russian Revolution, as well as the many documents from the Bulgarian-Macedonian front. In Hungary, too, there were open revolts and disobedience both in the rear and at the front. The Austrian collapse was largely brought on by Russian élan, and if the Russian Revolution had not broken out, neither of the Germanic empires—Germany and Austria-Hungary—would have broken up as early as 1918. The war would have lasted another year or two at least and, accordingly, it is an indubitable historical fact that the Russian Revolution had the immediate effect of halting the rhythm of international butchery. The numerous documents published by Franz Pfemfert in his journal *Die Aktion*, and also in *Clarté* in Paris under the editorship of Henri Barbusse, as well as the observations and statements by Henri Guilbaux, Marty, Otto Flake, Leonhard Frank, etc., confirm this theory.

Lenin's slogans were very simple. They called on the warring European proletariat to stop the senseless slaughter in its own interest, and when I spoke to Belgrade university students about the Russian Revolution several years ago (1922), I compared the historical events of 1917 with the mechanical state that occurs when a physical body that has been thrown into the air reaches a culmination point, where the effect of gravity is equal to zero.

The Russian Revolution's aggregate of problems had been flung by the force of wartime events to the height of taking political power, and Leninism, as an ideological foundation with the thesis of the dictatorship of the proletariat, retained that revolutionary dynamism at the height of political power and prevented it from falling back to the previous state due to the gravitation of reactionary forces. And indeed, in 1917, the fourth year of the world war, that reactionary gravitation came close to zero all over Europe due to a number of factors. But the European revolutionary mood, lacking a Leninist basis, collapsed back into the *status quo ante bellum,* thus confirming Lenin's theory that the twentieth century would be a century with cycles of imperialist wars.

After twelve million dead and 247,129,000,000 dollars of international debt, today, six years after the Treaty of Versailles, the European powers have around five-and-a-half million men under arms in standing armies, as an organizational cadre for a total of 18–40 million rifles. In addition, there are 84 dreadnoughts, 167 cruisers, 1,094 destroyers and torpedo gunboats, over 400 submarines, and around 10,000 aircraft (according to the League of Nations and the Federal Bureau of Statistics in Washington).

The *Daily Express* reports that around ninety large-tonnage warships are currently under construction in European shipyards, and the number being built at Japanese docks is probably the same. All states are arming themselves with gas, and the contours of a new chemical war are being sketched in international specialist literature.* The twelve million dead and 250 billion dollars of material damage in the span from 1914 to 1918 were "achieved" by old-fashioned means, with gunpowder and dynamite, in relatively restricted battlefield zones; chemical warfare does not distinguish between the front and the rear, and thus the resulting devastation in the scope of a new war will probably be disproportionately greater.

---

* **Professor Smithells, a British authority in the poison-gas field, says:** *The use of poison gases has been called ruthless and unnatural. But it should be acknowledged that every new method of warfare, even gunpowder, was initially considered barbarous, and only lost some of its horror gradually, over time. It is impossible for Great Britain to renounce gas.*

In 1920, the British prime minister declared to Parliament:

The USA*, France, and Italy are experimenting with gas as an offensive weapon. It would be mad for Great Britain to renounce gas.*

After the Washington Conference on Disarmament, Dr. I. Mills, an American military specialist at that conference, stated that "gas is the most humane weapon because it is the most effective, and therefore gas cannot be excluded by any agreement."

According to figures from Drs. Hanslian and Bergendorf, one air force squadron of twenty planes equipped with 4,000 lb. gas bombs is capable of destroying a city of one million inhabitants in an exceedingly short space of time.

The chaos in international production and the imperialist struggle for markets brought about the global conflagration of 1914, and all those ingredients are still at work today with the same, and in many respects with even greater force.[*]

The economic situation is fragile and looks set to further decline. Currencies are falling, prices of goods in Europe are rising together with unemployment, and no one at all knows a way out of the crisis. The bourgeois economic critic of Versailles, Keynes, speaks in the same tone as Rosa Luxemburg when she wrote *The Accumulation of Capital* on the eve of the world war. When the price of labor falls, the banks accumulate unheard-of riches.[**] Those riches are an international, mechanical, and financial force that functions according to the laws of its own logic, and state systems play a subordinate role to it. The state is only a decorative sham in its pretense to "belong to the people," when in fact it is an exponent of the bank. The bank is a machine that acts according to the sole regulatory factor, i.e. the pursuit of its own financial operations and profits, and the state's politics are just a tool in the hands of the banks' financial strategy. Just as profit and competition are parallel phenomena, so too wars are essentially economic and financial power struggles of individual financial competitors. As long as profit and competition are the only common denominator of international life, crises in international relations will continue to feature

[*] *The Observer*, the organ of the International Miners Union, gives the following statistics for coal: Europe, 1924, 9% less than 1923; America 2.6% less; Africa 50%; Asia and Australia 20% more. Thus the acute crisis in European mining and shipping and the reason for the unemployment of several million workers (at the end of 1925, there were around five million unemployed).

[**] In his speech in the French Chamber of Deputies on November 11, 1925, Marcel Cachin called banks the feudal lords of democracy. The Parisian banks hold around 80 billion francs in their vaults, and the same amount of financial reserves; in the last five years the 67 French banks reported 4,357, 617,820 francs of net gain in their balance sheets. This result does not include currency speculation, profits from stockbrokers' manoeuvers, business deals and private operations of the administrative apparatus, speculation on commissions, exchange discounts on international shares and exchange rates, incorrectly assessed real estate values, etc.

on the historical stage. Crises give rise to wars, and therefore the making of peace is logically followed by a new spiral of rearmament, which in turn leads to new cycles of wars. After the Treaty of Versailles, in the period from 1920 to 1924, a dozen European wars and armed interventions flared up,* and the cited figures on international armament and the emerging contours of chemical war are the prelude to new cataclysms. In addition to that constantly precarious financial strategy fraught with innumerable dangers, Europe is also faced with the volcanic colonial question. Today, more than eight hundred million colonial and semicolonial slaves are in thrall to financial Europe.** The life of those pauperized colonial slaves is an existence below the bedrock minimum of human dignity, and the objective penury, famines, and epidemics are indefensible. The agrarian regions of China and Japan accommodate 2,000 inhabitants per square kilometer, compared with 280 inhabitants per square kilometer in Belgium, the most densely

---

* The Anglo-French intervention in Russia, the occupation of the Ruhr and Cologne, the Albanian expedition of the Kingdom of Serbs, Croats, and Slovenes, various wars: Lithuanian-Polish, Polish-Russian, Greco-Turkish, and Greco-Bulgarian. German-Polish fascist actions, D'Annunzio's fiasco in Rijeka, the Italian occupation of Corfu. Uprisings in the colonies. Syria, Morocco, etc. The whole complex of unresolved questions in the Danube region and the Balkans, etc.

** According to information from Eddy Sherwood, Secretary of the English Youth Movement, a 12- to 18-hour working day is normal in the Chinese silk industry, for seven pennies a day (around 8 dinars). In the textile factories six-year-old children wash out the silk cocoons with scalding-hot water 16 hours a day. Twelve-year-old workers are an everyday occurrence in China. Six-year-old children work in the factories in Shanghai under international control.

Prof. Chen Han-sun, a member of Sun Yat-sen's Kuomintang Party, writes that every tenth man in Peking is a "rikshaw coolie," running in front of his vehicle. In addition to those 70,000 coolies, in Peking alone there are around 170,000 beggars on the streets.

The coolie washes once a year, in the period of the great religious festival. His face is yellow and stiff like a mask. Seminaked and squalid, he wears a sign around his neck that reads "Coolie." That is an animal of the lowest kind that runs all day in a harness, louses itself like a monkey, and stinks like a wild donkey. (HUELSENBECK, *Vorwärts*, Berlin)

populated and industrialized country in Europe. The situation is the same in India and the Malay Archipelago, where periodic, catastrophic famines and epidemics are a normal, everyday occurrence, and colonial labor is therefore disproportionately cheaper than European. The relationship of industrialized Europe to its colonies is that of a 50,000–ton iron, mastodonic hyperdreadnought with its 35cm caliber muzzles trained on the naked and barefoot, wretched and defenseless masses of colonial slaves. How can the flesh of pauperized and hungry Africans stand against European cannons?

While Abd el-Krim invokes the 1,000–years of Arabic culture and learning in his appeal to the South American universities, his naked and hungry shepherds are facing a Franco-Spanish armada of eleven heavy battleships and entire fleets of torpedo boats, submarines, and coastguard warships, and 260,000 infantry with state-of-the-art aircraft and tanks. The Syrian Sultan al-Atrash quotes Rousseau in his proclamation, but in vain; he invokes the Jacobins' "Rights of Man" and the slogans of the Great French Revolution about freedom and equality—also in vain. Rivers of oil flow through Syria, Morocco represents a great abundance of ore, and the Bank of Paris and the Netherlands needs coal, just as the Bank of Syria and Greater Lebanon needs oil. "All wars are just about plunder." (Voltaire).*

In the face of all those intertwined questions and relations of the many financial crises of imperialist politics, Leninism took the firm, iron, and logical attitude, as ruthless and unyielding as that of the conquerors and exploiters: an eye for an eye, a tooth for a tooth!

When the foundations of the alliance of French capital and Russian tsarism were laid in 1893, Lenin wrote his fundamental

---

*   **The logic of interest is an iron law and has nothing but scorn and disdain for the meat of Europe's colonial slaves. During the 1922 Black Congress in Brussels, the British press wrote derisively about tailcoated savages with red umbrellas and mouth organs, who demanded a Free Africa. The Ku Klux Klan in America lynches Blacks systematically, in line with its social code. Professor Amar wrote recently in *Echo de Paris*: "The colonial natives ought to be banned access to European culture because its influence in the colonies is harmful. The natives get carried away and adorn themselves with science, literature, and jurisprudence, and then, rising up to the European, oppose him with their own aspirations and challenge his authority."**

analysis "The Development of Capitalism in Russia." His intransigent stance in the framework of the London split of 1903 was dictated by bloody experience. (1894–95: the Japanese-Chinese War. Port Arthur changes into Russian hands. 1900–02: the Boer War. The fall of the Transvaal. 1900–02: the European-American expedition in China. The Boxer Rebellion.)

Lenin and Rosa Luxemburg's addition to the resolution of the social democratic congress in Stuttgart in 1907 was adopted after lengthy debate, and dictated by experience of the Russo-Japanese War and the Russian Revolution of 1904–05: *"Should war break out nonetheless, it is their duty to intervene in favor of its speedy termination and to do all in their power to utilize the economic and political crisis caused by the war to rouse the peoples and thereby to hasten the abolition of capitalist class rule."* From Stuttgart to Basel (1907–12), the life of Europe and Asia proceeded in the shadow of constant crises, diplomatic entanglements, and wars. (1908: annexation of Bosnia and the customs war between Serbia and Austria-Hungary. The Italian-Turkish war of 1911. Agadir. Liberation struggles of the Austro-Hungarian nationalities. The awaking of an integral South-Slavic liberating consciousness. The Young Turk Revolution. Morocco-Egypt-Tripoli. The Chinese Revolution 1911. The fall of the Manchu dynasty. Sun Yat-sen founds the Republic of China. The Balkan War of 1912.)

Lenin played an active role in the commissions of the Basel congress, so his stance from the collapse of the Second International in August 1914, via the Kiental and Zimmerwald congresses, to the April Theses of 1917, represents a logical development of the organizational conclusions and directives adopted at the congresses of the Second International. Lenin, therefore, did not drop out of the blue sky onto Nevsky Prospect to harangue the proletarian masses in Petrograd with nebulous demagogic slogans (as some in Philistine circles think). Rather, as a consistent Marxist and internationalist, he ideologically elaborated the copious material of his historical role for over thirty years, struggling without respite for the affirmation of socialist political theses in all forums of the Second International. His ideological and political achievements stand today before the world as the giant hyperdreadnought USSR, armed with guns of the heaviest caliber, and today that is no longer a text of Platonic resolutions before the opportunistic forums of the Second International but the economic and political force of a whole continent from the Pacific Ocean to Europe, which will play the historical role in the liberation movement of the colonial masses of the Near East, Orient, Indian subcontinent, Southeast Asia, and China, which Bonapartism played in the awaking of national consciousness among the peoples of feudal central Europe.

The picture that the European bourgeois intellect creates in its imagination of the historical and cultural development of Europe, contemporary civilization, and a whole series of phenomena connected with the cataclysm of 1914–18, and all its fatal future consequences, is blurred, confused, and barely coincides with reality. G. F. Nicolai, for example, one of the most brilliant European intellectuals, who morally prevailed over the unworthy prejudices of Western-European petty bourgeois nationalism and statism (which Nietzsche in his time called "cattle nationalism"), that Hippocrates and doctor of medicine became lost in utopian delusions, and later in the dubious languor of subjective disappointment.*

---

* In his famous book *The Biology of War* he printed a declaration full of love and Feuerbach's humanism, drawn up in mid October 1914 together with Wilhelm Foerster and Albert Einstein:
> *The war raging at present will scarcely end in a victory for any one, but probably only in defeat. Consequently, it would seem that educated men in all countries not only should, but absolutely must, exert all their influence to prevent the conditions of peace being the source of future wars, and this no matter what the present uncertain issue of the conflict may be. Above all they must direct their efforts to seeing that advantage is taken of the fact that this war has thrown all European conditions, as it were, into a melting-pot, to mold Europe into one organic whole, for which both technical and intellectual conditions are ripe.*

Those were the basic principles of the declaration published to counter the manifesto of German intellectuals who opposed the Entente powers' theories and denied that Germany was avidly preparing for the conflagration of 1914:
> *Es ist nicht wahr, daß Deutschland diesen Krieg verschuldet hat.* (*It is not true that Germany is guilty of having caused this war*).

Among the ninety-three prominent Germans who signed that pro-military statement were Peter Behrens, Max Klinger, Liebermann and Stuck, Haeckel, Röntgen, Dehmel, Hauptmann, Sudermann, Eucken, Riehl, Wundt, Wagner, Weingartner, and Reinhardt.

In vain G. F. Nicolai cited Homer: "A clanless, lawless, heartless man is he who loves the horror of war among his own people," and with this argument tried to turn the megalomaniac line of Germanic financial-capitalist and industrial development from Krupp's Essen to Goethe's Weimar. The movement of history follows iron laws, and the events of European reality proceed according to the iron logic of profits and dividends, 180 degrees contrary to the pious wishes of noble and idealistic individuals.

Lenin was always opposed to such utopianism on principle. Already on May 1, 1915, he wrote about three categories of pacifism: the rich's fear of revolution; the misty longing of the petty bourgeois and semiproletarians for a breathing space; and the conscious wish for peace, which does not want the democratic peace of petty bourgeois philanthropists but systematic anti-war action by the masses as the sole effective means of subduing and stopping the madness of war. From 1914–17, Lenin issued polemics against the petty bourgeois and utopian slogans of the United States of Europe in a whole series of articles, propagating the idea of the direct seizure of proletarian power in one country, or a whole group of countries, for a victorious war of those groups of proletarian states against the whole capitalist system (August 1915, *Sotsial-Demokrat*, no. 44). (A Jacobin position toward feudal Europe.)

Not in one of his anti-war articles did Lenin fall to the level of the phony declamatory passions for obscure geographic wholes, as did some geopolitical "Confusians" like Hanslick or Austro-Catholic sermonizers such as Hermann Bahr (Dr. Erwin Hanslick: *Österreich, Erde und Geist*, Vienna 1917). The pan-European nebulousness of Count Coudenhove-Kalergi, which appeared with twelve years' delay, is as equally odious to him as the cosmopolitical tone of the stockbrokers' press from Trafalgar Square.

Leninism is the principled negation of petty bourgeois Philistinism, be it in its social democratic hue[*] (Masaryk,

---

[*]   **Karl Renner's Austro-Marxism, with its supranational ideology and national autonomies, was a Danubian, black-and-yellow adjunct to Friedrich Naumann's *Mitteleuropa*, with the Baghdad Railway.**
        If we do not reach a solution quickly, not only will we have missed the chance, but the die will be cast over us. In a decade or two, the world will have been divided up!

Kautsky) or the inconsistent phrases in political and cultural fields.*

Friedrich Adler, son of the prominent Austro-Marxist ideologue Viktor Adler, and himself a socialist by conviction—a devotee of Empiriocriticism—took a Browning and shot Count von Stürgkh, the minister president of the Monarch's discretion, so that his assassination might alarm the bourgeois Austrian conscience; it was to be a demonstration before the eyes of the world against the policy of the German "drive to the East," and also against Renner's Austro-Marxist "socialist supranationality."

Leninism, in contrast to Friedrich Adler's gesture of individual terrorism, does not stand for an isolated, despair-filled revolver shot in the restaurant of the hotel Meissl & Schadn at an Austrian representative of feudal and financial politics. Rather, it is massed artillery with guns of the heaviest caliber deployed against international monetary artilleries according to all the

---

* The late Gustav Landauer voiced nervous and even irritated critiques of German social democracy and its mentality in his socialist pronouncement "Aufruf zum Sozialismus," in an elevated tone. All of Proudhon's and Landauer's theses were tragically confirmed on August 4, 1914. Jaurès was an idealist and Kantian, and still he was shot, like Landauer. Masaryk, as a Humean and agnostic, for whom Stenka Razin and Pugachev were just ordinary brigands (*Russland und Europa*, 1913), begins with a study on suicide but ends up in Prague Castle; Macdonald wines and dines with the English king. Noske kills Liebknecht; Hungarian, Bulgarian, Italian, Spanish, and Russian liberals (Oszkár Jászi, Nitti, Unamuno, Ibáñez, Struve, Burtsev) end up in the futility of emigration. The concept of Eurasia, of a cantonization of the Danube region along Swiss lines, an ideal democratic decentralization of the West (*L'Ère nouvelle*)—all of it is delusion. The syndicalist Georges Sorel ideologically opposes Nietzsche, a contemporary of Cecil Rhodes, as does the leader of the French royalists, Maurras, who wants to model France on the tradition of forty kings and is one of the adepts of Nietzscheism for whom Nietzsche himself is in no way responsible. Fascism, which Jack London presaged as early as 1905 in *The Iron Heel*, is today international reality. On top of that reality, all the democratic freedom-loving frenzy is paradoxical and false. The Russian tsar built a peace palace in The Hague, just as international bankers today lie and bloviate at the conference tables in Geneva and Locarno, and on the other hand arm themselves with gas and tanks.

rules of political strategy. Leninism comes to us as a striking confirmation of the theory that wars are an attendant phenomenon of the capitalist economic system, and that the twentieth century of imperialist wars is characterized by the historical emergence of Asia and the ever faster development of a social revolution, which will succeed in asserting itself first in one group of states, until it is finally and integrally victorious and in a position to implement a higher order of production on an international scale.

There are signs, to be sure, that bourgeois Europe is collapsing. Not only have international politics become a completely shameless trade-off of principles and ideas, prostitution for the sake of material power (Machiavellianism as the cult of political talent), but those same symptoms of anxiety, a racing pulse, and a palpitation of alarm from the desire for shallow gains, manifest themselves in all intellectual and artistic fields. Art has become industrialized, and in place of the romantic enthusiasm for beauty today commodities are produced. Neurasthenia, hysteria, and pornography as goods for neurasthenic and hysterical consumers. The absolute victory of the sexual! Today a woman finds her mission in infantile infatuation with the latest fashion. Hetera defeats the patriarchal mother! (Weininger-Strindberg.) Creative skill and art are transformed into decoration and mechanized art production. (From the Secession to Dada, the bluff rules Europe.) Music and literature are typically aristocratic and decadent, full of the sensations of dying patricians, when the barbarians appear on the fringes.* From Baudelaire and Verlaine to Anatole France and Marcel Proust, from Chopin to Gustav Mahler—one finds the same phenomena of "autumnal dying." The decline and fall of classical civilization coincides with the decay of contemporary bourgeois reality. (Spengler: *The Decline of the West*.)

Sophists, Cynics, Stoics, and Epicurus in antiquity, pseudo-materialists and decadents of various philosophical nuances today—the decay of taste in the ancient world corresponds exactly to our contemporary decline of taste. In painting, it is a

*   *I am the Kingdom at the end of its decline / That watches as big white Barbarians pass / That composes indolent acrostics / Of golden style where the sun's yearning dances.*
     (VERLAINE, "Langueur")

steep downward slope from Ingres to Paul Klee* and Kandinsky, and an architect like Fischer von Erlach stands out grandly compared to O. Wagner's bronze laurels and Secessionist caryatids, like Diderot in literature compared to any contemporary journalist and hack. (Names are secondary and odious.) Compare the lack of taste in the last centuries of imperial Rome, those eclectic compositions with Doric and Ionian gateways combined with Egyptian palm columns and sphinxes, with today's eclectic architectural absurdity of the huge bank buildings in big cities. Today the meandering adornment on the majolica of the English toilet and the destruction of form from the Parnassians to Expressionism is a symptom of chaos and decay. Ljubomir Micić coined the notion of the "Balkan Barbarogenius" and claimed Dante would be unfit to collaborate in the avant-garde magazine *Zenit*, and therefore Arabic music, African sculpture, Black dances, shimmy, foxtrot, ragtime, saxophones, are the favorite music of bourgeois Europeans after Bach, Mozart, and Beethoven. Fads and fashions—the cult of Africa, India, and Java. First there was the Alexandrian cult of form, and in that monotony a disintegration of talent occurred, and there ensued a period of the skeptical lyricism of decline.** Nine tenths of European lyrics are written in the smug minor of transience. A boring cult of the nuance brought forth absurdity, which devours beauty endlessly like a cancer consumes flesh. The chaos in cognitive theory is one more example of the general destruction of principles. Newton's Principles, as magnificent as Michelangelo's sculptures, vanish today like phantoms in this time of molecular mechanics. After Lavoisier's principle of the indestructibility of matter, one can conjecture a system of thought for which all that is not idea is nothing. Matter is dematerialized to its perception, and after the great romantic enthusiasm for material, when it seemed metaphysics had finally been taken off the agenda, people are writing about God again. (It cannot be proved that he doesn't exist, and vice versa.)*** In the mists of

---

* On Klee: Miroslav Krleža, *Kriza u slikarstvu* (The Crisis in Painting).

** *Of death, perchance! Alas, so lagging in desire! / Ah, all is drunk! Bathyllus, hast done laughing, pray? / Ah, all is drunk,—all eaten! Nothing more to say!* (VERLAINE, "Langueur")

*** Empiriocriticism, illusionism, pragmatism, meliorism, blurred and disturbed worldviews (all the currents in philosophy since the British empiricists and Kant), in the bloody and crazed interest of animals of the lowest sorts, which only pretend to walk like biped humans and in fact devour one another depravedly (tabular statistics on wars and economic disturbances), between caricatures of God, goodness, and beauty (all churches from Luther and Byzantium to Rome and the Salvation Army*), at that catastrophic pace and quantity across bourgeois Europe, like herds of furious biblical swine, into which someone compressed all the madness of the world. Ever newer sensations, lies, and bluffs shake society, ever newer sects and organizations, all with their principles, views, and flags, all with their programs and signposts on how to resolve the unsolvable problem of sick, warped Europe! Carnivores preach vegetarianism; illiterates learn Esperanto; professionals play international chess, roulette, and soccer; petty bourgeois enthusiasts of the Sokol movement, horsemen, nationalists, and virtuous patriots** yearn for war; spinsters and barren women build children's homes; exploiters collect for charity on street corners; liars hold lectures about a new Messiah who appeared in India; little old ladies believe in chiromancy, lay tarot cards, and read belletristic literature; drunkards propagate teetotalism. And so from Saint-Simonianism and anthroposophy in European parlors, from Max Stirner*** to the bankocracy, from solipsistic armchair philosophy to the professor's rostrum, **** and from the metropolitan production of books to industrialized art, from lies in the family to those in parliament—all of that is blood-

---

        militarism, fideism, conceptualism, and anti-intellectualism in contemporary philosophy, with several hundred philosophers' names in all European countries, correspond to analogous phenomena in literature and painting, from Impressionism and Pointillism to abstract painting. (Expressionism, Futurism, Surrealism, Imaginism, Unanimism, Primitivism, Dadaism, etc. There are over twenty theoretical-isms in contemporary Russian painting alone.)

*   See G. B. Shaw, *Major Barbara.*

**   "Whoever sees war and is not seized by horror, is not a man. He is a patriot!" (KURT TUCHOLSKY)

***   Max Stirner, *Der Einzige und sein Eigentum* (The Ego and His Own), a book very dear to individualist, bourgeois anarchists.

****   Cf. Schopenhauer and all his writing about philosophy professors.

187

stained and hopeless. Tolstoy wanted to resolve the problem through the passivity of suffering, but he died in the flight from reality; Romain Rolland propagates the idea of a synthesis of Western culture, in aesthetics and music, patterned on Bach and Beethoven, but lives as an émigré, accused of high treason in his homeland; Gauguin died in self-imposed exile, Van Gogh in an asylum; Bakunin wore himself out in years of fury between Siberia and London, and Goya and Marx died in emigration. The crisis of European intellect is becoming more acute by the day. Through their fiery agitation, tens of thousands of European minds are demonstrating the abnormal intensity of the protracted disease that has lasted from Schopenhauer to the end of the nineteenth century and on till today—without letup and seemingly without cure.

An intellectually daring move in the face of Western Europe's wartime blood and chaos, a move of marked, direct, and unyielding unilateralness against European moral and political lies and deceit, a move with the unshakable conviction that it was a matter of overcoming the inertia of centuries of backwardness—that is Leninism as it appeared in 1917 in the face of all the Western-European plans for peoples, states, and religions.

Leninism is a political plan of logic and intelligence, allowing the globe to approach the Cosmopolis at a steady speed, twenty-four hours a day. Leninism is Archimedes's political lever, sufficiently reliable to help the globe, including legitimist, finance-capitalist Europe, to rise to the heights of a brighter civilization, whose format would correspond to the imperative of the technocratic age. Leninism is Marxism, but there is huge difference between Lenin's Marxism and Western-European Marxists. In all the sixty years after Marx and Engels, there have been sixty years of Marxism in Europe and several million Marxists, but only one single Lenin, who lent that scheme his very own vigor. Galilei's truth was already evident long ago, in Ptolemaic times, and its accuracy has been verified scientifically for several hundred years already, but for millions and millions of anti-Galilean minds in contemporary Europe the naïve, biblical theory still applies that the earth is the center of the universe, and as such rests immobile. The Roman Catholic Church, for example, which the prominent thinker Georges Goyau called "the grand International of the moral strength of humanity," still occupies the anti-Galilean standpoint. And if that question was to be resolved by popular, secret ballot, the anti-Galileans would win by the huge, compact democratic majority of their votes and convictions.

Therefore, logically, Leninism is not a puritan sermon about the formalistic dribblings of so-called democratic, bourgeois parliamentarianism. Leninism proceeds from a fundamental hypothesis, which takes as an axiom that labor is an internationally inseparable whole, and as such one must bring down all the feudal and banking structures of this outdated economic system built on the backwardness of human consciousness. In distinction to social democratic, philanthropic, and pacifist declamations, Leninism aims to create living conditions that will bring forth the socialist psychology of a new social consciousness rooted in internationalist solidarity. In contrast to the 5,000–year efforts of various organized religions to shape more humane relations that would produce real and viable results, Leninism has demonstrated in practice that a socialistic psychology is not a prerequisite for socialist relations, but conversely, that socialist economic relations are the historical factor that gives birth to a socialist consciousness.

Leninism emerged at a time when the last phase of international capitalism was taking on symptoms of evident madness, which imperiled even the most fundamental preconditions for the civilized life of man, and the results of the wars of last fifty years leave no doubt as to this. The accumulation and concentration of capital is growing in geometric progression, the credit system is leveling the feudal remains of European statism with breathtaking speed, and, flanked by a gamut of the most idiotic contradictions, a shadow is increasingly growing on the horizon—that of an international magnate, a new feudal lord of industry, parliamentary democracy, and production.*

One characteristic of the final phase of imperialism is the acute contradiction between the development of science on the one hand, and the imbecilic mental inertia in the scope

---

*   **Cf. Hilferding's figures on the role of finance capital compared with the almost naïve innocence of the agrarian feudal system. According to Marx, the position of the slave in the ancient world was brilliant compared to that of the contemporary industrial slave.**

of the feudal bankocracy and outmoded economic relations on the other hand. Biological principles confirm the theory of class struggle, and in analysis of the genealogy of morals they give rise to ethical relativism (Darwin, Marx, Nietzsche). With reckless speed, science is closing in on the last secrets of material, which it penetrates analytically, and is on the path to uncovering the secret of organic and inorganic relations. The protuberances of the sun and the mists in Orion and Andromeda cast light from the most distant galaxies into the eyepieces of man-made instruments and can be seen just as clearly as bacteria in the bloodstream or diseased organs. Radium breaks down material and opens perspectives into the exceedingly fast movements of atoms, and the speed of electricity sets insuperable masses in motion and bends all expanses to the plans and will of man. Machines overcome all obstacles of detached geographical, continental, intercontinental, and planetary space, and a whole series of small inventions, from the postal service and telegraph wires to Marconi's antennae, give rise to the consciousness of the integral whole of the globe and the universe. The earth has long ceased to be the regionally limited Mediterranean Basin of antiquity or other isolated patches of geographically separate, individual civilizations (Chaldea, Syria, Egypt, the Arabic Mediterranean zone, Hellas, the Roman Empire, and feudal Europe); the globe appears in outline before man's eyes and the first signs of synthesis are showing. In the twilight of illiteracy and patriarchal psychology founded on elements of medieval manufacturing, at a time when anti-Galilean darkness still reigns in millions of European brains, when wooden saints and demigods are enshrined in churches and human souls are ruled by apparitions, with feudal sovereignty and the Roman principle of private law, when the relationship of masters and slaves from antiquity still reigns, and when the right of the sword and the principle of war still dominate Europe—amid the churnings of those grand quantities of stupidity and backwardness there arise, like long ago in Parsifal's time, knights of light and the fanatical belief in progress. And these knights of light march at the head of the masses, defying all the elements of obscurity and the antediluvian, troglodytic grossness of prejudice, and lead mankind to the victory of intelligence. That victory of human wits is not the mystery of an obscure ritual, like 1,000 years ago when Europe expected its downfall at the turn of the Millennia. That victory of the intelligence of today's man is not the successful mechanical reaction of bloodstained slaves and galley rowers under Spartacus, who rose up two millennia ago to break the chains and fetters of ancient thralldom. The victory of intelligence is a victory of contemporary cultural awareness, which has taken the world by storm. It is the conscious voluntarism of a unique culture, the geographically mixed, class-composite, nationally and linguistically unrestricted base for new efforts of all of humanity. There have been signs of a heterogeneous rebirth of consciousness for over 150 years. Gods and religions have been dying since the middle of the eighteenth century. The results of technological development in just one decade of the nineteenth century surpass the technical successes achieved in past millennia. The steady growth of material culture and the ever greater development of solidarity of the civilized classes are leading languages and peoples to amalgamate into a common, unitary condition at the turn of the twentieth century. Order and the supranational control of international production and commodity exchange become the underlying prerequisite for the regulation of civilized life, and these theses already emerged in the second decade of the twentieth century as political slogans of everyday struggle. The earth, in our time, has become a relatively small ball, whose equatorial belt amounts to barely a few days' travel. Distances are perfectly surmounted. Space and time, climes and climates, wealth, capital, money, goods, and machines shall pass into the power of man in the course of the twentieth century.

In the twenty-first century, man will be free and the earth will live and flourish like a well-maintained garden, with waterfalls, seas, and forests. The free selection of the abilities of gifted individuals to the advantage of the collective, the relationship of man to man equal, the dignity of humankind restored, homo homini homo est, and no longer a wolf as in Hobbes's time—those are the prospects for the decades to come. Humanism is no longer a moralistic hobbyhorse of philanthropists, maniacs, charlatans, and organized creeds, but a necessary consequence of our living conditions. The thesis that the philosophers have only interpreted the world will be realized. The point is to change it. In these developments, Lenin is the light that beamed forth in the darkness on Europe's horizons and shines forth clearer from day to day, like the titanism in the epilog of Kranjčević's poem "Thought of the World."

THE TOMB OF VLADIMIR ILYICH ULYANOV (LENIN)

The desperate, Austrian, black-and-yellow, Ricardian, mad slaughter went on; the sky was black and sullen, it rained, and the streets resounded to the noise of heavy guns and the tramp of armed soldiers. In the dim, Calvarian half-light squads marched through the city day and night; there was a constant clatter of arms, bayonets were honed in barracks, sick mothers stood drenched in the rain for days on end, waiting on the streets for a handful of moldy flour, church bells rang, funeral processions crawled one after another into infinity, and everything was sick, grey, and without hope. Everything was putrid like death in wartime putrefies. Everything became tainted in the corruption of the tangible and the intangible, condemned to death and downfall on an international scale.

The desperate, Austrian, black-and-yellow, mad slaughter went on, and the sky was sinister, black, and sullen; it rained and everything was in shambles, and life a putrid corpse at the bottom of the grave, in a coffin nailed shut with a hundred spikes of malediction, madness, despair, calumny, the venal press, and the criminal machinations that international command centers mendaciously sold to their subjects as victories.

Then one night, the radio sparks from the antennae of Kronstadt fortress lit up the five letters of his name on all the world's frequencies, and all the Morse keys on all continents and telegraph lines of the globe sent those five letters around the planet—that name blew like the wind and fluttered like a flag over all expanses, also in the trenches awash with blood, where men killed and died. The name of Vladimir Ilyich Lenin.

Vladimir Ilyich Lenin appeared on the European stage as an embodiment of Fortinbras and Richmond from Shakespeare's dramas, and whoever does not have the fantasy to envision his heroic figure against the bloodstained background of the European butchery as a standard-bearer of the avengers has not experienced our time and will never understand it. Whoever does not have the fantasy to perceive Lenin's figure as a symbol of revenge does not have the imagination to comprehend the essential meaning of the European drama, if it has a deeper meaning at all.

Whoever did not feel the passionate dynamism of that event during the desperate Kronstadt days of 1917, when the slaughter had been underway for three years already, when Lenin proclaimed his slogans to the world for the first time; whoever has not realized with all their heart and guts that here, for the first time in human history, it was about the idea of reconciliation and the symbolic triumph of a man with an olive branch in his hand; whoever felt no urge to spread out his clothes before the triumphal entry of that phenomenon, to bow down and cry out hosanna—he will never sense the embrace of that name and its significance, because he is deaf and blind to the meaning of our sad and bloody time in Europe.

In 1917, Lenin's name was a lighthouse beam over the shipwreck of international civilization, and from then until now not a single day has passed without the Morse keys sending the name of that man across all the world's telegraph lines, and not a single day has passed without those telegraphs reporting the occasional lie, muck, and calumny about him.

All the dark forces of this world—all the banks, stock exchanges, capital cities, trusts, and cartels mobilized a mighty armada against that name: the press and rotary printers and hectoliters of ink, battalions of mercenary pens, shortsighted tradition, monumental stupidity, tanks, generals, and guns— and from murder and arson to dissolute madness and the lust for carnage, there is no trick they have not used in their attempts to besmirch, dishonor, and obliterate that name. And yet, after six long years of hard, bloody struggle (which make the Renaissance condottiere wars and the European wars from the Thirty Years' War to Bonaparte and Bismarck look theatrical), that name rose above Europe like the ball of the sun, still bloodshot and blurred from the gloom and mist of dawn, but it grows unrestrained and gigantically, from minute to minute, like the morning light.

Nameless millions of slaves and tormented wretches, from the civilized European worker (whose bondage is termed "selling his labor power") to the colonial subject who slaves away without such decorative formality even today—millions of simple and uneducated people felt with the impulse of a beaten draft animal that an arm had moved to cast off the 1,000-year yoke, and, from the Black colonies of the Congo to the Arko liqueur factory on Zagreb's Vlaška Street, a whisper full of messianic trust and hope spread and gathered strength.

A traveler who returned from Spain noted recently that in El Escorial, the sepulchral complex of the Spanish kings, where the Spanish sovereigns from Charles V to the Austrian Don Juan lie buried in monumental sarcophagi, he found Lenin's name written in chalk above a royal tomb: *Viva el Lenin!* Lenin's name, scrawled above the crypt of Spanish kings in El Escorial, clearly tells us what we can read on the church walls of our city; that name is carved into the stone of Egyptian pyramids and the bark of trees in the Indian jungle, and that means that Lenin's name has become a legend that will outlive all those powers that wanted to stamp it out and smother it.

Lenin's name was born like the wave of a storm, and with such tempestuous names a man's private life represents an insignificant episode that fades away and disappears, just as drops of rain run off and disappear in the rivers. Lenin was not happy in his private life.

That great builder of the magnitude of Peter the Great or Bonaparte (what poor comparisons!) did not live to set a dome atop his grand design. For forty-eight years he waited like a Cromwell for his mission, and after the revolutionary fever from April to October 1917 he became the armor that twenty wars broke against, only for that victorious cuirass to be pierced by the bullet of an unfortunate young woman and, suffering from that wound that never properly healed, he collapsed onto the rubber-lined wheelchair of a sarcastic, demonic, Strindbergish apparition.

Since we had heard every second day for a year or two that he was dying, and because the international telegraph agencies of the bankers and bandits had maliciously announced to us at least fifty times that he was already dead, and because we kept seeing him sick, drained, and weary in photographs, the news of his death did not take us completely by surprise. Lenin's death did not have any disastrousness to it like the rumble of a mined quarry; it came in a sourdine way, like a snapping violin string. Lenin lived in poverty, as humbly as a servant, and died for the cause. His physical form sank in front of us like a ship that we knew was damaged, so its going down seemed to us more a logical consequence of protracted suffering than a catastrophe.

If a Beethoven of the future writes an *Eroica* of the European revolution, he will not have to erase the dedication to Lenin, as Ludwig van Beethoven did with his dedication to Bonaparte, hearing that he had crowned himself emperor of France.

An intellectual worker and ideologue, Lenin stands before history with his twenty books, aware that his talent has found fertile soil. A brilliant fighter and builder, Lenin can say with a clear conscience that he was the first man since Archimedes who dared to lift the world out of its cosmic inertia. As a man, Lenin marked the typical tragic course of a martyr, whom the gods tied to a crag in the Caucasus and ordered the eagles to peck out his liver.

As an ideologue, builder, and man, Lenin is a luminary of our time: a hero who showed how one should live in the midst of chaos, when the old forms of decrepit civilization can be seen to break beneath the weight of new questions at every step, and all moral-political schemes and plans are simply inadequate to correspond to the ever more calamitous rhythm of technological development.

As an ideologue, Lenin realized that the Marxist conception of the London-Manchester process in the European textile industry (from the second half of the nineteenth century) was just the first octagonal in a web of sociological diagnoses, and his undeniable service in the scope of Marxism is that, with his innate truculence, he prevented the Russian Marxist formula from degenerating into that of Western European reformism. And as the capitalist phase in the history socialism up until the world conflagration of 1914 bears Marx's name, today it is clear that the historical period from 1914 until today will be designated with Lenin's name. Marxism has turned into Leninism.

Lenin observed the entire catastrophic collapse of Western European civilization in 1914 from the perspective of the thirtieth century. He assessed the events between the Russo-Japanese War, the First Russian Revolution, and the breakdown of Western European socialism from a real and unshakable retrospective, from that utopian distance, solemnly and clearly, and only this can explain why he frontally attacked the whole theoretical, abstractly formulated reformism, with its hopes, slogans, and illusions as furiously as a wild boar—at a time when having such opinions seemed maniacal and excessive.

That thirtieth-century perspective gave him the strength to stand firm in the difficult, critical days of 1914–15 when, like a hermit in his room at 12 Spiegelgasse in Zürich, he preached a course of events that no one believed in at the time. From his little room on the third floor, which he rented from the shoemaker Kammerer, he set out with Bakuninesque singularity of purpose on his famous and victorious campaign from Kronstadt and Petrograd to Moscow and Vladivostok, so as to instill new hope in the masses of slaves from Hong Kong and Panama to Madagascar and Morocco, and to dig the first sturdy foundations for the Cosmopolis amid the wide Russian lands.

And when humanity one day is no longer a putrid and ragged wound as it is today, and when the Soviet republic is not the only ship sailing for the Cosmopolis but whole fleets of peoples and classes shall sail in that direction, it is certain that Vladimir Ilyich Lenin will be waiting on that other shore, like a giant lighthouse, to welcome the ships as they enter the harbor, like a monument to the man who first disembarked on the other shore.

HOME GUARDSMEN GEBEŠ AND
BENČINA TALK ABOUT LENIN

It was a warm, late fall. The windows of the sick bay (known as "marod zimmer" in the imperial Austrian and royal Hungarian regiments) were open and the damp smell of early evening fluttered in through the wrought-iron bars. The fields in front of the barracks were sodden with grey meltwater, and as it thawed under the blasts of the southerly wind, rags of snow glimmered between the dry maize stalks as if they had been streaked here and there, asymmetrically, with the dirty brush of Postimpressionist technique. The banging of coaches and the squeals of steam engines at the southern station came with clear acoustics, and an anvil reverberated in a nearby blacksmith shop. An orderly was chopping wood in the hall, and I lay there with a temperature on the hard straw mattress, so in that soft and heavy silence of the fall evening I was carried away by an unspeakable pining for broad, blue expanses. I stared out through the wrought-iron bars, listened to some children's cheerful shouting in the twilight, and dreamed effeminately of how good it would be if this man were a bird rather than rotting in those damp and dirty blankets, did not fall ill, was not a colonial soldier, and had not been flung headlong into this mindless war, but flew high over misty willow groves, over the river quietly flowing, and over railroad tracks with their signal lights red and green.

In the heavy, suffocating semidarkness, in the helpless struggle to escape from those vile and leaden spaces, in the compassionate aspiration to lift up all our poor and wretched lives with one solid, hard lever, there resounded, like the blare of a knightly, heroic horn, the voice of home guardsman Gebeš, from Stubica in northwestern Croatia, who had returned several days earlier via Stockholm and Berlin from captivity in Russia. Mirko Gebeš, a home guardsman with pockmarked features and pale, tubercular cheeks, had been shot through several times; he fell into Russian hands in a mad Austrian attack at the Dniester, roamed the Asian and Siberian prison camps, and returned to barracks as one of the first harbingers of the Russian tempest. He had attended mass meetings during the Russian Revolution ("learned that revolutionary trade"), and what he told us about that—that he had heard Lenin speaking from the top of barrels and boxes in a Petrograd warehouse—will stay ingrained in my memory for a long time.

Gebeš portrayed Lenin for us there in the *marod zimmer* as an ordinary Russian muzhik, who spoke to the peasant soldiers about peasants' uprisings, barracks, and war, and said it was dishonorable to hold a rifle, to give one's blood in an imperialist war, and to shoot *for* the gentry, rather than *at* them!

Oh, how every simple word of pockmarked and tubercular Gebeš accorded with my own passive, heartfelt dreams about leaving, breaking out of, or being rescued from, that sick bay, that ague, and those moral contradictions that occur in a man in barracks, when he is at war for others and against his convictions, and when there is nothing else for him to do but daydream in his sickbed about dusk and about birds. Oh, how the life of contemporary man is reduced to roguish minimums, when his ideal is just to become a sparrow and to warble at dusk above civilization and the barracks' roofs! In my own personal misfortune and that cheerless dejection, the words of home guardsman Gebeš boomed in that dirty, malodorous room like the beating of a drum. It was as if I saw the colossal outline of fiery medieval peasant leader Matija Gubec there in the semidarkness of the hazy room as he set out with a huge scythe in hand and strode like a giant over the barracks and the town.

Fiery Matija Gubec arose, our glorious compatriot from Stubica, and all the Gebešes rose with him, everywhere from Krško and Sevnica in Slovenia to Mokrice in Croatia and the Sused fortress near Zagreb; they set out with the smoke of fires and the tolling of church bells to show that they exist, to destroy that malodorous Austrian, Habsburg, symbolic *marod zimmer*, and to break all the bars, frames, pacts, addresses in the Sabor, majorities, minorities, paragraphs, phrases, lies, follies, and the grief of our hopeless situation. To break out, to leave all that behind, to overcome.

I don't recall the details, I just remember that everything grew dark in the room and the men on their beds sighed quietly in ominous silence. We felt the dark weight of the absurdity of our lives, and Gebeš's words thundered in our souls like an explosion to bring down the concrete walls of that whole barracked, soldierly life that was our deadly reality, the reality of the Austrian-Habsburg war, the likelihood of a nasty and senseless end for that evident folly.

"Lenin stood on top of the barrel in the warehouse and said loudly and clearly, so we could all hear him, that the real war was the one being waged on the streets and in the stores, not at the front."

"Yeah, sure. An uprising. The right of the peasants. War on the streets against the gentry. That's all Jewish balderdash— shut yer trap!"

It was Sergeant Benčina, an old front-line veteran. Twice critically wounded and decorated, he showed his trench coat shot through by seven machine-gun bullets as a trophy, with great pride. Benčina felt that Gebeš was exceeding the bounds of order and discipline so now he joined in to tell him to shut his gob and not blurt senseless tripe.

"Those are all lies made up by the Jews!" He had read in the paper that the Russian Jews wanted to wreck the whole of Russia and sell it off to foreigners and profiteers for golden sequins.

Gebeš was unimpressed by Sergeant Benčina's outburst. Instinctively, he felt that it threatened not only his personal reputation as a home guardsman but also the prestige of the notion he called "soldierly freedom and equality": "NCOs won't give us free advice no more! Russian Jews haven't sold anything to anyone, that's just what's written in the stupid newspapers that Benčina reads. That's what the Jews here write out of fear that soldiers could plunder their storerooms!"

And he started to explain to Benčina with skill and a convincing method what a wretched life he led, that he had been sent to the front five times, that his trench coat had been riddled by twenty machine-gun bullets, that he had nine wounds like a scarecrow, and now, in spite of everything, they were driving him to the front again, like a dog, with his crooked rubber jaw.

"The front is bunkum, Lenin said loudly and clearly on the barrel, and every man who goes there is a blockhead!"

The argument grew ever more heated and reckless; Benčina jumped up from his bed infuriated, and things were on the brink of ending in a brawl, with Gebeš being arrested by the sentry. I don't remember if it was illustrious Gebeš's impertinent aggressiveness, my own rotten mood (which I myself was sick of), or if it was because Benčina's superior, sergeantly abuse gave me an uncanny feeling of jackbooted north-Croatian Vendée loyalists, but for the sake of all the men in the *marod zimmer* I didn't want Gebeš to have to back down. So I drew the brunt of the quarrel onto myself and incurred the rage of the sergeant.

After much further argument, the matter ended in bribery and corruption, and when we were onto the second liter of vermouth we forgot that Gebeš had wanted to agitate the *marod zimmer* and incite the revolution of the Russian muzhiks. I don't know what on earth brought about the change, but Benčina started to whistle the famous aria from Albini's operetta *Baron Trenk*: a tiger one minute, a lamb the next.

One rainy fall evening the following year, a soldier stopped me on the street. I was already in civvies, and he dashed up to me from behind, like a shadow, and grabbed my sleeve. With an open umbrella in one hand and books in the other, I was somewhat encumbered in my movements and flinched at the touch of that nameless shadow, in instinctive helplessness. It was Benčina.

"Oh, it's you, Benčina, hello! How are you?"

"I've been on the Italian front! A constant barrage of artillery and gas down there! Yourself?"

"Well enough, thank you! Demobilized, as you see!"

"Do you remember that crazy Gebeš, who we had a row with one evening in the *marod zimmer*? He was shot on the Italian front!"

"The poor fellow! Why didn't he look after himself?"

"No, he wasn't killed at the front—they shot him. There was a court-martial and he got the firing squad. For hitting an officer on the head with his gas mask! Afterward we poured lime over him in a lime pit. I can still see his knee today, sticking out of the lime... It was unbearable with him. I always told him: *You'll dangle at the end of a rope for that kike balderdash of yours!* And now, I ask you, why didn't they circumdederunt him? What did he get out of it?"

A month later, Sergeant Benčina himself was shot by mercenary condottieres of the National Council—he, at least, was "circumdederunted."

THE MUSEUM OF
THE RUSSIAN REVOLUTION

Like one who comes from Croatia,
Perhaps to see our cloth of Veronica
And is not sated with looking because of its ancient fame.

But, as long as it is visible, says, in thought:
"Lord Jesus Christ, true God, |
Was this then your face?"
DANTE, PARADISE, XXXI, 103–108.

The house of the Counts Rostov on Povarskaya Street, famous since *War and Peace* lyceum days, served until recently as the Museum of Painting. To study the anarchy in contemporary painting, that historico-cultural material so important today has been moved to the Museum of Asian Fine Art, Ars Asiatica, and the house of the Counts Rostov has been used to house a police station for Povarskaya Street, which has recently been renamed after Vatslav Vorovsky, the assassinated Russian ambassador to Switzerland. Apart from having converted some aristocratic palaces into museums and renamed some old Moscow streets after dead revolutionaries, the Revolution seems to show a high degree of deference toward the past in this regard.

In Alexandrovsky Park, today People's Park, in front of the Arsenal Tower of the Kremlin, the Romanov obelisk erected here to commemorate the 300th anniversary of the dynasty has been pulled down. Today the defiant Obelisk of the Revolution stands in place of it, and on that marble column, where the gold-lettered names of Russian tsars once gleamed, are now chiseled the names of revolutionaries of all centuries and nationalities: from the Encyclopedists and Voltaire to Mikhailovsky, from Lavrov and Plekhanov to Lenin, and here also are Robespierre and Babeuf, Herzen and Kropotkin.

The infamous palace of Moscow's governor-general on Tverskaya, today Soviet Square, is where the city's bodies of governance meet, and in front of the palace, where a monument to General Skobelev once stood, there is now the Monument of the Soviet Constitution: an obelisk with a peace-bringing angel and the inevitable academic palm and copper slabs of the Constitution (petty bourgeois and banal as a work of art).

The tsarist governorate prison on the other side of Soviet Square has been razed to the foundations, but the Ionian, Empire-style gateways, which served as a decorative entrance to the old prison building, dominate the space like a triumphal arch raised to mark the victorious Revolution. The monument to Tsar Alexander III in front of the Cathedral of Christ the Savior has been knocked down, and its monumental, red marble plinth will be the foundation for a future monument to the "Liberation of Labor." The bronze figure of Tsar Alexander II on Ivanovskaya Square in the Kremlin is gone, but the pseudo-monumental framework of the monument with its marble arcade and Venetian mosaics still spoils the architecturally unique ensemble of the Kremlin's walls.

Of the new monuments on Moscow's streets, a granite Dostoyevsky and Timiryazev, and a bronze Vorovsky, stand in front of the Commissariat for Foreign Affairs. On Moscow's former Theater Square (now Sverdlov Square) there are four foundation stones for monuments to Griboyedov, Ostrovsky, Karl Liebknecht, and Marx. Prince Dolgoruky's famous palace is home to the Marx-Engels Institute, and the mansion of Count Razumovsky, with the parlors of the English Club, is now home to the Museum of the Russian Revolution.

As in all museums, the marble-and-wallpaper halls of the English Club smell of naphthalene. The numerous displays reveal an impressive effort to restrain time in its incessant, termite-like gnawing at all that man wanted and initiated, completed or intended to complete. Suspending time is the diabolical theme of all Faustian motifs, as futile in the scope of museums' undertakings as it is in poetry.

Half-rotten, printed paper, old-fashioned bulldog revolvers with nickel-plated drums, Cossacks' whips on heavy green cloth abundantly strewn with naphthalene tabs to combat insects, faded photographs, and countless death masks—all of this is a kind of columbarium or ritual mortuary, where oppressors and victims alike are turned into corpses, and corpses into dead objects on display. What, in the end, are the various things a man had in his hands reduced to, if not wooden, plaster, and metal testimonies to technical skills, to the decaying paper of manuscripts, and to the junk of archives gathered on the roads a man travels from the beginning, through fire and misfortune, in moonlight or in the rain? All that remains of wretched human testimony after such raging winds and large-scale historical blazes (and the Russian Revolution of 1917 is by all means a historical fire of massive proportions) is just a fistful of ash and dust.

Without the poetic imagination that manifests itself as instrumentation around all human testimonies to a dead time, no reminiscence of any distant, bygone event can be aroused that would be a fitting expression of dead objects and things that otherwise are as silent as an empty stage. A man who enters the halls of this museum without his own personal, lyrical, subjective inspiration about those dramatic battles will not discover any particular sensations in these rooms. Odd objects, writings, and photo portraits, worn-out pots and pans used by convicts, photographs of the last Calvarian walk to the gallows, a glass Muravyev drank out of, a most banal signature of the tsar on someone's death sentence, pointed brass knuckles used by the tsarist police, rifles, or porcelain from contemporary revolutionary manufacture—all of this is arranged under plates of glass with the same impassive solemnity, depicting crime and punishment with the same undertakerish criteria. All these objects are dead, all these people are dead, and the museum guards the dead objects just as graves are guarded by the law of mental inertia that is deathly boring to everyone concerned. Letters to wives and mothers, written before execution, letters written in pencil on crumpled paper in tragic moments when revolutionaries were about to be murdered, the scalp of a Red Army soldier killed by Petlyura's cavalrymen, and ragged old threadbare ties do not speak a single word by themselves. For a person not attuned to this type of tragic poetry, these long-forgotten murders and the century of blood that poured in cascades over the Russian lands will not bring a single line of a poetry to their inner ear. When Marshal Murat enters Moscow in *War and Peace*, the evening bells in the Kremlin are sounding. The King of Naples halts with a detachment of Württemberg hussars at the Church of Saint Nikola Yavlensky in Arbat, and Tolstoy, describing the deployment of the French artillery over Arbat with the muzzles of its cannons trained on the Borovitskaya and Troitskaya gates of the Kremlin, emphasizes that, for the French artillery from Marshal Murat to the

last anonymous gunner, Moscow's terrain meant neither Vozd-
vizhenka nor Mokhovaya streets, Kutafya Tower was not Kutafya
Tower, nor was the Kremlin's Troitskaya Gate the gate that leads
into the Kremlin; rather, Moscow's terrain was nothing but a set of
ballistic circumstances for the French gunners, ordinary terrain
where batteries maneuver and open fire on command.

If a man comes to the Museum of the Russian Revolution
as a foreigner, as the French gunners before the Kremlin's walls
were foreigners—to whom Moscow meant nothing—he will not
see, understand, or feel much of all that in this museum.

So, roaming Moscow's streets with Monsieur Philippe (a
correspondent of a Western European tabloid), I often recalled
Tolstoy's description of Napoleon's cannon fire, which touches on
an intricate and no less important psychological question that, at
its broadest, encompasses understanding, or the lack thereof—the
conceptualization of a phenomenon or subject—without sufficient
background knowledge. Reading Dante without a commentary
to an audience that has no idea of the Florentine and Italian tre-
cento, is a reading of an empty and boring text in a vacuum. The
many different worldviews, moral and intellectual principles and
convictions are all based on networks of assumptions, and if these
are not known, all this represents boring ballast for the ignorant.
Monsieur Philippe, for example, a typical intellectual adventurer
of the Western European ilk, inwardly, most privately and secretly,
in his heart of hearts a nonconformist in his attitude toward the
problems of the world war, got snagged at the edge of certain political realizations, albeit as an indifferent bystander. Around 1918,
he was a Leninist sympathizer in a vague, romantic sort of way and,
as such, was able to get his head around some concepts to such a
degree that, deep inside, he was convinced he was a "socialist." A
"socialist" of the Western European ilk, for whom everything that
happens east of the Rhine, and especially east of the Vistula and
the Danube, is utterly enigmatic and obscure, and his view to the
Russian plains east of the Kremlin did not differ much from that of
Murat or Bonaparte's artillerymen when they trained their guns'
muzzles on that bastion. Everything that is "Slavic," and in particular Russian, was so foreign to Monsieur Philippe that even what
little romantic inclination he had for Leninism from 1918 went up
in smoke in the ominous vacuum of his nonadaptation.

We roamed the half-lit streets in the early evening without any particular plan; tearooms steamed next to barbershops, huge fish lay in shop windows, balalaikas echoed in underground hovels, and geysers of thick steam spouted from Chinese laundries. Monsieur Philippe was disgusted at "Asia." He spoke about the West, civilization, democracy, the crisis of communism, and about all those chaotic phenomena that strike the Monsieur Philippes of this world as contrasts between their paltry schemes and reality. When Monsieur Philippe spoke the word "democracy," he imagined it as the witty impertinence of a Parisian taxi driver who travels home for lunch and will not take passengers whose direction does not coincide with his own. How far is Moscow (in Monsieur Philippe's perception) from that high level of taxi drivers' libertarian democracy when there are no taxis here, let alone taxi drivers, and when the first carriage and its nags appeared on the streets only last year?

When Monsieur Philippe pronounced the word "civilization," for him it meant the rich restaurants on the boulevards of the left and right bank of the Seine. But what civilization was there to speak of here, in these canteens, where the only food served was cabbage? Monsieur Philippe was greatly worried by one crucial question: Was secrecy of the post guaranteed in this country, where until yesterday ninety-nine percent of the population did not write at all? The freedom of assembly, opinion, freedom of the press, the right to express one's negative convictions, and so on—all of that troubled Monsieur Philippe, who pined for every lost minute of mourning for his Parisian drivers, his Parisian dinners, his friends, for Montparnasse, for the Dôme, the Rotonde, the Closerie des Lilas, for all the amiable nooks of his Paris, where the ancient Celts had already been engravers of great refinement. Like for Murat's artillerymen, for Monsieur Philippe (and the vast majority of those gentlemen) Moscow today represents nothing but terrain created for journalistic-cum-ballistic purposes, and its quarters like Arbat, its cathedrals, streets, basilicas, the Kremlin—all of that is barbaric, boring, and at best the basis for a profitable report.

Count Tolstoy's house, the modest study on the mezzanine with the floor of simple fir boards, where Tolstoy's famous desk stands next to a little iron stove at the window (Repin painted the old Count writing there), left Monsieur Philippe completely cold, without any association whatsoever, indifferent. The frayed, black-oilcloth armchairs studded with little white nails ("mauvais goût"), the towels over the washbasin, the mass of baroque porcelain in the dining room, and the photographs on Makart-style bamboo stands in the parlor—everything seemed to Monsieur Philippe "un poco povero," and a bit ridiculous, shabby and long demoded. "Why show such pathetic testimonies to retrograde taste and provincial privation?"

The only thing that could engage Monsieur Philippe's attention in Leo Tolstoy's house were the calling cards on a silver plate in the paws of a young she-bear in the hall on the first floor. He looked long and pensively at the visiting card of a French marquise who had been there and honored the count with her visit in this distant, backward, barbaric country. One can visit Chekhov's grave, Skryabin's or Rubinstein's room, imagine the figure of Solovyov, or gaze into the sad face of the Iveron Mother of God with a certain feeling of sadness: Look, that is the unhappy Iveron Mother of God, who generations of Russian unfortunates have knelt before, and her look is as melancholic as these meadows. But Monsieur Philippe was bored because he was not sipping aperitifs on the Champs-Élysées. And so Monsieur Philippe strolled through the many rooms of the English Club in his tedium, unable to understand why I was looking for so long at ragged bits of paper that, for him, were just covered in dislikeable, enigmatic hieroglyphs.

"What point is there in contemplating broken, old, wooden, and rustic chairs from Vyatka just because Chernyshevsky had sat on one of them? Who was this Chernyshevsky anyway, and why should we talk about him like some Prometheus, as if Mr. Chernyshevsky discovered fire? Take Béranger—he was a poet the same as Chernyshevsky, and people would unharness their horses for Béranger in order to drive him through Paris in triumph like a laurel-wreathed poet. But who in their right mind would mention Béranger's name today when it comes to poetry?"

For Monsieur Philippe it was simply enigmatic, or more than that—utterly incomprehensible why I had come to this wretched panorama of smelly and singed rags for the third time, while he was simply dying to free himself of this misery and get out in the sunshine, under the blue sky on Tverskaya, where people were buying red balloons, dogs were barking, and it did not smell of naphthalene, death sentences, blood, soot, smoke, and murder.

I do not know if the material amassed in the Museum of the Russian Revolution will have its Dante, but it is beyond doubt that the epic poetry of these bloodstained Russian days, which lasted more than 250 years from Stenka Razin to Lenin, cries out for artists with sufficient Sistine fantasy to sing the deeds of this "Last Judgment," this "Day of Wrath" in Russian history. From Pugachev to the Decembrists, from Radishchev to Chaadayev, from Herzen and Chernyshevsky to Bukharin and Leon Trotsky—there is no Russian who would not feel deeply a solemn, sublime revolutionary catharsis when confronted by the tragic Russian reality. Russian intellectuals plodded in columns, one in the shadow of the other, over the icy Siberian plains, and those endlessly long winter nights in exile, in penal servitude, final breaths beneath the gallows, suicides in despair and the anguish of emigration, a giant quantity of the most subtle nervous energy: that is the power that is electrifying Russia today.

Gallows, the nightly pronouncement of death sentences in the gleam of oil lamps, stealthy agreements in the half-light, conspiratorial terrorist raids with dynamite and firearms—all those are symbols of the Russian drama that lies under glass today as historical material in this diabolical wax museum. The thousands and thousands of unknown, nameless dead are signposts for the movement that emerged in the Russian underground over the last hundred years as a constant subterranean rumble, which, in this museum unique in the world, ends in the triumphal hall of Lenin's funeral. Here are the halls on the revolutionary movements of the 1860s, 70s, and 80s, arranged chronologically, with letters, photographs, and individual items of furniture and clothing, guns, an illegal printing press, pamphlets and books. From N. V. Tchaikovsky and the Tchaikovskians (1873–74) to the inception of the Bolshevik party (1903) and the Revolution of 1905, those events meant continuous carnage, hangings, dead bodies by the roadside and in pits, the horrors of Siberia, fire, and death...

Here the army fired volley after volley at angry crowds and hundreds of innocent people bled to death in one minute. Here are the bloody searches, nighttime arrests, mass political trials, galloping Cossack cavalry with sabers drawn, the rattle of convicts' chains, dead children, mothers in mortal fear, bloodstained men, bloody swords, blood-spattered roads—blood, blood, and more blood. From the Balkan blood, with which Vsevolod Garshin wrote his story "Four Days" (a work significant for the Russian comprehension of militarism, like Lavoslav Vukelić's elegy "Solferino" is characteristically Yugoslav), from Shipka and the Balkans to Manchuria and Port Arthur (Andreyev, *Red Laughter*), it was always the same leitmotif: nighttime searches and arrests, beatings in prisons, political trials, and hangings. In the age of Dostoyevsky and Gorky, from the Decembrists to the massacre in front of the Winter Palace (Father Gapon), from Stepan Khalturin to Lieutenant Pyotr Schmidt, the commander of the mutinous Black Sea Fleet, it was always the same leitmotif: the massacre on Nevsky Prospect, the shootings at the Lena River, the massacre in Odessa. Red streaks of blood on the decks of battleships, red flags in the hands of children, bloodstained snow, candid nighttime photographs of infantry battalions in columns, sabers, hooves, cavalrymen, machine-guns, campfires on the streets, overturned trams, and barricades. Spontaneous and unorganized revolts of the peasant masses, holdups of trains, assassination attempts, agents provocateurs, whips, brass knuckles, rifles, and more machine-guns, more pamphlets and dailies, the first tsarist proclamations after the repressed uprisings—all of that speaks in the mute tongue of dead things, which is often stronger and more obstinate than the liveliest and most plastic speech. Innumerable suffering masses have passed along the roads of Russia's dramatic destiny for three whole decades, waving flags, falling from the blows of the knout, buckshot, and heavy, cavalry sabers. Companies in light grey tsarist uniforms camped on the streets, and morose generals, always wreathed in a fine, hazy ring of gunpowder smoke, fired professionally at enraged crowds. One strike after another failed, the movements of the masses ebbed and flowed rhythmically, and so that bloody struggle lasted for decades and ended with the seizure of political and economic power by the proletarian masses themselves. At first scarcely visible in such a clime, and mysterious, but later ever more fiery, from the depths of Russian life there erupted a bright new flame born of Russian pain and suffering: Bolshevism.

The development of Russian Marxism was marked by massacres, hangings, and pogroms, and that process over the last five or six decades has not been just a political, intellectual plan with parliamentary combinations like that in Europe, not just a political program, but a fanatical worldview based on negative Russian experience, as if the notion of a "worldview" did not already imply a degree of fanaticism. Russian revolutionary fanaticism began as romantic messianism of belletristically varied ethical principles, as an exaltation of humanistic ideals and a defiant faith in the victory of man, as all convictions are defiant that are born in wars, blood, and beneath the gallows—as a higher, human negation of wars, blood, and gallows.

Russian Marxism grew in the consciousness of many in the vast expanses from the Mongolian wastelands to Warsaw and Riga, to the roll of funeral drums, the fires of anti-Semitic pogroms, and the crying of widows and mothers. In the Museum of the Russian Revolution the wise and poetic eyes of Russian revolutionaries look at us from the photographs and paintings, men who began their Calvarian path while still children. The drums of Cromwell's Puritans thunder and the incandescent theatrics of Jacobin days flare up in the consciousness of such young people. In the mists of Orthodox childhood, that enigmatic world of golden-grey Byzantine icons and transcendental hazy magic, where supernatural authorities spread their shadows in the skullcaps of church domes—in that lightdark of glimmering coals between two worlds, Slavophile and Western, the first beams of European beacons appear in that gloom: Darwin and Marx; flashes from distant, rich financial-economic systems, where technology is highly developed and outmoded feudal and metaphysical images of life are dying in the swift birth-rhythm of new realizations. The fundamental question was thus resolved in the consciousness of the first Russian Marxist generation. Turmoil gave way to tranquility, and chaos yielded to systematic order on the basis of the simple conviction that that is how things are, and that is the only way they can be. In the catastrophic downfall of supernatural authorities, all saints with halos, generals with golden collars, and the tsar and boyars in brocade were turned into monkeys with tails, and as Marx demonstrated that profit is not an inexplicable force (as was thought in Condillac's time), but that profit stems from labor in a very simple and natural way, a monumental dome of materialism was raised in the minds of the first generation of Russian Marxists on the ruins of the tsarist, Orthodox, militaristic hierarchy, with icon lamps of new icons: Gassendi, Hobbes, La Mettrie, Feuerbach, Strauss, Vogt, and Büchner. The contemporaries of Mazzini and Proudhon, Bakunin and Herzen, created platforms of Western-style, European integral orientation in the Russian intellectual world, and the Marxist children of the 1890s, fascinated by materialist passion from the first days of their childhood, believed the activist theory that the class contradiction is the mechanism that inherently bears all the possibilities for transcending gory Russian reality and rising to a higher level of development.

From the moment the Russian youth of the 1890s reached out their hands to the Russian proletariat, in the deep conviction that their will, as solid as stone, would allow them to overcome all the barriers on the road to victory, there began the last gigantic battle of the last thirty years, and it was fateful not only for Russia but also for the Second International. That class necessity led to a sheer enormous force of Russian revolutionary will, mental persistence in action, and calm fixity of purpose—all those fundamental elements of political strategy that finally, for the first time in world history, brought down capitalism and smashed it with cannons. The beginnings of Lenin's thirty years of unswerving dedication were already clearly manifested in his high school years in Kazan, when he gave a critique of individual terrorism beneath the gallows of his elder brother,* and his focus was just as clear thirty years later as a proletarian politician when he wrote his theses against anarchism, or when in Swiss exile, after the defeat of the First Russian Revolution, he published obituaries of now forgotten revolutionaries—victims of the reactionary backlash of 1905–06. This Russian revolutionary clarity in Lenin and thousands of other revolutionary minds before and after Le-

---

*   **Alexander Ulyanov, hung in Shlisselburg fortress in the spring of 1887 for involvment in an assassination attempt on Tsar Alexander. Lenin, in his seventh year at high school, opposed individual terrorism. According to his sister, Maria Ilyichna, he took the firm position that it would not lead to the desired end.**

nin was unshakable in its fundamental beliefs, in theoretical discussions on the development of capitalism in Russia and on the religious problem, as well as in the question of seizing political power by force of arms, in the shot of the *Aurora* in Petrograd, on Petrograd's and Moscow's streets, and throughout the country, and also later in the protracted and bloody revolutionary wars.

Reams of printed speeches, resolutions, and theses, banned and newly launched underground newspapers printed illegally, using primitive machines, countless lithographed minutes of congresses, conferences, and meetings, polemical writings and resolutions, pamphlets, and the thick tomes of today's lavishly produced, luxurious state editions—all that graphical mass cast in typesetter's lead represents the foundations of revolutionary politics today, bearing the unique stamp of Russian revolutionary will, of activism developed through experience and bloody resistance in the framework of a logical coordination of ideas.

Amiable, intelligent faces of Russian revolutionaries look at us from oval, black frames, figures with high brows and bright eyes, who consistently and heroically stood at the forefront of revolutionary activity amid the European disarray of atomic decay, electron theory, and revived Humean agnosticism. Western Europe's fashionable idealism in thought was in a state of disintegration, which was also reflected in Russian culture, music, religion, poetry, and the nationalist romanticism of Slavophilia, and later in the many fine differentiations of Russian neo-Kantianism; but these Russian revolutionaries, in their philosophical discussions, stubbornly and diligently, with fanatical, persistent simplicity, continued to defend the everyday, seemingly insignificant material interests of the broad masses of humanity. After Engels's *Anti-Dühring*, they wrote endless polemics in prison and Siberian banishment against the idealistic revision of Marxism, pointing again and again to the objective reality of hunger, tsarism, firing squads and gallows, Siberian exile, and capitalist exploitation. The Russian revolutionary interpretation of Kant's "thing-in-itself" is in no way otherworldly but coincides entirely with the conception of tsarist Russian reality and its Black Hundreds' "in-itself"; at every step of the torment and suffering of the Russian man it is an image of the unnatural death of the masses

213

and becomes the collective awareness of one monolithically organized revolutionary party. That party wants to take political power in the interests of the tormented and suffering, and in the given circumstances it wishes nothing other than to devote itself exclusively to the question of taking political power in an economically and culturally backward country, with a uniform plan for overcoming that economic and cultural backwardness in as short a time as possible. That party fought with ideas, theory, and cannons for the principle of the objective reality of the Russian political and economic state of affairs, because if that state of affairs is not objectively real, and if proletarian class consciousness, as a negation of the barbaric and primitive violence of the boyars, is not the force that bears within it all the possibilities of lifting Russia's backward reality up to a higher category of civilized life, then there is nothing left but the belletristic absurdity of Andreyev's anarchism. Then all skeptical possibilities would be open and this catastrophic failure of economic and intellectual systems would leave no further possibility for a revival of politics, trade, or industry.

When a man visits the Museum of the Russian Revolution, the violent fanatics of Russian reality look at him from the pictures, figures in whose vocabulary the name Hamlet sounds like an insult. That one-sided orthodoxy in questions of Russian revolutionary conceptions, total political and ideological encirclement, that steadfast foundation of Russian revolutionary conviction held the Russian Marxists at their high internationalist level of political consciousness in August 1914, when they defended the dignity of European Marxist convictions in practice. From the Russian socialist perspective, to go to war as a Marxist politician beneath the banners of tsarism would have meant nothing but death for the Russian revolutionary concept. And when the Second International failed in August 1914, the Russian revolutionary fanatics remained in their Swiss exile, illustrious like eagles above the peaks of the Alps, ready to swoop down on the boyars' Russian execution site one day and put an end to it within twenty-four hours.

The political and personal biographies of the Russian revolutionaries reveal none of the moral vacuum that Carlyle's Robespierre feels just before death. In Lunacharsky's play *Oliver*

Cromwell there are flashes of dangerous Carlyle-esque emptiness from physical and moral exhaustion, when consciousness gapes into the great nothing and consigns itself to fate. But Lunacharsky's Cromwell, whom Kerzhentsev labeled a counterrevolutionary, despite his moral indolence, calmly cooks his scrambled eggs and, quoting the Bible, strikes off one head after another with a kind of peasant simplicity. Cromwell's revolutionary simplicity is based largely on the conviction that the validity of the policy of revolutionary violence coincides with the interests of the broad proletarian masses, and that elementary unshakable consciousness of the validity of one's political orientation is also determined by an elementary faith in the interests of the masses. The way of thinking about objects and phenomena is simple: those activists do not doubt the objectivity of Russian reality, and their intellectual profiles are as bony and dark as the puritanical profiles of the miners from the underworld of the Don Basin. In contrast with the effeminate, lyrical, warm, sensual confusion of the metropolitan intellect mollified by Western European comfort and corroded by the moral and material corruption of the political bazaar in a wealthy, aristocratic environment, the Russian revolutionary scheme represents a puritanical one-sidedness without the slightest caustic inclination to understand "spiritual nuances" in a decadent Western European sense. It is not *l'art pour l'art*-ish, spiderweb-like fantasizing on the verge of lyricism; it is often a crude and naïve rejoicing of the consciousness at the rightness of one's voluntary trajectory, the simplicity of the peasant who knows what he wants, and the only thing he wants is to stop being a backward and simple peasant. The giant Russian muzhik in these people got rid of their past at any price, scratched the back of their heads, and, in typical peasant fashion, from their own point of view, sarcastically spat on all kinds of so-called European "charlatanism, scandals, and stupidity."

"What the hell? We know what we want, we know where we are, and where we're going! We rifle-butted the banks in the head, we liquidated the aristocracy, the feudals, and the big landowners. We broke up the Russian village into three classes: the kulaks, the peasants of average means, and the poor. Together with the poor, we have to finish off the kulaks, that terrible Russian parasite. Russia needs to be electrified! What good are those

215

European wars to us? Let the bankers fight each other there in the West, and we'll take our cavalry and artillery across the Himalayas to liberate Asia! We've killed tsarist generals, razed the Great Wall of China, and today every cat in Peking knows what our flag means. We've captured one sixth of the globe, so there are five sixths more to go. We'll give the earth a good plowing, and Boris is your uncle."

All very simple and clear! And then this is what a man meets when he goes through the halls of the Museum of the Russian Revolution, looking at the innumerable pictures of people who sacrificed their lives for the realization of these theories in the deep conviction that their sacrifices were necessary and of cardinal importance for the fate of the Russian people: waffling and often sentimental phrases about humanity, humaneness, and the moral principles that are opposed to the exploitation of man by man. In Western European belles lettres those philanthropic phrases are diluted down to slobbery rhetoric and decorative, pseudo-Christian, mystical weaknesses, when novelette protagonists weep at the suffering of their neighbors but pharisaically roll their eyes at the real state of affairs, with a lastingly perverse tendency to evade the relevant question: What does the world of international political reality revolve around today? Was the bourgeois and feudal machinery of state created for the material exploitation of the weaker classes or not? Tolstoy and Dostoyevsky preach the idea of higher, superhuman passivity in suffering; they say nothing about the most fundamental truth— the main reason for the distortion and dehumanization of life. Claudel and Ghéon (to mention just two contemporary Catholics) write free verse and dramas following George Sand's thesis: kiss and say goodbye, without forgetting to flirt with the legitimist right wing, to whose apologists they in fact belong.

But there is another logic, one also inspired in essence by pain and suffering, and that other, nonbelletristic, nonlyrical logic does not declaim about the ethical problem in novels and free verse. That Russian-revolutionary logic is not sentimental, and it observes things in a simple way, consistently and clearly: "If it is true that over 500 peasant uprisings were drowned in blood under Nicholas I alone, and if it is true that Nicholas II killed several million people from Port Arthur to Lvov, from 1905 to 1917, then the logical conclusion that inexorably follows from those facts, and differs in principle from the sermons about passive suffering, is that man must resist the evil that produces dehumanization and the unnatural pestilential death of millions through active, collective organization of the masses themselves, in their own interest. That collective organization, a deep belief in progress based on the collective organization of the masses and contrary to Reclus's anarchist thesis that progress is not an axiom, propagates its own political and party credo: we do not believe that suffering is unquestionable and we know that it can be abolished!"

That is how a new consciousness is born and how spontaneous uprisings of the masses gather momentum; unorganized, spontaneous mass revolts give rise to parties, the parties to Lenin, Lenin to Leninism, and, after Lenin's death, as a retrospective panorama, to this museum with its flags, trophies, and honored dead.

From Stenka Razin, who gained control of all Russian lands from the Volga to the Caucasus and Persia, to Yemelyan Pugachev and the terrorists of the 1870s, through the trials and tribulations of Russian life, despite all obstacles, a negative formulation of suffering made its way to victory, a simple and legitimate formulation: we do not believe that suffering is inevitable! The emancipation process of the Russian masses lasted a full 250 years, with their tenacious striving to break free from their suffering; and from Radishchev, who poisoned himself in despair, from the dead Decembrists, Bakunin, and Kropotkin, to the last romanticists of Stepnyakov's *Underground Russia*, proletarians perished on the gallows and in exile with the deep conviction that suffering is not an axiom. Through the series of suicides, emigration, and desperate assassination attempts, two catchphrases to be found in all the pamphlets, the illegal press, and private correspondence: the liquidation of tsarism and the agrarian problem. From the Tchaikovskians and The People's Will, through Tkachev, Sheviryov, Ulyanov, and Khalturin, to Osinsky and all the terrorist groups and programs of the 1870s and 80s, the liquidation of tsarism and the agrarian problem are the two fundamental questions constantly on the agenda of Russian society. Propaganda circles, terrorist raids, illegal pamphlets, assassination attempts, and political monster trials for thirty long years stand at the fore of Russian life.

The "Trial of the Ten" in 1877, the "Trial of the Hundred and Twenty-Three" in 1878, the countless criminal charges brought against the "Land and Freedom" group, the series of assassination attempts between 1880–81, the "Trial of the Fourteen" in 1887, the trials of the South-Russian Workers' Union and of the North-Russian Workers' Union, and much more judicial repression in the first days of unionism, economic strikes, and agrarian unrest—all those testimonies in the museum seem so dramatic in their specific weight, and no one can deny on the way out of this crypt that Bolshevism is one stage in the long historical process coinciding with the last two centuries of Russian history. The gun muzzle on the *Aurora* gave out an internationalist call founded on the thesis of the Second International that proletarians have no fatherland, but after winning power in Petrograd, in the Russian sector of international capitalism, there appeared a huge mass of new, specifically Russian problems, for which a good part of the Western European proletariat, unfortunately, showed little understanding.

There is a yawning gulf between Hobbes (who as a counterrevolutionary émigré in Paris became a republican) and Lenin's room in that fantastic museum. The conscious revolutionary volition at a superior level of social and moral awareness was articulated in the middle of the eighteenth century already, and between then and all this clutter in the rooms of Moscow's English Club—how many generations have fallen in the hard and bloody struggle toward realms of sense suffused with light and worthy of man?

All those individuals who perished were shooting stars in the long Russian and European night. They vanished, borne away by the unintelligible rhythm of death, but they were shooting stars that flashed in the darkness with their meteoritic radiance, as if the eastern brightness of dawn was ignited. Thousands of these Russians who faced a certain death, who made a personal sacrifice for the victory of humanitarian principles and the interests of the international proletariat, disappeared, stolen away on the black wing of the hardest death, an end at the gallows or against an execution-yard wall. The walk through this graveyard of the Revolution tells us that all these brave revolutionaries would have been hopelessly disconsolate if their faith in the progress of humankind as an axiom was not really an axiom.

218

When a man walks through these marble halls, a sense of sepulchral silence arises in him such as reigns in all churches and mausoleums. Here, under glass, in the smell of bloodstained rags and torn pamphlets, of rotten fabrics and faded photographs, lie testimonies to self-effacing devotion and heroism. Tokens of those last generations of romantic realists sleep beneath the folds of the red flag, and those pale, noble profiles, those warm eyes in amiable faces—all of that lives a solemn life in glass cases. Reflections of light flash in the eyes of the visitor, and history is mute beneath the trembling glass in the terrible silence of a great dead thing. One's breath stops, and then a sound comes, as if from somewhere in the room, and yet from afar, from the Caucasus, the cries of the eagles. Glory to you, o Promethean eternity!

IMPERIALISM AND
THE SIGNIFICANCE OF
THE RUSSIAN REVOLUTION

What is imperialism?

In his popular text on imperialism, written in 1917, Lenin defines imperialism as the monopolistic stage of capitalism:

But very brief definitions, although convenient, for they sum up the main points, are nevertheless inadequate, since we have to deduce from them some especially important features of the phenomenon that has to be defined. We must give a definition of imperialism that will include the following five basic features:

(1) the concentration of production and capital has developed to such a high stage that it has created monopolies that play a decisive role in economic life; (2) the merging of bank capital with industrial capital, and the creation, on the basis of this "finance capital," of a financial oligarchy; (3) the export of capital as distinguished from the export of commodities acquires exceptional importance; (4) the formation of international monopolist capitalist associations, which share the world among themselves, and (5) the territorial division of the whole world among the biggest capitalist powers is completed.

We can assume that the inevitable mechanics of imperialistic catastrophes have been explained convincingly in this analysis of the capitalist mode of production. The same law of the production of capital, which causes crises of individual firms and enterprises on a small scale, through competition, acts on an international scale according to the same principles and leads to the development of political crises and wars.[*]

In contemporary industrialized life there is no doubt that goods are not produced for the sake of the goods themselves, but

---

[*] As we know, the capitalist mode of production has Money and Commodities as its main constituents. The formula Commodity-Money-Commodity (when an excess Commodity is sold in order to buy a needed one) does not yield any profit because the Commodity remains in the form of equivalent exchange. Profit originates on the basis of the speculative formula: Money-Commodity-Money plus Profit, a formula opposite to the first, a trading formula, when a trader only buys in order to sell more dearly. Marxists, economists, counter-Marxists, and even the sparrows on the roof know that Marx refuted the classical view, i.e. the old-fashioned

for profit. Virgil's "Accursed hunger for gold." That ancient (and also Marxian) holy thirst for gold is of such elemental force that it verily rages around the globe in its frantic vortices, like a perpetuum mobile, because of the ongoing and ever greater increase of production, in ever more desperate attempts to find new and convenient markets for finished goods. We live in a time of blind economic anarchy, a period whose purpose is not the production of any particular goods, but the constant and mechanical, voracious reproduction of capital—a most banal, blind, and ravenous striving for profit.

Keynes, the bourgeois economic critic of the Treaty of Versailles, compared the situation of European industry today with a mad automobile that races along the roads of profit without a driver, and Sismondi described the unavoidable periodicity of crises (due to overproduction) as a spiral that twists higher and higher, from one cycle to the next, only to collapse disastrously at one time, and then, after the catastrophe, that stupid mechanical process of constant rises and falls begins automatically all over again.*

The insane thirst for ever greater wealth, a constant gold fever, the blind and fateful rotation of profit and super-profit, commodities and overproduction, the dense mists of political and economic crises, colonial conquests, wars, revolutions, and

opinion now long discarded by the left and the right that Profit arises exclusively from Speculation and Fraud, because Marx's discovery of Surplus Value laid the foundations of Economic Science. We know that Labor is a Commodity sold for less than its equivalent, that in capitalist production "the atoms of time are profit's elements of its creation." We know that, but it needs to be repeated (just as it needs to be repeated every day that the earth is round and rotates, because a mass of people still do not believe this truth) that the value of a certain Commodity is determined by the time required for its production, and that Labor in capitalist markets is bought for a significantly lower price than its actual worth. Labor gives disproportionately greater Value per diem than its consumption actually costs, and its quantitative productive capacity grows at an exponential rate as a consequence of technological development, professional perfection, better-organized cooperation, etc., etc.

* The factual state of affairs in imperialism has been analyzed by Kautsky, Hilferding, O. Bauer, R. Luxemburg, Baranovsky, Bukharin, and Lenin. Many of the figures are cited from Sternberg's book on imperialism (1926).

catastrophes—all of that becomes an ever more unearthly and sinister menace to our civilization, like the smoke of a volcano before eruption.

Billions in profit create ever newer and greedier billions, armies and navies with their modern armaments consume ever greater investments, larger and ever more valuable quantities of rubber, oil, and coal are transported from one continent to another, and the prospects of that mad rhythm become ever more turbid, ever less clear. Along with pauperism, the decline of living standards, the growth of unemployment and international debt, and the general arms race there comes the iron thunder of machines, and billowing black clouds of poison gas that threaten to destroy the biological substance of entire cities can be glimpsed. Symptoms appear of new conflagrations and new cycles of wars, the tragic and unnatural death of millions on the battlefields, from fire, famine, and epidemics.

The Hellenes imagined Europa as a beautiful goddess who traveled on the back of Zeus, a divine bull, but today (if we wanted to express the problem of that abduction allegorically) Europa, that old whore, rampages in blood and has no inclination to bear Zeus a son under a plane tree on Crete! The furies of madness and crime that have threatened the feeble-minded systems of bourgeois industry, banks, and cartels for over fifty years will rend this European carcass before our eyes like rabid she-dogs, and they will feast on a battlefield of human bones.

The wars and crises of imperialism over the last fifty years

If a man contemplates for a moment the bloody chaos that has continued for the last fifty years, and if he has doubts about the innate social instincts propounded by Kropotkin, it is easy to think for a minute: perhaps Reclus* was right to question the axiom of human progress.

From Peter the Great to Nicholas I, a staggering total of seven Russo-Turkish wars were fought for the Bosporus. The

* **Élisée Reclus expressed his skepsis in his classic letter to V. Buurmans of September 25, 1878:**

Eastern Question, accompanied by the political disintegration of the Ottoman Empire, is manifested in an acute crisis lasting until the First Balkan War in 1912, with Pan-Slavism, Slavophilia, Russian political crises, and the collapse of Austria-Hungary, with the related ferment in Slavic Europe. The Eastern Question stands in the foreground from the victory of the counterrevolution in 1848 through the victorious counterrevolution of 1918. The political turmoil in Egypt lasts the entire nineteenth century until Great Britain finally finds a temporary solution with its occupation in 1881.

After the conquest of Algeria in 1830, France extends its sphere of influence on the African continent ever more energetically, and after capturing Senegambia and Congo in 1870 the bloody problem continued uninterrupted up until Abd el-Krim in 1925–26. In 1883, France seizes Annam. In 1884, Germany conquers East Africa, and in 1885 it takes the Caroline Islands in the Pacific. 1885: establishment of Belgian Congo. 1885: the Battle of Slivnitsa (in the words of G. B. Shaw: an Austro-Russian war fought by Serbian and Bulgarian troops). 1888: Wilhelm II's ascension to power, 1890 the fall of Bismarck. Tensions in Anglo-German relations. Program of the German fleet and competition between the two powers. 1888–96: thirteen French loans to Russia to the value of five and a half billion francs. 1891: Russian-French alliance. 1901: two billion in new French loans. The amount of French capital invested in Russia totals seventeen billion francs.

The question of the Asian Race manifests itself in the 1890s. Korea. The Japanese-Chinese War of 1894–98. Germany makes Tsingtao its base in the Far East. The question of the Trans-Siberian Railroad. Growing Russian influence in the Far East. 1894–96: Armenian unrest. Constant massacres in Asia Minor. 1897: Greco-Turkish War.

If I could give back to you courage by saying that we shall triumph some day, that the conscience of justice will develop within all men, that we shall become equals and brothers, I should do this with pleasure, but I confess, my friend, that I am far from believing in progress as an axiom. For my part, I struggle for what I know to be the good cause, because I am thus conforming myself to my sense of justice.

British Empire's breakthrough into southern Africa, Egypt, and Sudan. Kitchener. Mass slaughter. Unrest and so-called pacification. 1895: the Italians in Eritrea. 1896: Italians defeated at Battle of Adwa. Menelik II ruler of Ethiopia. Franco-British tensions begin the epoch of 1896–99. Fashoda Incident. The Congo. Belgian-British tensions. Unrest in the Dutch colonies in Java. The Germany fleet grows according to plan. The Baghdad Railway with the plan of an anti-British, Islamic, and anti-Slavic penetration. America. The Spanish-American War of 1898. 1899: The Hague. Manchuria. Korea, Tibet, the Russian affair on the Yalu River, and the Boer War in 1900–02. 1900: Port Arthur passes into Russian hands. The Boxer Rebellion in 1900 in China. International intervention. The Chinese Question in the Far East. The Anglo-Japanese Alliance, American-Japanese tensions. The Pacific Ocean Question. Ever worsening Austro-Hungarian crises in the early twentieth century. Macedonian unrest and the Abdul-Hamid Question. Russo-Japanese War of 1904–05 and the First Russian Revolution. From the First Russian Revolution of 1905 to the Turkish Revolution (under the Young Turks), from the Turkish Revolution to the Chinese Revolution of 1911, the constantly critical state of Austria-Hungary, to the Balkan League and the Balkan War, and finally to the conflagration of 1914–18—all that could be called one organic whole. We were its witnesses, and the results of the last conflagration of 1914–18 are well known.

What is the meaning of this continuous carnage, bloodshed, and violence on all continents over the last fifty years? The answer is very simple: all of that together represents the chaotic inability of an economic system that amasses commodities and breeds overpopulation on the one hand, and accumulates profits and new markets on the other, to resolve any of the political and economic crises in a methodical way. Civil war due to overpopulation or colonial expansion—that is the alternative that drives European statesmen into ever more hazardous military adventures and the conquest of new markets. The destruction of overproduced commodities, or military and economic crises, which cause periodic intervals of depression in the otherwise unbroken cycle.

Wickham Steed, a close friend of Cecil Rhodes, the conquistador of Southern Africa, founder of Rhodesia, and inspirer of the Boer War, recorded this episode in 1895:

"I was in the East End of London [a working-class area; м. к.] yesterday and attended a meeting of the unemployed," Rhodes told Steed during a stay in London. "I listened to the wild speeches, which were just a cry for 'bread! bread!' and on my way home I pondered over the scene and I became more than ever convinced of the importance of imperialism... My cherished idea is a solution for the social problem, i.e., in order to save the 40 million inhabitants of the United Kingdom from a bloody civil war, we colonial statesmen must acquire new lands to settle the surplus population, to provide new markets for the goods produced in the factories and mines. The Empire, as I have always said, is a bread and butter question. If you want to avoid civil war, you must become imperialists." (Quoted by Lenin.)

The power of monopolies, cartels, and finance capital

It is common knowledge that the monopolies with finance capital actually run the world, and Lenin provided a mass of figures from bourgeois economic statistics in his book about imperialism to substantiate this thesis. Tobacco, iron, petroleum, coal, rubber, and textile production are branches that have been monopolized on an international scale.* The bourgeois national economist Eduard Heimann writes:

Those enormous coal companies with production figures in the millions of tons, firmly organized in their syndicates, those

---

*   In North America, more than 80% of all production is in the hands of cartels. Over 20 years, the Standard Oil Company has paid out 889 million dollars of net yield and 606 million dollars in dividends. The United States Steel Corporation has 210,180 employees and 66% of the total production of iron.
        According to information from 1907, there were 3,260,000 businesses in Germany, and 30,000 of them were large-scale enterprises. Of the total of 14 million workers, 5.7 million were employed by those enterprises, i.e. 39.5%, and of the 88 million horsepower, their share was 66 million, i.e. 75%, and of the 1.5 million kilowatt (кw) of electrical energy—1.2 million кw, i.e. 80%. "In other words, 3,230,000 German businesses meant nothing, and 30,000 enterprises everything." (LENIN)

*ventures with their tens of thousands of workers, with their own
railroads and ports—those gigantic enterprises are typical today
of the German iron industry. And the process of concentration is
still continuing. Germany's current industry, financed by a handful of Berlin banks, is ripe for expropriation.*

It is only natural that a financial oligarchy develop
alongside the banks, and in 1910 the overall amount of secu-
rities was estimated at 600 billion gold francs, of which more
than 80%, i.e. 479 billion gold francs, was concentrated in
four countries: England, the United States, France, and Germany. Those four banking oligarchies have exported capital
to the value of 200 billion gold francs over the last two decades, which at a 5% interest rate bears up to 10 billion gold
francs annually. That capital is invested securely, guaranteed
by commercial contracts that compel small debtors to buy
merchandise from the creditor at dictated prices, which independent of the interest rate means fantastic profits. (All
the Balkan, Levantine, and Asian mini-states arm themselves
thanks to Krupp, Schneider, Škoda, or Armstrong, using money borrowed from those very state firms; the purveying of
munitions to the Kingdom of Serbs, Croats, and Slovenes
via the "Omnium-Serbe" consortium is a splendid example
of this thesis.)

The imperialism of Great Britain

The frenzy of that rolling avalanche of British wealth, labor, and
commodities is neatly illustrated by the data given by A. Supan
in *The Territorial Development of the European Colonies*. The British Empire penetrated India with great speed:

> 1765: conquest of Bengal, 436,200 km^2
> 1799: end of the Anglo-Mysore Wars, 431,000 km^2
> 1818: the Anglo-Maratha War, 268,400 km^2
> 1826: occupation of Indochina and Malaya,
> 320,000 km^2
> In sixty years, a total of 1,455,600 km^2
> with over 30 million inhabitants.

At that time, the population of Great Britain and Wales numbered 12,200,000. Thus began the concentration process of British capital and industry.[*]

A century ago, in 1823, the states of South and Central America freed themselves from Spanish and Portuguese domination and thus the rich territory became a huge realm of countless new markets for British merchandise, money, and credits. Between 1821 and 1825, British exports to the republics of South America grew from two billion to six and a half billion pounds sterling, and the purchasing power there grew exclusively because of the British loan, which, naturally, bore high rates of interest. Those extraordinary financial and trade deals of the British Empire with South and Central America lasted up until the end of the fourth decade of the nineteenth century, when the North American Union emerged as a serious competitor in the markets directly to its south, leading to periods of crisis in British industry with the Chartist movement—powerful evidence that revolutionary situations are causally related to economic crises. But at the same time, the triumphant epoch of the railroad system began, which guaranteed British industry's primacy for the following seven decades, resulting in the conclusive conquest of Africa, Cecil Rhodes's conception of a railroad linking Alexandria, Cairo, and Cape Town, and enormous investments of British capital that from 1880 to 1900 alone totaled 45 billion gold marks. According to G. Peish and figures of the Royal Statistical Society from 1880, British wealth amounted to 3,191,836,000 pounds sterling (65 billion gold marks), which earned around 180 million pounds of interest annually. Before the war, those interest payments totaled 210 million pounds. In 1904, exports were valued at 4.8 billion gold marks and by 1914 they had grown by 60% (figures from Fritz Sternberg). An accompanying phenomenon of that gigantic

[*] **The figures given by Manabendra Nath Roy show very clearly that the penetration of British industry in two decades completely destroyed Indian textile production, which pauperized millions of workers in the Indian textile industry and caused mass deaths from starvation. Only recently has independent Indian industry begun to develop again, and its progress, again, has a certain negative influence on the British domestic labor market.**

economic development was above all the powerful growth of small investors, the increase in the living standards of broad sections of the working class, the growth of wages, a general betterment of the situation of the proletarian masses, and the development of a certain psychology—the mind-set of a working-class aristocracy.

The number of beggars and paupers dropped, unemployment disappeared, and the number of rentiers with an income of over 60,000 dinars monthly climbed to 1.5 million. That was a time when the size of "playgrounds" (land for amusement such as tennis, horse races, sport, etc.) in southern and central England was significantly larger than the agricultural area under cultivation. Until 1914, England spent 14 million pounds sterling annually on foxhunting and other equestrian sport. Hobson, otherwise a very sober critic of British imperialism, imagined Europe after the final division of the Chinese market between the Western great powers as one big playground with villas, hotels, and idlers.[*]

The rivalry of imperialist groups and Anglo-German relations

The adherents of the pan-European movement all imagine Europe as fantastically as Hobson. They believe it is possible for all the cartels of the European industrial and financial oligarchy to concur in one enormous shareholders' company, a "Pan-European Stock Corporation," which in unity and harmony would usher in a new century (1930–2030) of exploitation of the other continents, in the company of America and the British Empire.

The amateurishness and frivolousness of Count Coudenhove-Kalergi's hypotheses and similar conjectures are neatly exposed by the figures presented by Heinrich Friedjung, the noted Austrian historian, who played a pitiful and ludicrous role as an agent provocateur for Austrian imperialism in the Supilo-Friedjung-Aerenthal trial of 1911. Friedjung, in his pan-Germanic

[*]   **The largest part of Western Europe would have the same character as southern England, the Riviera, Italy, and Switzerland do today. Society would consist of rich rentiers and merchants, and industrial products would flood in from the colonies as tribute (quoted by LENIN).**

work on imperialism (1921), provides the following data on Anglo-German rivalry and competition, two decades before the catastrophe:

GERMAN PRODUCTION OF CRUDE IRON:
1890—4 million tons,
1910—17.8 million tons = 344% increase
British production of crude iron:
1890—7.7 million tons,
1910—9 million tons = 17% increase
German production 327% more!

GERMAN PRODUCTION OF COAL:
1910—255 million tons = 240% increase
British production of coal:
1890—?
1910— = 60% increase
German production of coal 180% more!

GERMAN MERCHANT NAVY:
1896—1,970,000 tons,
1913—5,082,000 tons = 160% increase
British merchant navy:
1896—13,146,000 tons,
1913—18,700,000 tons = 40% increase
Germany 120% more!

BRITISH EXPORTS:
1896—29 billion,
1913—73 billion = 150% increase
German exports grew by 240% in the same period.
German exports 90% more!

COMPARE THIS SITUATION WITH NAVAL FORCES IN 1897:
The British navy: 1,320,000 tons, with 97,000 crew, and
The German navy: 270,000 tons, with 24,000 crew.

When one takes into account that despite this impressive impetus of industry Germany was only the sixth maritime power in the world (England, France, America, Russia, Italy, and then Germany), there is nothing more logical than the plan of pan-Germanic maritime expansion. Tirpitz's plan of rapid naval armament, the plan of imperialist antipolitics by the Triple Entente with encirclement of Germany, the war, Churchill as First Lord of the Admiralty 1911–15, Scapa Flow, the catastrophe and collapse of the German Empire, and then the game begins all over again.

On December 7, 1897, Chancellor Bülow declared, when submitting the bill for the enlargement of the German imperial fleet: *The days when Germans granted one neighbor the earth, the other the sea, and reserved for themselves the sky, where pure doctrine reigns—those days are over. In short, we do not want to put anyone in our shadow, but we also demand our place in the sun.*

Already in March of the following year, 1898, China leased Tsingtao to Germany for ninety-nine years, and the German chancellor stated on that occasion: *Without a territorial base all German ventures in China would be of more use to others than to ourselves.*

The minds of men such as Admiral Tirpitz and Wilhelm II hatched the plan of doubling Germany's navy with the fastest speed of production of all state arsenals: two enormous new battleships were to be built annually (34 warships in 16 years) as the maritime formula of commercial rivalry. Admirals exist in order to ensure profits, i.e. dividends, for the merchant navy.

Admiral Tirpitz, inspired by the upswing of German naval power, said on February 10, 1900, as Secretary of State of the Imperial Naval Office: *We believe that our navy, according to the new bill, will be so strong that the North Sea will be free. Our naval battles need to be fought in the North Sea.*

Tirpitz, Count Zeppelin, Wilhelm ii, Krupp, Siemens-Schuckert, Ballin, etc., or Lord Cromer, Governor of Egypt, Edward vii, Cecil Rhodes, director of Rhodesia, Lord Minto, the colonizer of Canada, Kitchener, the victor of Egypt and the Transvaal, or Von der Goltz, the German chief instructor of the Turkish military—all of them were "engineers of death" and the gravediggers of European civilization. When the pyramids of rubber tires and sewing machines, and presses and mines, are backed by bank vaults, and when those bank vaults are supported by barracks, battalions, and heavy guns, it is clear that the consequence is catastrophe, and that simple, plain truth produces the results of 1914–18, 1926–36–48... When is it all going to end?

The result of imperialism—anarchy

The capitalist mode of production is accompanied by the disastrous consequences of the accumulation of commodities and profit on the one hand, and overpopulation and pauperism on the other, and that economic system, by the force of its fatal rotation of value (dynamic in all its parts, in contrast to the static nature of ancient and feudal economies), destroys old civilizations and ploughs up continents like an armored tank furrows a battlefield, moving always and exclusively toward the greatest profit. Because the Egyptian, Roman, and Hellenic slaves, as well as feudal serfs, all gave their labor to their exploiters for less than its equivalent, and the surplus value, as the product of their labor, was used to build the Roman Forum, the Pantheon, the Egyptian pyramids, or Medvedgrad fortress above Zagreb. But neither in the ancient world nor in feudalism, typically parasitical economic systems, was it the case that the greatest percentage of profit automatically returned to economic activity as capital, and there was no reproduction of capital in such a blind and insatiable form that occurs today.

In the ancient world and feudalism the masters were parasites who ruled over endless quantities of slaves and continents, enjoyed their annuities, and spent the greatest part of their surplus income for their own comfort and enjoyment. Today's capitalist spends a relatively small part of his profits for his own personal benefit and ploughs the other part, much more sizeable, into his business and enterprises, which in that way grow enormously. Moreover, as the number of capitalist slaves grows, noncapitalist spaces become smaller by the day, and thus the relation between production and consumption shifts significantly, and there are periodically recurring crises, which our system of production has been unable to emerge from for the last fifty or sixty years. (R. Luxemburg's example of the downfall of the small farmer in the US is a classic.) The consequence of all that is, because of the capitalist structure of the very system that engenders a disproportion between production and consumption, overpopulation and overproduction. A situation has to arise where capitalist systems expand into noncapitalist spaces (while they still exist as such), and those different financial and military-political spheres of interest and ventures unavoidably come into conflict with one another. The examples given clearly show the quality of those crises, and the experience of the last seventy years is incontestable: when banks are behind the machinery of state, such assistance inevitably and inescapably leads to war. Just as there are *l'art pour l'art* painters and others, who are convinced that art exists for the sake of art, a type of economist-cum-politician has developed in the capitalist mode of production today, who is convinced that "war as such," "war in itself," has become the only politico-economic means.

There is no doubt that chaos reigns in the world of capitalist production. From back at the time of the July Revolution of 1830 and Proudhon's era of 1848, when all petty bourgeois utopian socialists, in opposition to the reactionary tendencies of their era, dreamed of an economic superstructure, we find a mass of testimonies that all strive idealistically for a new and higher economic order. The European subject observed the mechanism of the imperialist system soberly and rationally, and it was clear to him that it was high time for human intelligence to take control of the economic machine instead of the interest and profit of the rentiers, as seen in this instructive quotation from Saint-Simon:

The present anarchy of production, which corresponds to the fact that economic relations are developing without uniform regulation, must make way for organization in production. Production will no longer be directed by isolated manufacturers, independent of each other and ignorant of man's economic needs; that will be done by a certain public institution. A central committee of management, being able to survey the large field of social economy from a more elevated point of view, will regulate it for the benefit of the whole of society, will put the means of production into suitable hands, and above all will take care that there be constant harmony between production and consumption.

The results of the Russian Revolution

The history of social struggle in Europe is a history of the protracted, painful maturing of subjective consciousness regarding the anarchic and undignified state in the mode of production, the exploitation of labor, and all the portentous consequences of those underlying antisocial relations. The history of social struggle in Europe is reflected in a whole series of systems of thought and political options of how the initiative can be transferred from individual owners of the means of production and money to a higher, social entity, and how the sanguinary relationships of slaves and masters can be turned into social bonds worthy of man. Seventy years rushed by from Saint-Simon and Marx to the Russian Revolution, and the organizations that originated in the "Bolshevik experiment" today are positive innovations of inestimable value for everyone who views the torn and anarchic state of European economic forces from a socialist perspective.

The Bolsheviks' seizure of power was decried as a Bakuninist putsch that would collapse by itself within forty-eight hours. It suffices to cast a most superficial glance at Bakunin's path in life and recall his words: "I believe in nothing, I read nothing, I think of only one thing: how to get myself hung and to leave this world without a trace," to assure oneself that the stocktaking after a decade of the "Bolshevik experiment" (1926) has nothing whatsoever to do with the tragedy of that romantic amateur revolutionary. As opposed to the Geneva-based League of Nations, armed to the teeth, racked by enormous industrial crises and anarchy in production, with an irresolvable colonial problem, 250 billion of wartime debt, and the unquestionable economic and military superiority of the US, the USSR stands before the eyes of the world today as a direct outcome of the Russian Revolution, as a strong counterweight, perhaps not yet equal in diplomatic and military terms but, beyond any doubt, superior in an ideological and political sense.

The Russian Revolution is of invaluable practical significance. From the innumerable theoretical debates in the First and Second International and Philistine social democratic beer-hall declamations for May 1 to parliamentary ministerialisms and Party or factional quarrels in political synagogues with talks and texts about revisionism, the concentration of capital, and monopolism as preconditions for nationalization, the ever stronger increase in the living standard of the American and Western European proletariat, the strengthening of a Philistine "class-consciousness" as a direct result of that prosperity, and the expropriation of the expropriators by democratic and parliamentary means—the road to organized state power seized by force of arms is long. Instead of all the eloquent phrases about relative prosperity, the periodicity of crises, and the possibilities of peaceful development, and in place of the enormous heap of words about democratization of the proletarian masses and the freedom of man, the USSR stands defiant today with its positive results as well-nigh irrefutable proof that everything that has happened and is happening in Russia is no longer some kind of experiment, but a fact: socialism has passed from theory into practice. A book, a phrase, and a resolution became a state administration with police, courts, and positive legislation. A speech in parliament, an evening course in Marxism, a newspaper editorial, or polemics with the bankers' press gave rise to the realities of coinage, armored vehicles, artillery, modern aviation, and diplomatic relations on an international basis.

Because, if the statistical data we gave at the beginning is accurate, if it is true that the contemporary economic machinery devours itself like Saturn his children, and if Keynes's automobile without a driver is not an exaggerated allegory of a bourgeois economic skeptic but really the truth, then it is also true that the results of the Russian Revolution convincingly show that the anarchy of capitalist production and forcible conquest of markets has ended in one part of the world, and a new group of political, state, and economic forces is going ahead with a plan of socialist construction. In the vicious circle of contemporary financial exploitation, in the witches' brew of industrial and military crises, an internationally recognized political subject has emerged, whose functions are no longer reformist in nature and no longer a journalistic homily with theoretical instructions for the betterment of a certain, economically backward, antiquated, anarchic state of affairs in international political relations, but a social force organized on the basis of state power with the firsthand task of creating a classless economic system on the ground.

International social democracy (and particularly its political center) criticizes the October Revolution for appearing prematurely. After twelve million war dead in the international conflagration of 1914–18, the October Revolution can hardly be considered a premature putsch in an international sense, although on a Russian scale, taking into account the backwardness of the huge agrarian complex in Asia today, after nine years of negative experience, that heroic swoop certainly looks bold. The realization of communism in an international context is only conceivable if the anarchy of production in the whole world were to be removed in a systematic and unitary way, and if, with a correct exchange of goods and raw materials, the international arms race and periodic crises with mass unemployment and social tensions were to stop. But since the territory of the victorious October Revolution amounts to just one sixth of the globe and that one sixth with its 130 million inhabitants is relatively under industrialized, its technical shortcomings (the consequences of wars and civil strife), the shortage of ready capital, and the very intensive boycott by the capitalist oligarchy mean that a cycle of economic, and thus also political, crises is a normal and logical occurrence. Produced goods were unable to be marketed, and NEP is a risky attempt to create an internal market and enable proper circulation of goods and capital, production and consumption.

The 2,744 billion gold rubles of gross production at the end of 1925 (which amounts to 90% of the gross production of 1913) suggests that the danger zone has been passed and that there can be no word of a premature experiment, even on a purely Russian scale. As can be seen from the table below, the factual state of affairs is not hopeless, and the figures cited show an upward trend.

AGRICULTURAL AREA UNDER CULTIVATION:
1922: 67.8% of the prewar area was under cultivation,
1924: 87% of the prewar area was under cultivation.

INDUSTRIAL PRODUCTION IN MILLIONS OF POODS
(OR ARSHINS):

	1921	1925
Coal	464	1,048
Oil	232	396
Iron	7	76
Steel	19	102
Canvas (arshins)	40	296
Fabric (arshins)	21	66

TOTAL VALUE OF GROSS PRODUCTION:
1923: 1,134 billion gold rubles
1924: 1,857 billion gold rubles
1925: 2,744 billion gold rubles (10% less than 1913).

This does not mean that communism has been achieved, but nor is it anarchy. It means that capitalism exists, but state capitalism, in a state whose system is governed by the International. Accumulation functions in the interest of strengthening the international system, and despite the dangers of bureaucratization and the triggering of an economic crisis, the entire machine is still heading toward the realization of its goals. The problems of the increasing wealth of the middle and upper stratum of farmers, the figure of the NEPman, and a certain differentiation within the Party apparatus are problems of dictatorship and democracy, problems of the construction of socialism on an international scale or in a particular country—all those are natural and normal phenomena in a process of such dimensions and importance, which today is engulfed in the turmoil of open questions that the Revolution placed on the agenda. Compared to the crisis that began in 1917 and the five hard years of war communism, all those problems signify only that the thesis has been affirmed and that a new economic and political subject is taking shape between China and the Baltic that shall play a historical role in the economic chaos of Western Europe. The fact that this subject (with all its deficiencies) exists at all is proof that the October Revolution did not flare up too early.

The question that arises by itself in connection with the designation "too late" or "too early," and which F. Sternberg elaborated negatively and critically in his book about imperialism, is an open question. But it could also be formulated quite differently: Will it be too late for a European-scale social revolution after the next conflagration? Because the twelve million dead and around 100 billion in wartime damages from 1914 to 1918 have largely been offset now, in 1926, and Europe stands again before new cycles of open political and military crises like on the eve of the blaze of 1914. The next conflagration conducted with destructive means, with air forces and poisonous gas, whose effects make dynamite and gunpowder look quaint and old-fashioned, will not be waged only in relatively under industrialized zones (Galicia, Champagne, and the Balkans), but also in the heart of old civilizations (the Rhine and Britain). The result of the next conflagration could well be catastrophic and of such dimensions that any reparations would be out of the question. Along with the obliterated means of production, given the fierce vehemence of European civil war, the famine and epidemics, the prospects for the construction of socialism in Europe after the next conflagration are much more dismal than those in Russia today. The very fact that there exists a base today that is beyond those dangers and can assume a role of constructive assistance in such catastrophic circumstances on a European scale is of the greatest importance, and in that respect the October Revolution did not come about prematurely; rather, its political conceptions anticipate the political development of the world.

In a nutshell

Imperialism is the monopolist stage of capitalism. The wars and crises of imperialism over the last fifty years are proof of its anarchy in economic, political, and cultural terms. Capital reproduces itself according to familiar laws, and the ever more intensive accumulation creates disparities between production and consumption. Because of overpopulation and competition, as well as the periodicity of its crises, imperialism penetrates noncapitalist (feudal and colonial) spaces, revolutionizes production, and exclusively follows the path of ongoing destruction and ever greater profit. The rivalry of particular groups within the financial oligarchy is of such enormous proportions that any attempt to artificially prevail over this blindly competitive, impassioned battle of the great powers is naïvely utopian. The historical significance of Marxism lies above all in its scientific critique of utopian socialism and in placing organizational emphasis on international labor. That international labor, as meat, as the object of exploitation, is constructive and integral in its own interests. In the anarchy of international economic relations, international labor is a reliable guarantee that humanity will emerge intact from this madhouse. The historical significance of the October Revolution is that it passed from theory into practice. After fifty years of expectation, it became a fact—a fact with 130 million inhabitants and one sixth of the globe. Despite the huge obstacles in its path, that fact has been confirmed in practice and, with the elasticity of NEP, it has created its own market independent of Western capital and thus largely raised its production to the prewar level. Despite the many unresolved questions and internal problems, that fact of the October Revolution entails a gradual and ever greater overcoming of resistance and the organizational strengthening of those political, economic, and military forces that will play an ever greater and more important role in Western imperialist conflagrations. Thus the October Revolution did not come prematurely; it is a guarantee that the Revolution will not come too late, even in Europe, and that the existence of the most modern, destructive weapons will not result in an ahistorical period, as occurred with Egypt and Rome. It is clear that the impact of the October Revolution in terms of the International, in terms of international and trade-union politics, as well as regarding the colonies, will be of ever greater influence and significance in the next decade, or decades, because rights vested by revolution act historically as catalysts, and wishing to return them to the previous state is just as infantile as it would be naïve to want to return a river to its source.

About the Translator

Will Firth was born in 1965 in Newcastle, Australia. He studied German and Slavic languages in Canberra, Zagreb, and Moscow. Since 1991 he has been living in Berlin, Germany, where he works as a freelance translator of literature and the humanities. Firth translates from Russian, Macedonian, and all variants of Serbo-Croatian. His best-received translations of recent years have been Robert Perišić's *Our Man in Iraq*, Andrej Nikolaidis's *Till Kingdom Come*, and Faruk Šehić's *Quiet Flows the Una*.

www.willfirth.de